FOURTH EDITION

Daytrips
GERMANY

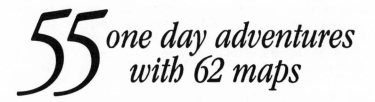

55 *one day adventures*
with 62 maps

EARL STEINBICKER

HASTINGS HOUSE
Book Publishers
Mamaroneck, New York

We are always grateful for comments from readers, which are extremely helpful in preparing future editions. Please write directly to the author, Earl Steinbicker, c/o Hastings House, 141 Halstead Avenue, Mamaroneck, NY 10543; or FAX (914) 835-1037. Thank you.

The author would like to thank the following people, whose generous help and encouragement made this book possible:
Hedy Wuerz, of the German National Tourist Office.
Lucille Hoshabjian, of Lufthansa German Airlines.
Beatrix Sturm, of the German Railroad.

All photos and maps are by the author except as noted.

Distributed to the trade by Publishers Group West, Emeryville, CA

ISBN: 0-8038-9369-8
Library of Congress Catalog Card Number 94-072932

Printed in the United States of America
10 9 8 7 6 5 4 3 2 1

Contents

Introduction

Visitors to Germany can choose from an enormous range of experiences. There are magnificent cities and medieval towns to be explored, mountains to be climbed, history to be relived, and wines to be tasted. Few nations can match its scope of art, architecture, music, or natural splendor. What's more, the overwhelming majority of Germany's most exciting attractions can easily be enjoyed on a daytrip basis with absolutely no need for frequent hotel changes. This book takes a careful look at 55 of the most intriguing destinations and describes, in step-by-step detail, a simple and natural way to go about probing them on your own.

Daytrips in Germany is not intended to be a comprehensive guide to the entire nation. It focuses, instead, on four broad areas of maximum tourist interest—Bavaria, The Rhineland, The North, and The East. Each of these has one major city that, for reasons of transportation and accommodation, makes the most logical base for daytrips in its region. These are Munich, Frankfurt, Hamburg, and Berlin. Other towns, of course, could be substituted as bases; and these possibilities are suggested in the text whenever practical.

Daytrips have many advantages over the usual point-to-point touring, especially for short-term visitors. You can sample a far greater range in the same time by seeing only those places that really interest you instead of "doing" the region town by town. This can lead to a more varied diet of sights, such as spending one day high in the Alps, the next in Munich, and the third in medieval Rothenburg. Daytrips are also ideal for business travelers with a free day or so interspersed between meetings.

The benefits of staying in one hotel for a while are obvious. Weekly rates are often more economical than overnight stays, especially in conjunction with airline package plans. You also gain a sense of place, of having established a temporary home-away-from-home in a city where you can get to know the restaurants and enjoy the nightlife. Then, too, you won't waste time searching for a room every night. Your luggage remains in one place while you go out on carefree daytrips.

There is no need to pre-plan every moment of your vacation since with daytrips you are always free to venture wherever you please. Feel like seeing Würzburg today? Ah, but this is Monday, when its sights are closed, so maybe it would be better to head for the Black Forest instead, or take a stroll through Wiesbaden. Is rain predicted for the entire day? You certainly don't want to be on the Rhine in a shower, so why not try the wonderful museums in Cologne? The operative word here is flexibility; the freedom of not being tied to a schedule or route.

All of the daytrips in this book may be taken by train or by car. Full information for doing this is given in the "Getting There" section of each trip. A suggested do-it-yourself walking tour is outlined in both the text and on the street map. Practical considerations such as time and weather are included, along with price-keyed restaurant recommendations and background information.

The trips have been arranged in a geographical sequence following convenient transportation routes. In several cases it is possible to combine two trips in the same day. These opportunities are noted whenever they are practical.

Destinations were chosen to appeal to a wide variety of interests, and include fresh discoveries along with the proven favorites. In addition to the usual cathedrals, castles, and museums there are mountain peaks, wine villages, boat cruises, Roman ruins, country walks, salt mines, elegant spas, great seaports, places where history was made just yesterday, and places that are vibrantly alive today.

Most of the attractions have a nominal entrance fee—those that are free will come as a pleasant surprise. Cathedrals and churches will appreciate a few coins in the collection box to help with their maintenance costs.

Finally, a gentle disclaimer. Places have a way of changing without warning, and errors do creep into print. If your heart is absolutely set on a particular sight, you should check first to make sure that the opening times are still valid. Phone numbers for the local tourist information offices are included for this purpose.

One last thought—it isn't really necessary to see everything at any given destination. Be selective. Your one-day adventures in Germany should be fun, not an endurance test. If it starts becoming that, just stroll over to the nearest café or beer garden, sit down, and enjoy yourself. There will always be another day.

Happy Daytripping!

Section I

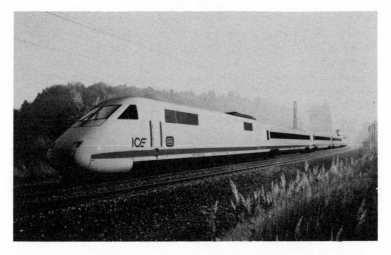

GETTING AROUND

Getting around Germany on your own is really quite easy once you know a few of the practicalities. This first section discusses transportation, package deals, holidays, food and drink, some hints on the suggested tours, and sources of additional information. The book then goes on to describe 55 of the most exciting daytrip possibilities in Germany. All of these excursions can be made by rail, or by car. In choosing a form of transportation you should consider the following:

BY RAIL:

The **German Railroad** *(Deutsche Bahn, or DB)* is among the finest in the world. It operates thousands of passenger trains a day over some 25,000 miles of routes serving nearly 8,000 communities, as well as an extensive bus network connecting small villages and rural areas with the rail network. The system is presently being expanded to accommodate additional high-speed service between major cities.

There are very few places in Germany that cannot be reached by rail. Equipment now in use varies from the sleek *InterCity Express (ICE)* trains to some rather quaint railcars. If you enjoy riding trains you will savor each type for the special and diverse experiences it offers.

Seasoned travelers often consider riding trains to be one of the best ways of meeting the local people and making new friends. It is not unusual to strike up an engaging conversation that makes your trip all the more memorable. You also get a marvelous view of the passing countryside from the large windows, and have time to catch up on your reading. Then too, you are spared the worries of driving, especially after sampling the local beers and wines.

All trains operated by the German Railroad belong to one of the following categories:

EC—*EuroCity.* Fast international luxury expresses. Both first- and second-class seating is offered, and there is a supplementary fare called a *Zuschlag* that is covered by the various railpasses. Reservations are suggested during peak travel times.

ICE—*InterCity Express.* Offering state-of-the-art travel at speeds of up to 155 mph, these luxury trains connect major cities within Germany at convenient intervals, synchronizing their arrivals with connecting trains. Speed comes at a price, as a fairly hefty surcharge is made to all but railpass holders. Both first- and second-class seating is available. Reservations are not required, but advisable during peak travel periods.

IC—*InterCity.* These swift, modern trains run at hourly intervals between principal cities and towns and to neighboring countries. Connections with other expresses are very convenient, with many IC trains stopping at the Frankfurt airport for the benefit of air passengers. All trains of this category carry both first- and second-class cars, with a choice of compartment or open seating. There is a modest additional charge to ride IC trains, called a *Zuschlag,* but this does not apply to railpass users. Reservations are a good idea during peak travel times.

IR—*InterRegio.* A new class of very modern, comfortable air-conditioned expresses connecting cities with smaller destinations. There is mixed open and compartment seating in both first and second class, with a *"Bistro-Café"* car for light meals and drinks. A supplementary fare *(Zuschlag)* is charged for distances of up to 50 kilometers, but not to railpass users.

D—*Express.* Sometimes made up of older equipment, these expresses serve more towns than the ECs, ICEs, ICs, or IRs, albeit at a slower pace. There is usually an extra charge for distances of up to 50 kilometers, although this does not apply to railpass users. Seats may be reserved if desired. All trains in this category carry both first- and second-class cars, but don't expect air conditioning.

E—*Eilzug.* These semi-express trains frequently use older equipment, rarely offer food or beverage service, and primarily serve smaller towns.

S—*Schnell Bahn.* Usually made up of modern-but-utilitarian equipment, these commuter locals serve the outlying areas near large cities, and operate as subways within the city.

N—*Nahverker.* Usually not given any particular designation on schedules, these locals make many stops and can take you to very rural locations. Much of the equipment is old and sometimes rather quaint, although there are modern N-trains. They are often second-class only.

Buses—operated by or for the German Railroad, marked "DB," connect rural areas with train stations in larger towns, and fill in for rail service during off-peak hours. Railpasses are accepted.

SCHEDULES for train services can be consulted at the information offices *(Auskunft)* in stations. While there, be sure to check the return schedules as well to avoid any possibility of getting stranded. Tables of **departures** (*Abfahrt,* on yellow paper) and **arrivals** (*Ankunft,* on white paper) are posted throughout the stations; and are stated in terms of the 24-hour clock. Thus, a departure at 3:32 p.m. would be marked as 15.32. Be sure that you are looking at the correct table, not one for a nearby city. Some stations, notably Munich's *Hauptbahnhof,* have free printed schedules for popular destinations. Watch out for the word *"Umsteigen,"* or the letter "U," which indicates a change of trains. A complete schedule book, called a *Kursbuch,* can be purchased at the stations, but it's too big to carry around. The compact **Thomas Cook European Timetable**, sold in some travel book stores in America, by mail from the Forsyth Travel Library (P.O. Box 2975, Shawnee Mission, Kansas 66201-1375, phone toll-free 1-800-FOR-SYTH), or at Thomas Cook offices in Britain, is very useful although it does not list *every* local service.

RESERVATIONS are desirable for travel on EC, ICE, or IC trains during peak periods, and can also be made for IR and D trains. Railpass holders must pay a small fee for this. The reservation will assign you to a specific car and seat, which you must claim within 15 minutes after departure. You can choose between compartments and open-seating cars, window or aisle seats, and smoking or non-smoking areas. Those traveling without reservations should be careful not to sit in someone else's reserved seat, which is marked by a card at the compartment entrance or above the seat. Careful observation of these may gain you a seat when the entire train is full, as most passengers seem to believe that a reservation card always means that the seat is taken. Not so. It only indicates that the seat is reserved from a certain station to another certain station, and these are marked on the card. Outside of that specific trip segment the seat is free.

A RAIL TRAVELER'S GLOSSARY

Abfahrt	Departure
Ankunft	Arrival
Anschluss	Connection
Ausgang	Exit
Auskunft	Information
Ausland	Foreign
Ausser	Except
Bahnhof	Train station
Bahnhofwirtshaft	Station restaurant
Bahnsteig	Platform
Bergbahn	Mountain railway
Besetzt	Occupied
Besonderheiten	Special particulars
Bestellung	Reservation
Binnen	Inland (domestic)
Damen	Women
DB, Deutsche Bahn	German Railroad
Eilzug	Semi-express train
Einfache	One-way
Eingang	Entrance
Einsteigen	Board (the train)
Eisenbahn	Railway
Erste Klasse	First class
Fahrgast	Passenger
Fahrkarte/ Fahrschein	Ticket
Fahrplan	Timetable
Fahrpreise	Fare
Fahrrad am Bahnhof	Bicycle rental in station
Fahrt	Journey
Feiertage	Holidays
Fensterplatz	Window seat
Fernzug	Long distance train
Frauen	Women
Fremdenverkehrsverein	Tourist information office
Fundbüro	Lost-and-found
Garderobe	Checkroom
Gefähr	Danger
Gepäck	Luggage
Gepäckabfertigung	Baggage check room
Gepäckträger	Porter
Gleis	Track
Haüptbahnhof (Hbf)	Main train station
Herren	Men
Hin und zurück	There and back (round trip)

Kofferkuli	Luggage cart
Kursbuch	Offical timetable book
Kurswagen	Through car to indicated destination
Liegewagen	Inexpensive sleeping car with bunks (Couchette)
Männer	Men
Münz-Zugtelefon	Pay phone on train
Nahverkehr	Local train
Nichtraucher	No smoking
Nur	Only
Ohne	Without
Platzreservierung	Seat reservation
Postamt	Post office
Raucher	Smoking
Reisebüro	Travel agency
Reiseproviant	Food & drinks to take along
Reserviert	Reserved
Richtung	Direction
Rückfahrkarte	Round trip
S-Bahn	Commuter rail line, may operate as subway inside large cities
Schaffner	Ticket collector
Schalter	Ticket window in station
Schlafwagen	Sleeping car
Schliessfach	Luggage locker
Schnellzug	Express train
Sitzplatz	Seat
Sonderrückfahrkarte	Reduced price excursion ticket
Speisewagen	Dining car
Täglich	Daily
Triebwagen	Rail car
Tunnelbahnhof	Underground train station
U-Bahn	Subway, Métro, Underground
Umsteigen	Change (of trains)
Verbindung	Connection
Verboten	Forbidden
Verkehrsbüro, Verkehrsverein,	
Verkehrsamt	Tourist information office
Wagen	Car (of train)
Wagenstandanzeiger	Train make-up diagram
Wartesaal	Waiting room
WC	Rest rooms
Wechselstube	Money exchange place
Werktage	Weekdays (Mon. Sat.)
Zoll	Customs
Zu	To
Zug	Train
Zuschlag	Supplementary fare
Zutritt verboten	Do not enter
Zweite klasse	Second class

It is always best to arrive at the station *(Bahnhof)* a few minutes before departure time and go directly to the track platform *(Gleis)* shown for your train on the departure board. There you will usually find a sign marked *Wagenstandanzeiger* that shows the exact makeup of every express leaving from that platform, including the location of each car. This serves two major purposes. First, you won't have to make a last-minute dash when you discover that the first-class cars stop at the opposite end of a long platform. Secondly, and more important, it shows which—if any—cars are dropped off en route to your destination.

The **routing** and final destination of each car is shown just outside its door as well as in its vestibule. First-class cars are marked with the numeral "1" near the door, and sometimes with a yellow stripe above the windows.

Most express trains offer a **food and beverage service** of some sort, as shown on the schedules. Riding in a regular dining car or self-service café car can be a delightful experience, but beware the pushcarts in other cars that sell well-shaken cans of warm beer. You are much better off stocking up on snacks and refreshments at the station and bringing them with you, as most Europeans do.

RAILPASSES can be a bargain if you intend to do any real amount of train travel. Ask your travel agent about them before going to Germany, as they are difficult if not impossible to purchase once there. The German Railroad **(DB)** accepts the following passes:

EURAILPASS—The best-known pass, allows unlimited first-class travel throughout 17 European countries, excluding Great Britain. It is available for periods of 15 or 21 consecutive days, or 1, 2, or 3 months. The Eurailpass includes a wide variety of fringe benefits including free rides on Rhine River steamers, some buses, free international ferry steamers, discounts on popular mountain railways and cable cars, and a discount on EuroStar Channel Tunnel service.

EURAIL FLEXIPASS—Allows unlimited first-class travel on *any* 5, 10, or 15 days within a 2-month period. It is valid in the same 17 countries and has the same benefits as the regular Eurailpass. This is an attractive deal if you intend to spend time exploring the base cities as well as making daytrips from them.

EURAIL SAVERPASS—An economical version of the Eurailpass offering the same first-class benefits for groups of three or more people traveling together. Between October 1st and March 31st the group can be as small as two persons. This pass is available for periods of 15 or 21 days, or one month, and the travel must *always* be done as a group.

EURAIL YOUTHPASS—This low-cost version of the Eurailpass is available to anyone under the age of 26 and allows unlimited *second-class* travel in the same 17 countries for periods of 15 days, or 1 or 2 months. There is also a **Eurail Youth Flexipass** valid for any 5, 10, or 15 days within a 2-month period.

EURAIL DRIVE PASS—A complex program that combines rail travel with car rentals at an attractive price, tailored to meet your specific needs.

EUROPASS—This mini-Eurailpass allows unlimited rail travel in your choice of 3, 4, or 5 of the following countries: France, Germany, Switzerland, Italy, or Spain. The countries chosen must be adjacent. Adults and children travel in first class; the youth rate (under 26) is for second class. For an extra price, the following countries may be added: Belgium and Luxembourg, Austria, and Portugal. Durations of any 5 to 15 days within a 2-month period may be selected. There is also a **Europass Drive** arrangement combining rail travel with car rentals.

GERMAN FLEXIPASS—is valid for unlimited travel throughout Germany only, on *any* 5, 10, or 15 days within a one-month period, and offers a substantial saving over the Eurailpass. It is available in both first- and second-class versions for adults, or in second class for youths under the age of 26. There is also an economical **Twinpass** version for two adults traveling together, as well as a **rail/drive** arrangement for combining rail travel with a car rental.

BRITGERMAN RAILPASS—Combines 5 or 10 days of unlimited first-class travel within a one-month period in both Britain and Germany, but does not include travel between the countries. Children 5-15 get a 50% discount.

All railpasses must be **validated** in Europe before their initial use. The first and last day of validity will be entered on the pass at that time. Be certain that you agree with the dates *before* allowing the validating station agent to write them in. Read the specific instructions that come with each railpass and follow them exactly to get all of the benefits you're entitled to.

If you intend to take several of the daytrips in this book, and especially if at least one of them is to a distant location such as Berchtesgaden, Trier, or Goslar, a railpass will probably wind up saving you a considerable amount of money. Even if the savings are less than that, a pass should still be considered for the convenience it offers in not having to line up for tickets (only to find that you're in the wrong line!), and for the freedom of just hopping aboard almost any train at whim. Possession of a railpass makes practical the use of extra-fare expresses (*EC, ICE, IC, IR,* or *D* types) for even short distances, and encourages you to become more adventurous, to seek out distant and offbeat destinations. You can also use them to save money by "going native" and staying at inexpensive inns in the suburbs instead of costlier city hotels, commuting each day by train. And, should you ever manage to get on the wrong train by mistake (or change your plans en route), your only cost will be your time—not an extra fare back!

The passes described above are sold by most travel agents, who also have current information and prices, and by mail from the Forsyth Travel Library mentioned on page 11. Alternatively, you could contact the nearest office of the German Railroad's North American agent, **DER Tours Inc.**, at 9501 West Devon Avenue, Rosemont, IL 60018, phone (800) 782-2424 (toll free) or (708) 692-6300; 122 East 42nd St., New York NY 10168, phone (212) 308-3100; 11933 Wilshire Blvd., Los Angeles CA 90025, phone (310) 479-2772; or 904 The East Mall, Etobicoke, Ontario M9B 6K2, Canada, phone (416) 695-1211.

If you've decided against a railpass, or live in Germany and therefore can't buy one, you still have some money-saving options. Before purchasing a full-fare ticket you should always ask about special one-day excursion fares *(Ausflugskarte)* that might be applicable to your journey. 24-hour passes are usually available for use on the S-Bahn trains and local public transportation in and around major cities. Remember that there's a premium fare for rides on all ICE trains, and that a surcharge (the dreaded *Zuschlag*) is required for rides on all EC or IC trains, or on IR or D trains for distances up to 50 kilometers (31 miles). Railpass users don't pay these extra charges.

Germany also has a few privately owned small railroads, which do not accept railpasses but may grant discounts to their holders. The only ones that pertain to the daytrips in this book are the rack-railways to the Zugspitze and Wendelstein peaks, and the steam train at Chiemsee.

BY CAR:

Many tourists prefer to explore Germany by car, especially when several people are traveling together. The country's extensive network of superhighways *(Autobahnen)* is world-famous for its virtually unlimited speeds. And Germans do tend to drive *very* fast, frequently over 100 miles per hour. Autobahn routes are marked by the letter "A" preceding their number, while the letter "E" indicates international routes. Secondary roads, including those of the "B" category, have strictly enforced speed limits. The use of seat belts is mandatory at all times, and penalties for driving while intoxicated can be quite severe. Driving in German towns is often tricky, what with the one-way streets

(Einbahnstrassen) and numerous pedestrian zones. German cars now use unleaded gasoline *(bleifrei Benzin).*

A brief glossary for drivers is provided on page 18. For more comprehensive automotive terms, you may want to use a pocket-sized phrase book, such as *German for Travellers* by Berlitz.

Cars may be rented from a large number of agencies at airports and in major towns, including some familiar American firms. The German Railroad (DB) makes arrangements for car rentals at major train stations, reservations for which can be made at the stations or even on board some trains. The **fly/drive plans** offered in conjunction with transatlantic flights on **Lufthansa** and some other carriers can save you a great deal of money over what it would cost to purchase these services separately. Full details on current offerings are available from your local travel agent, who should be consulted as far ahead as possible since advance purchase is required.

BY AIR:

Lufthansa operates an extensive **domestic air service** that is very useful in traveling between the base cities, such as Munich to Hamburg or Frankfurt to Berlin. Since reunification, the airline now connects Berlin with all major German cities.

As to **transatlantic service**, Lufthansa offers more flights between Germany and North America than any other carrier, serving a total of 16 North American cities including 11 in the U.S.A. The majority of these land at Frankfurt; one of the largest, most modern, and busiest airports in the world. This is the hub of Lufthansa's world-wide service—where easy connections can be made to virtually all major cities in Europe and around the globe. The airline also has direct flights from North America to Munich, Düsseldorf, and Hamburg.

The **Frankfurt Airport** has commuter train *(S-Bahn)* service to Frankfurt's main station as well as to other points in the city. These run at 10-minute intervals and take only 11 minutes for the ride. Departures are from a station located on the lower level of the terminal building, near the luggage claim area. Tickets should be purchased from the vending machines, which have instructions in English (see page 153 for details). Commuter trains to Mainz and Wiesbaden also leave from here, as do InterCity express trains to other cities in Germany and beyond. The railroad offers a handy baggage delivery service to and from other destinations in Germany. Those wishing to take a taxi to downtown Frankfurt will find the fares to be reasonable.

BY BICYCLE:

Not for traveling from a base city, of course, but once you've gotten to your destination by train or car you may want to **rent a bicycle**

A DRIVER'S GLOSSARY

Achtung .... Caution
Anfang .... Start, entrance
Anlieger Frei .... Local residents only
Ausfahrt Freihalten .... No parking in driveway
Ausgang .... Exit
Aussichtspunkt .... Look-out point
Autobahn .... High-speed limited-access highway, indicated by letter "A" preceding route number
Autovermietung .... Car rental
Baustelle .... Road construction
Benzin .... Gasoline (Petrol)
Blaue Zone .... Time-indicator disc required for park-
Bleifrei .... ing Unleaded gasoline
Bremsen .... Brakes
Brücke .... Bridge
Bundesstrasse .... Main road, indicated by letter "B" preceding route number
Durchfahrt Verboten .... No thoroughfare
Durchgangsverkehr .... Through traffic
Einbahnstrasse .... One-way street
Einordnen .... Follow in line
Ende .... End
Ende des Parkverbots .... End of no-parking zone
Engstelle .... Road narrows
Fähre .... Ferry
Freie Fahrt .... No speed limit
Führerschein .... Driver's license
Fussgänger .... Pedestrians
Gefahr .... Danger
Gefährliches Gefälle .... Dangerous descent
Gefährliche Steigung .... Steep hill
Gegenverkehr .... Two-way traffic
Geradeaus .... Straight ahead
Halt .... Stop
Kein Durchgang .... No thoroughfare
Kurzparkzone .... Short-term parking
Kurve .... Bend in road
Langsam .... Slow
Links .... Left
Links Fahren .... Keep to the left
LKW .... Truck
Mietwagen .... Rental car
Münztank .... Coin-operated gasoline pump
Nebel .... Fog

Öl	Oil
Parken Verboten	No parking
Parkplatz	Parking place
PKW	Private car
Rechts	Right
Rechts Fahren	Keep to the right
Reifen	Tire
Sackgasse	Dead-end street (cul-de-sac)
Schlechte Fahrbahn	Rough road surface
Schule	School zone
Steinschlag	Falling rocks
Stadtmitte	Town center
Strasse	Road
Strasse Gesperrt	Road closed
Strassenarbeiten	Road construction
Strassenkarte	Road map
Tankstelle	Gasoline (Petrol) station
Überholen Verboten	No passing
Umleitung	Detour (Diversion)
Unfall	Accident
Verengte Fahrbahn	Road narrows
Vorfahrt	Priority
Vorsicht	Attention
Wagen	Automobile
Wasser	Water
Zoll	Customs

DAYS OF THE WEEK:

Montag	Monday
Dienstag	Tuesday
Mittwoch	Wednesday
Donnerstag	Thursday
Freitag	Friday
Samstag (Sonnabend)	Saturday
Sonntag	Sunday
Heute	Today
Morgen	Tomorrow
Feiertag	Holiday

SEASONS:

Jahreszeit	Season
Frühling	Spring
Sommer	Summer
Herbst	Autumn
Winter	Winter

APPROXIMATE CONVERSIONS

1 Mile = 1.6 km

1 KM = 0.6 miles

1 U.S. Gallon = 3.78 liters

1 Liter = 0.26 U.S. gallons

(Fahrradverleihung) to use on the suggested tour instead of walking or taking local buses. Bikes can be rented in nearly all towns; just ask at the local tourist office for current details.

A particularly good deal is offered by the Federal Railroad, which rents bicycles at over 270 of its stations. These may even be returned to another station if desired. Those coming by train get a substantial discount on the already low prices of this service, called *Fahrrad am Bahnhof,* which operates from April through October. Don't expect any 15-speed racing bikes, however. Participating train stations, where applicable, are listed in the "Practicalities" section of each day-trip in this book.

Bikes may also be taken along with you on any train equipped with a baggage car *(Gepäckwagen)* for a small extra fee, called a *Fahrradkarte.* This does not apply to EC, ICE, or IC expresses, or to some local trains.

PACKAGE PLANS:

The cost of your German trip can be cut substantially by selecting one of the many attractive plans that combine transatlantic airfares with hotel accommodations, car rentals, or railpasses. An especially wide choice is available in conjunction with Lufthansa flights, as well as with some other carriers. Since the offerings change frequently and advance purchase is necessary, you should consult with a travel agent well ahead of time.

HOLIDAYS:

Legal holidays *(Feiertage)* in West Germany are:
January 1 *(Neujahr)*
Good Friday *(Karfreitag)*
Easter Monday *(Ostermontag)*
May 1 (Labor Day) *(Tag der Arbeit)*
Ascension Day (40 days after Easter) *(Christi Himmelfahrt)*
Pentecost Monday (2nd Monday after Ascension) *(Pfingstmontag)*
Corpus Christi (variable, southern Germany only)
August 15 (Assumption Day)
October 3 (German Unity Day) *(Tag der Deutschen Einheit)*
November 1 (All Saints' Day, some southern and Rhineland states)
Repentance Day (variable date in November) *(Busstag)*
December 25 & 26 (Christmas) *(Weihnachstage)*

FOOD AND DRINK:

Several choice restaurants are listed for each destination in this book. Most of these are long-time favorites of experienced travelers and serve classical German cuisine. Their approximate price range, based on the least expensive complete meal offered, is shown as:

$ — Inexpensive, but may have fancier dishes available.

$$ — Reasonable. These establishments may also feature less expensive daily specials.

$$$ — Luxurious and expensive.

X: — Days or periods closed.

If you're really serious about dining you should consult an up-to-date restaurant and hotel guide such as the classic red-cover *Michelin Deutschland,* issued annually in February and generally available in good bookstores; or the annual *Gault-Millau Guide Deutschland für Gourmets,* usually found only in German bookstores.

It is always wise to check the posted **menu** outside the restaurant before entering, paying particular attention to any daily specials listed on the *Tageskarte,* which are often offered only at lunch *(Mittagsessen).* **Fixed-price complete meals** are either called *Gedecke* or *Menus* (in the French sense of the word), while the regular **à la carte** menu is called a *Speisekarte.* The use of a pocket-sized translator book such as the *Marling Menu Master* will encourage you to try unfamiliar dishes without fear. Most restaurants have a weekly *Ruhetag,* a day on which they are closed. You are generally free to sit at any table except one that is marked *Reserviert,* or at the *Stammtisch,* which is set aside for regulars and is usually decorated with a fancy sign. In crowded restaurants you may be asked to share a table with strangers, a common and perfectly acceptable practice. A **service charge** *(Bedienung)* and taxes are included in the price, but it is customary to round out the amount to the nearest mark or give a small additional tip directly to the waiter.

If you're in a hurry to get on with sightseeing, you can save both time and money by eating lunch at an **Imbiss**, usually a stand-up counter where tasty sausages and similar dishes are dispensed along with beer and other beverages. **Department-store restaurants** are another good choice for economical and quick lunches, as are **outdoor farmers' markets** such as the Viktualien Markt in central Munich and the one by the cathedral in Freiburg. American-style **fast-food chains** have invaded Germany with a vengeance, and can be found in just about every town along with the ubiquitous **pizzerias**. On the slightly more elegant side, **ethnic restaurants** featuring Italian, Balkan, Turkish, and other foreign cuisines at inexpensive prices have become immensely popular in the larger cities as Germany becomes more and more of a multi-cultural society.

Beer remains the national beverage of Germany, and comes in a bewildering variety of tastes. Its purity is protected by the famous *Reinheitsgebot*, the world's oldest food-protection law, enacted in Bavaria in 1516 and strictly enforced throughout the nation. This guarantees that nothing can go into German beer made for domestic consumption except malt, hops, yeast, and water; the sole exception being wheat for some specialty beers. No chemical preservatives of any kind are allowed.

The most common types of German beers are *Export*—the closest thing to an American brew—and *Pils*, which is considerably more bitter. Another popular favorite is *Weizenbier*, a refreshingly tart beverage made from wheat. Traditional old-fashioned beers still flourish in isolated pockets; including *Kölsch* in Cologne, *Alt* in Düsseldorf, and *Rauchbier* in Bamberg—three beer-lovers' daytrip destinations in this book. Some of the other excursions that are especially attractive for the quality of the local beers are to Munich, the Ammersee, and Bremen.

Wine is Germany's other beverage, and may be even more popular than beer in some regions. The superior (and slightly sweet) whites of the *Rheingau* district, extending along the northern bank of the Rhine from near Wiesbaden to above Rüdesheim, are considered to be the best of their type in the world. Wine lovers will surely enjoy the daytrips to Würzburg and Rüdesheim!

RAINY-DAY TRIPS:

Alas, it does occasionally rain! If that happens while you're in **Munich**, you'll still have plenty of places to visit including the great museums described on pages 31 through 40, or the many indoor beer halls. However, with a railpass ticking away its validity you might still feel the urge for a daytrip, showers or not. **Augsburg** and **Nürnberg** are particularly well suited to wet weather explorations, as both have excellent museums and other indoor attractions that can be easily reached by public transportation.

Those staying in **Frankfurt** can while away any rainy spells along the Schaumainkai, which features nearly a mile of wall-to-wall museums. The best wet-weather daytrip possibilities are to **Mainz, Cologne**, and **Düsseldorf** because they also have wonderful museums linked by public transportation; and to **Freiburg** because, as the sunshine capital of Germany, it probably isn't raining there. If you're in **Hamburg** during one of its periodic wet spells, you could do worse than to visit its museums or go shopping in its many midtown indoor arcades. None of the daytrips from that city can be recommended for rainy days, however.

SUGGESTED TOURS:

The do-it-yourself walking tours in this book are relatively short and easy to follow. They always begin at the local train station since most readers will be traveling by train. Those going by car can make a simple adjustment. Suggested routes are shown by heavy broken lines on the maps, while the circled numbers refer to major attractions or points of reference along the way, with corresponding numbers in the text.

Trying to see everything in any given town could easily become an exhausting marathon. You will certainly enjoy yourself more by being selective and passing up anything that doesn't catch your fancy in favor of a friendly *Bierstube*. Forgiveness will be granted if you fail to visit *every* church.

Practical information, such as the opening times of various attractions, is as accurate as was possible at the time of writing. Everything is, of course, subject to change. You should always check with the local tourist office if seeing a particular sight is crucially important to you.

You can estimate the amount of time that any segment of a walking tour will take by looking at the scaled map and figuring that the average person covers about 100 yards a minute.

*OUTSTANDING ATTRACTIONS:

An *asterisk before any attraction, be it an entire daytrip or just one painting in a museum, denotes a special treat that in the author's opinion should not be missed. Asterisks are used very sparingly in this book; even so, you'll probably disagree with some of the choices, but on balance these should appeal to most travelers most of the time.

TOURIST INFORMATION:

Virtually every town, or even *Dorf*, of any tourist interest in Germany has its own information office that can help you with specific questions or book local accommodations. Usually identified by the words *Verkehrsbüro, Verkehrsverein, Verkehrsamt, Kurverwaltung*, or simply by the letter "**i**," they almost invariably have English-speaking personnel on staff. The smaller ones are frequently closed on Saturday afternoons and all day on Sundays.

The locations of these offices are shown on the town maps by the word "**info.**," and repeated along with the phone number under the "Practicalities" section for each trip. To phone ahead from another town in Germany you must first dial the area code, which always begins with 0 and is shown in parentheses, followed by the local number. Calling ahead is useful if the whole reason for your daytrip hinges on seeing a particular sight that might possibly be closed, or perhaps to check the weather. Most public phones accept the *Telefonkarte,* a convenient pre-paid calling card sold in various denominations at post offices and elsewhere. Many also accept coins, and return those that are not used.

ADVANCE PLANNING INFORMATION:

The **German National Tourist Office** (DZT) has branches throughout the world that will gladly provide help in planning your trip. In North America these are located at:

122 East 42nd St.,
New York, NY 10168-0072
Phone (212) 661-7200, FAX (212) 661-7174

11766 Wilshire Blvd.,
Los Angeles, CA 90025
Phone (310) 575-9799, FAX (310) 575-1565

175 Bloor Street East,
Toronto, Ont. M4W 3R8, Canada
Phone (416) 968-1570, FAX (416) 958-1986

In England, they are at 65 Curzon Street, **London** W1Y 7PE, phone (0171) 495-3990, FAX (0171) 495-6129.

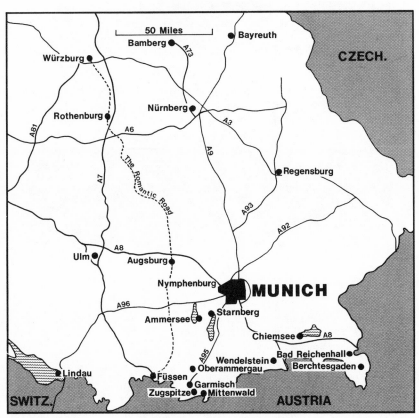

Bavaria

The enormous state, or *Land,* of Bavaria with its splendid capital of Munich did not really become a part of Germany until the last century, and then only with reluctance. It still fancies itself as an almost sepa-rate nation, a fact made abundantly clear by the border signs proudly proclaiming *Freistaat Bayern.* With customs, manners, traditions, and even a dialect that is alien to the rest of the Federal Republic, Bavari-ans are a race apart; genuinely friendly, open and warm-hearted to strangers—yet hide-bound conservatives at heart. This is the land of

The Karwendel Mountain at Mittenwald

fantastic castles, snow-capped mountains, clear blue lakes, and magnificent cities. In the eyes of many tourists it is the very essence and soul of Germany.

You may want to start your Bavarian adventures with an exploration of Munich, for which two walking tours are described in the next few pages. Following that are 20 carefully selected destinations, all within easy daytrip range of the city. It is not actually necessary to stay in Munich itself to make these trips—many will prefer basing themselves in the outlying districts, which are often more charming and less expensive. Munich's superb *S-Bahn* commuter trains make this a highly attractive alternative.

Another good option is to stay in Augsburg, which has excellent hotels, is close to Munich, and has direct transportation to most of the destinations. Garmisch-Partenkirchen makes a superb base for exploring much of the Alps, as does Würzburg for Franconia.

Four of the daytrips from Munich can also be made from Frankfurt. These are Rothenburg, Würzburg, Nürnberg, and Bamberg. Two other Bavarian towns, Miltenberg and Aschaffenburg, are included in Section III as they are much closer to Frankfurt and The Rhineland than to Munich.

Munich

(München)

*The Old City

Everyone loves Munich. It is Germany's favorite good-time city, a place that is both elegant and sophisticated and yet seems to be perpetually drenched in a beery earthiness. Bavaria's capital lives in the best of two worlds—in some ways a southern city almost belonging to the Mediterranean, and in others an affluent northern metropolis. Many of its streets are reminiscent of Rome or Athens, but under those cobblestones runs a transit system of Teutonic efficiency. Buildings that appear to be from earlier centuries are often post-World-War-II reconstructions, built from the ashes of destruction and already imbued with the patina of age.

Not really old as German cities go, Munich was founded in 1158 as a place to collect taxes from the lucrative salt trade. Its site, next to a 9th-century Benedictine abbey, gave it the appellation *zu den Mönchen*—"Place of the Monks"—which easily corrupted into the present German name of *München*. A little child-monk, the *Münchner Kindl*, still adorns the city's coat of arms. By 1180 the new settlement came under the control of the Wittelsbach family, who as dukes, and later kings, made it their capital. From here they ruled Bavaria until 1918, a span of over 700 years. It was this unbroken dynasty of art-loving sovereigns that was responsible for the splendid city of today.

Munich is famous throughout the world for its once-a-year *Oktoberfest*—16 days of beer-sodden revelry beginning in late September. Equally exuberant is *Fasching*, a bizarre carnival held just before Lent. Both epitomize the meaning of that untranslatable word, *Gemütlichkeit*, which for many tourists neatly sums up the special magic that is Munich's.

You cannot possibly see all of the city in a single day, or a week for that matter. The following tour was designed to take you past most of the major sights that can be reached on foot. Which of these you decide to actually visit will depend on the time available and, of course, your particular interests. The tour's length can be substantially reduced without sacrificing too much by skipping directly from Odeons Platz (7) to the nearby Hofgarten (14). Many will want to surrender to the lure of the Hofbräuhaus (15) and call it quits in that beer-lovers' paradise.

GETTING THERE:

Trains from all over Germany and Europe arrive at Munich's busy **Hauptbahnhof**, the main train station and probably the only one you'll be using. Local trains usually arrive on tracks 1–10 or 27–36, known respectively as the Holzkirchner Bahnhof and the Starnberger Bahnhof although they're all part of the same complex. S-Bahn commuter trains and U-Bahn subways stop at the underground levels, while long-distance buses use the platforms along the Arnulfstrasse side. The main part of the station houses the Munich Tourist Office, a post office, a hotel, several restaurants, a money-exchange bank, and numerous shops and services.

By car, Munich is at the hub of a network of Autobahns and major highways radiating out to all of Germany and the neighboring countries. To find your way to the city center, just follow the *Stadtmitte* signs.

By air, Munich's sparkling new **Flughafen München**, the international airport, handles frequent flights from major German cities, all of Europe, and much of the world including non-stops from North America. Fast, frequent S-Bahn commuter trains (route S-8) go directly to the main train station in about 40 minutes flat, with intermediate stops at the East Station and in the Old City. You could also take a taxi directly to your hotel.

GETTING AROUND:

Although this tour was intended for walking, you may want to use public transportation at some point. The system consists of subways, buses, and streetcars. A free **map** with **instructions** in English is available at the tourist office.

The city has *two* subway systems; the **U-Bahn** which remains underground, and the **S-Bahn** that pops up to the surface once beyond the inner city and continues on as a suburban commuter rail network. Railpasses are valid on the S-Bahn, *but very definitely not on the U-Bahn, streetcars, or buses.* Before boarding these (or the S-Bahn if you have no pass), it is necessary to buy a **ticket** or **Day Ticket** at one of the coin-operated ticket-vending machines in subway stations, by streetcar or bus stops, or on board those vehicles marked with a white letter "K." These are valid for the U- or S-Bahns, streetcars, or buses, or any combination going in a direct route to your destination. They must be canceled *(entwerten)* at the time of use by inserting them in a small time-stamping machine at subway entrances or on board the streetcar or bus. Your trip must then be completed within two hours. Failure to have a valid stamped ticket or pass could result in a fine.

The system is divided into fare zones, as shown on the maps, but all or virtually all of your travels will probably be within the basic inner-city zone. Note that fares are different for adults *(Erwachsene)* and children from ages 4 through 14 *(Kinder)*, indicated by pictograms on the vending machines. Both single-trip *(Einzelfahrkarte)* and the more economical multiple "strip" tickets *(Streifenkarten)* tickets are available.

If all this sounds confusing, you can relax. There is an easy way out. All you have to do is purchase an economical Day Ticket *(Tageskarte)* from the machine and cancel it. You can then travel at will from 9 a.m. until 4 a.m. the following morning, as long as you stay within the inner zone *(Innenraum)*. An *Aussenraum* version, good only in the outer zones, is also offered.

System-wide Day Tickets *(Gesamttarifgebiet)*, allowing you to travel to the farthest reaches of the combined systems, are available for about twice the price. These are a good deal for people staying in the suburbs who do not have railpasses. Incidentally, on weekends and holidays all adult Day Tickets are valid all day long and cover not just one person, but two adults, two children, *and a dog!*

PRACTICALITIES:

Munich is a city for all seasons. It is best to avoid making this trip on a Monday, when many of the important sights are closed. The local **Tourist Information Office** *(Fremdenverkehrsamt)*, phone (089) 239-1256, is located opposite Track 11 at the main train station. There is also a branch at the airport, phone (089) 97-59-28-15. Munich has a population of about 1,300,000, making it Germany's third-largest city.

FOOD AND DRINK:

Munich offers all sorts of places to eat, from three-star temples of gastronomy to the rowdiest of beer halls. Some good choices for a not-too-lengthy lunch along the walking tour route are:

Alois Dallmayr (Dienerstr. 14, a block north of the Neues Rathaus, upstairs) French-influenced cuisine above a renowned delicatessen shop. Phone (089) 213-5100. X: Sat. eve., Sun. $$$

Mövenpick (Lenbachplatz 8, a block northeast of Karlsplatz) Several dining rooms with different menus, outdoor tables in a garden setting. Excellent Swiss/German specialties. Phone (089) 22-03-13. $$ and $$$

Ratskeller (in the Neues Rathaus on Marienplatz) Authentic Bavarian specialties in several basement rooms, some of which are quite appealing. Phone (089) 22-03-13. $$

Franzikaner Fuchsenstuben (Peruastr. 5, a block southwest of the Residenz) Among Munich's best beerhalls, excellent food in colorful surroundings. Phone (089) 231-8120. $$

Spatenhaus (Residenzstr. 12, across from the Residenz) Continental and German cuisine in an old-fashioned beer hall with cozy corners. Phone (089) 290-7060. $$

Weisses Bräuhaus (Tal 10, 2 blocks southeast of Marienplatz) A traditional Bavarian inn since the 15th century, noted for home-brewed beer and roast pork. Phone (089) 29-98-75. $$

Augustiner (Neuhauserstr. 16, near St. Michael's Church) An old-fashioned restaurant with a separate beer hall, unchanged since 1896. Outdoor tables in the pedestrian zone. Phone (089) 55-19-92-57. $ and $$

Nürnberger Bratwurstglöckl am Dom (by the rear of the Frauenkirche) Traditional Bavarian sausages and grills in a crowded but enjoyable atmosphere. Phone (089) 22-03-85. X: Sun. $ and $$

Mathäser Bierstadt (Bayerstr. 5, between the main station and Karlsplatz) The world's largest beer hall is rough, rowdy, cheap, and fun. Go upstairs to the big hall *(Schwemme)* where there's live oom-pah music. Phone (089) 59-28-96. $

Pfälzer Weinprobierstube (Residenzstr. 1, part of the Residenz) An old wine cellar with hearty local dishes and plenty of atmosphere. Phone (089) 22-56-28. $

Hofbräuhaus (Platzl 9, 4 blocks northeast of Marienplatz) One of Germany's great tourist attractions, where beer triumphs over food. Check out the noisy ground-floor *Schwemme* hall, but you may prefer the central outdoor garden. Avoid the tour groups on the upper floors. Phone (089) 22-16-76. $

Haxnbauer (Munzstr. 2, a block southeast of the Hofbräuhaus) A traditional beer restaurant with unusually good Bavarian food and local ambiance. Phone (089) 22-19-22. $

Straubinger Hof (Blumenstr. 5, just south of the Viktualienmarkt) Small and very popular, has a nice outdoor beer garden and authentic local dishes. Phone (089) 260-8444. $

You can also eat outdoors around the Chinese Pagoda in the English Garden (11) or in the Viktualienmarkt (17), both very inexpensive and fast.

SUGGESTED TOUR:

You might find it convenient to start your tour at the main train station, the **Hauptbahnhof** (1), where the city tourist office is located. From there it is only a short stroll down Schützenstrasse to the real beginning of the walk, **Karlsplatz** (2). Popularly known as **Stachus**, this busy intersection should be crossed via the underground passageway.

Enter the **Altstadt** (Old Town) through the 14th-century city gate, the **Karlstor**, and walk along the pedestrianized Neuhauser Strasse to **St. Michael's Church** *(Michaelskirche)* (3). Built in the 16th century along Italian lines, it is one of the finest examples of Renaissance architecture in Germany. The bronze fountain to the left of its entrance commemorates the composer Richard Strauss, who was born in Munich in 1864. Step inside and visit the **crypt**, which contains the tombs of some thirty-odd members of the ruling Wittelsbach family, including that of King Ludwig II. Often called the "mad" king, whose extravagant fantasies nearly bankrupted the state, Ludwig was never really insane by any objective standards. His enigmatic life and tragic death in 1886 were full of mysteries; yet he left his country with an artistic heritage that continues to draw millions of visitors from all over the globe. As you travel throughout Bavaria you will frequently be exposed to his legacy, from the wildly romantic castles of Neuschwanstein, Linderhof, and Herrenchiemsee to the operas of Richard Wagner at Bayreuth. The crypt is open on Mondays through Fridays, from 10 a.m. to 1 p.m. and 2–4 p.m.; and on Saturdays from 10 a.m. to 3 p.m.

Continue on past the **Hunting and Fishing Museum** *(Deutsches Jagd-und-Fischereimuseum)*, which displays stuffed animals, weapons, equipment, and paintings of the sport, to say nothing of the world's largest collection of fishing hooks, in a former Augustinian church originally built in the 13th century and later remodeled in the Baroque style. It is open on Mondays through Saturdays from 9:30 a.m. to 5 p.m., remaining open until 9 p.m. on Mondays and Thursdays.

A left turn leads to the **Frauenkirche** (Church of Our Lady) (4), also known as the **Dom**, which has served as Munich's cathedral since 1821. Its **twin towers** are regarded as the city's trademark and look, appropriately enough, like two gigantic old-fashioned beer steins. The 325-foot-high **south tower** may be ascended—by elevator—for a good view of the city and even, on a clear day, of the Alps.

Built in the 15th century and badly damaged during the last war, this strikingly austere cathedral has since been restored. The original Gothic **stained-glass windows** had been put away for safekeeping before the bombs fell, and are now back in place along with other art

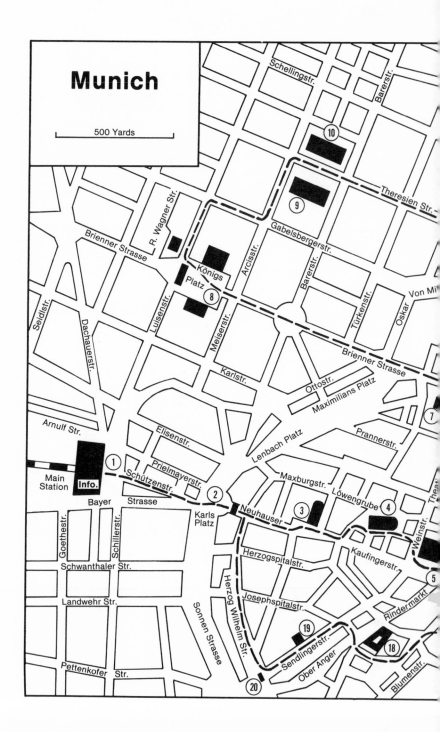

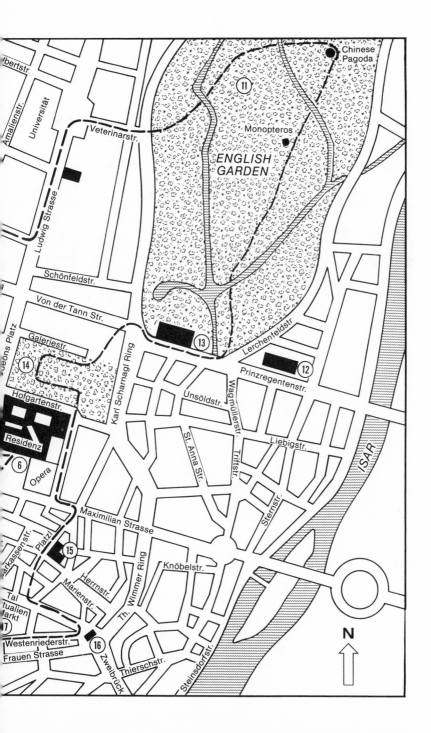

In the Marienplatz

treasures. These include the 17th-century **tomb** of Emperor Ludwig the Bavarian (1282–1347), by the south tower, and a modern **crypt** containing the remains of several Wittelsbach princes.

Continue past the rear of the church and turn right on Weinstrasse to **Marienplatz** (5). If you arrive by 11 a.m. you will be treated to a free show, complete with glockenspiel and mechanical figures reenacting a wedding of 1568 and a dance celebrating the end of a plague in 1517, given daily on the façade of the **Neues Rathaus** (New Town Hall). In summer, there are repeat performances at noon, 5 p.m., and 9 p.m. This richly decorated neo-Gothic structure was erected in the late 19th century and forms the northern wall of one of the most attractive squares in Germany, where you can sit down at one of several **outdoor cafés** while enjoying the passing parade. The Town Hall's **tower**, like that of the Frauenkirche, may be ascended by elevator for a splendid view.

In the center of the *Platz* stands the **Mariensäule**, a column dating from 1638 atop which the Virgin Mary watches out over Munich. A tiny casket inside its base allegedly contains a fragment of the True Cross. Near the northeast corner of the square is the **Fischbrunnen**, a reproduction of an old fountain where, each year on Shrove Tuesday, the city's apprentice butchers were dressed in sheepskins, put into the fountain, and made to throw nuts at people and splash them. They certainly had fun in those days!

To complete the scene with a romantic touch there is the turreted 15th-century **Altes Rathaus** (Old Town Hall) standing guard over the eastern end. This toy-like structure now houses the marvelous **Spielzeugmuseum**, where children's playthings from around the world may be seen daily, from 10 a.m. to 5 p.m.

St. Peter's Church *(Peterskirche),* just south of the square, is the oldest in Munich and actually predates the founding of the town. Rebuilt many times over the centuries, it has a lovely interior that is well worth visiting. The **tower**, affectionately known *Der Alter Peter,* may be climbed—on foot—for an unmatched **view** of the Marienplatz, Old Town, and possibly even the Alps.

From here, Dienerstrasse and Residenzstrasse lead to Max-Joseph-Platz, whose eastern end is dominated by the **National Theater**, home of the Bavarian State Opera. The premiers of several operas by Richard Wagner took place here during the reign of Ludwig II. First built in 1818, it was destroyed during the war and completely reconstructed to the original design in 1963.

The **Residenz** (6), fronting the north side of the square, was the royal palace of the Wittelsbach family from the 16th century until the end of the kingdom in 1918. It is a vast, incoherent complex of adjoining buildings in various styles; difficult to comprehend in a single visit, but well worth the effort if only for a tiny glimpse at the life to which royalty was accustomed. A visit to the Residenz is divided into three separate parts, each with its own admission.

First, there is the ***Schatzkammer** (Treasury), entered directly from Max-Joseph-Platz. A dazzling collection of Wittelsbach heirlooms, some over a thousand years old, fills ten rooms with crowns, gold, crystal, rubies, diamonds, and just about everything else that glitters.

Following this you may want to visit the **Residenz Museum**, a long trek through about a hundred rooms, many restored to their original appearance and others used as art galleries. While it is possible to rush through this in an hour or so, it is better saved for a rainy day when enough time can be devoted to a proper digestion of the riches on display. Rather lengthy guided tours are offered, or you can just stroll through on your own. The entrance is the same as for the Schatzkammer (above), and both are open on Tuesdays through Sundays, from 10 a.m. to 4:30 p.m. Both attractions are closed on Mondays and on some holidays.

The third highlight of the Residenz is the ***Cuvilliés Theater** *(Altes Residenztheater).* Originally built by the famed architect François de Cuvilliés in 1753, it was dismantled in 1943, just before the firebombs fell, and later reassembled in its present location. Lavishly decorated in gold, this small but exquisite theater is just about the ultimate in rococo décor. It is entered by way of a courtyard off Residenzstrasse, and is open on Mondays through Saturdays, from 2–5 p.m.; and on Sundays from 10 a.m. to 5 p.m., but closed on some holidays.

Continue along Residenzstrasse to the **Theatinerkirche** (7), an Italian Baroque church from the 17th century with a later façade by Cuvilliés. Its name derives from a small order of monks called the Theatines, founded by St. Kajetan. The restrained interior is especially beautiful and should not be missed. To the right of its chancel is the entrance to the **crypt**, where several of the Wittelsbachs are buried.

Just opposite the church is the **Feldherrnhalle**, an open loggia modeled after the famous one in Florence, which shelters statues of two Bavarian military leaders. From here the massive Odeonsplatz, scene of Hitler's abortive Beer Hall Putsch of 1923, opens the way to Munich's newer sections to the north.

If you feel up to it, you might want to make a lengthy **side trip** through a fashionable part of town, passing seven major museums and including a refreshing walk through a magnificent park. To do so, just follow the map past points 8 through 13. Otherwise, enter the nearby Hofgarten (14) and continue on from there.

The elegant Brienner Strasse leads to **Königsplatz** (8), a little bit of classical Greece in Munich. At the west end of the square stands the **Propyläen**, inspired by the entrance to the Acropolis in Athens. This and the surrounding pseudo-temples were all the doings of King Ludwig I (not to be confused with his grandson, "mad" Ludwig II), who had a peculiar passion for the Hellenic Age. Oddly enough, his second son, Otto, actually became king of Greece in 1832. The Grecian motif is continued on the north side by the **Glyptothek**, and on the south by the **Antikensammlungen**. Both are museums; the former specializing in Greek and Roman sculpture, the latter in small works of ancient art. Opposite the Glyptothek, on Arcisstrasse, is a large and rather pompous building in which the ignominious Munich Agreement of 1938 was reached between Hitler, Mussolini, Britain's Chamberlain, and France's Daladier. Now in somewhat seedy condition, it serves as a music academy.

The charming **Villa Lenbach** on Luisenstrasse, to the right of the Propyläen, provides a welcome touch of relief from all that grandeur. Formerly the home of the fashionable 19th-century painter Franz von Lenbach, it is now a small museum *(Städtische Galerie)* specializing in turn-of-the-century art, particularly that of Kandinsky, Klee, and others of the "Blue Rider" school. The museum is open on Tuesdays through Sundays, from 10 a.m. to 6 p.m.

Follow the map to the ***Alte Pinakothek** (9) on Theresienstrasse. This is one of the greatest art museums in the world, and by far the most famous in Munich. It houses the awesome collection of Old Masters put together over a period of centuries by the Wittelsbachs,

The Chinese Pagoda in the Englischer Garten

including works by Rembrandt, Rubens, Dürer, Van Dyck, El Greco, and so on. Allow plenty of time for this or, better still, come back another day. *The museum is closed for renovations until 1997, but its treasures may be seen at the Neue Pinakothek, below.*

Directly across the street is the very modern **Neue Pinakothek** (10), a stunning contemporary addition to Munich's architecture. Its collections encompass the 18th and 19th centuries, with fine selections of Impressionist and *Jugendstil* works along with the German Romantics. Again, it is worth several hours of your time and might be better combined with a revisit to the Alte Pinakothek. It is open on Tuesdays through Sundays, from 10 a.m. to 5 p.m., remaining open on Tuesdays and Thursdays until 8 p.m.

Continue down Theresienstrasse and turn left up Ludwigstrasse. Make a right on Veterinärstrasse just opposite the university and enter one of Europe's best city parks, the **Englischer Garten** (English Garden) (11). Laid out in 1789 by an American with British sympathies, the enormous and very beautiful landscape is a favorite retreat for *Münchners* of all ages, and a good place to watch them at play. On weekends, **bicycles** may be rented near the entrance. Following the map on foot or bike will lead you to the **Chinese Pagoda**, a strange wooden structure first erected in 1790 and rebuilt in 1951. It is surrounded by a popular **beer garden**, the perfect spot for a refreshment break. On the return stroll you will pass the **Monopteros**, a Grecian love temple from 1838 set atop a grassy knoll. Don't be surprised to see naked bodies lying about as sunbathing in the buff is quite common here.

Leave the park at Prinzregentenstrasse. To the left is the **Bayerisches Nationalmuseum** (Bavarian National Museum) (12) with its gigantic collections of just about everything that could loosely be termed art—an entire cultural history of Bavaria from Roman times until the 19th century. Especially noteworthy is the Tilman Riemenschneider room, devoted to that great 15th-century sculptor from Würzburg. The museum is open on Tuesdays through Sundays, from 9:30 a.m. to 5 p.m.

The **Haus der Kunst** (13) is yet another art gallery, this time erected not by the Wittelsbachs but by Adolf Hitler as a temple of official Nazi art. Somehow the bombs missed and it now houses the **Staatsgalerie Moderner Kunst**, a fine collection of significant international art of the 20th century, in the west wing, and special exhibitions in the east wing. Visits may be made on Tuesdays through Sundays, from 10 a.m. to 5 p.m., remaining open on Thursdays until 8 p.m.

Cross the busy intersection via the underground passageway and walk over to the **Hofgarten** (14), a formal garden from the 17th century. From here follow the map past the rear of the Residenz (6) to that tiny square so well known to generations of tourists, the **Platzl**. It was close to this spot that a brewery was set up for the royal court in 1589, expanding onto Platzl in 1644. When this was later moved, the space was filled by the world-famous **Hofbräuhaus** (15), built by the Wittelsbachs in 1896 to provide the poorer citizens of Munich with a place where they could drink cheaply, thereby avoiding revolutions. Today it is mostly visitors—millions of them a year—who guzzle down the one-liter mugs to the beat of an oom-pah band playing *In München steht ein Hofbräuhaus*. Whether you like this sort of thing or not, it is at least an interesting phenomenon; one that might very well bring your walk to an end right there. The ground-floor *Schwemme* (watering place) is the rowdiest (and most fun) level; if this gets to be too much you can always go outside to the courtyard garden. Leave the upper floors to the tour groups.

Survivors of the Hofbräuhaus—and those who avoided it—may want to carry on by following Orlandostrasse and a passageway through a building to Tal, a busy street leading to the **Isartor** (16). This 14th-century town gate, nicely restored, opens the way to the Deutsches Museum (see Additional Sights, below), which really requires an entire day in itself.

Follow the map to the **Viktualienmarkt** (17), a fabulous open-air market where all sorts of food delicacies have been sold since 1807. Near its center is a boisterous **beer garden**, a great spot for some late-

In the Hofbräuhaus

afternoon refreshments. Go to the kiosk for a mug of beer and join the natives at one of the long, plain tables. The small section with tablecloths is for waitress service, but only tourists go there. Inexpensive takeout food, mostly *Wurst*, is sold at several of the surrounding stands. Instead of regular beer, you might try *Radler*, a light beer/ lemonade mixture that's refreshing and won't make you groggy.

A few more steps will bring you to the **Münchner Stadtmuseum** (Municipal Museum) (18) on St.-Jakobs-Platz. Those who venture inside will be amply rewarded with a history of the city, puppets and musical instruments, and a splendid exhibition on the **history of photography** and movies. Don't miss the 15th-century **wooden carvings** of the Moorish dancers on the ground floor. The museum is open on Tuesdays through Sundays, from 10 a.m. to 5 p.m., remaining open on Wednesdays until 8:30 p.m.

Wander over to Sendlinger Strasse and visit the ***Asamkirche** (19), also known as the Church of St. John of Nepomuk. It was built by the Asam Brothers, Egid Quirin and Cosmas Damian, for their own use in the 18th century and is simply the most joyous riot of rococo décor to be found in Munich. The Asam Brothers' own house, next door at number 61, is nearly as fanciful.

Continue down the street to the 14th-century **Sendlinger Tor** (20), another medieval town gate, and follow the map back to the starting point at Karlsplatz (2).

ADDITIONAL SIGHTS:

Munich has several other attractions, mostly beyond walking distance of the center. One of these, Nymphenburg, is covered in the next chapter. Other suggestions for an extended stay include:

*Deutsches Museum—probably the world's greatest museum of science and technology; where exhibits are presented in an enjoyable and easy-to-understand manner. Allow plenty of time. The museum is open daily from 9 a.m. to 5 p.m., but closes on certain holidays. Located on an island in the Isar, its closest subway stop is the S-Bahn at Isartor Platz (16).

Schleissheim—another Baroque palace with great gardens, this one is nine miles north of Munich. Reach it on the S-1 line of the S-Bahn, getting off at Oberschleissheim. It is open daily except on Mondays and some holidays.

Theresienwiese—the site of the annual Oktoberfest, with a comically monstrous statue of *Bavaria*. The nearest subway is at Goetheplatz on the U-3 and U-6 lines.

Schwabing—often compared to Greenwich Village or Chelsea, but really a very different place, is best seen at night. Take the U-Bahn, lines U-3 or U-6, to Münchener Freiheit station and wander around on foot.

Olympic Park—a modern sports complex built for the 1972 Olympics, whose striking architecture is slowly fading. There is the usual revolving restaurant on a high tower, a feature common to many German cities. Car enthusiasts may want to visit the nearby **BMW Museum**. The fastest way to get there is by subway, on the U-2 or U-3 lines, to Olympiazentrum station.

Dachau—A pretty suburban village noted for its infamous Nazi concentration camp, now a museum, which is open on Tuesdays through Sundays, from 9 a.m. to 5 p.m. A disturbing documentary film in English is shown at 11:30 a.m. and 3:30 p.m. Take the S-Bahn, line S-2, to Dachau station, then bus number 722 to the site.

Munich
(München)
Nymphenburg

Another fascinating excursion to make while in Munich is a delightful half-day stroll through the Nymphenburg Palace and its surrounding park. This summer home of the Wittelsbachs is one of the most splendid royal palaces of Europe, in many ways outshining their downtown Residenz itself.

Begun in 1664 as a simple Italianate villa, Nymphenburg gradually expanded over the next century and a half as succeeding generations added their own ideas of how royalty should live. In much the same way as Versailles, the main palace is only part of the attraction. Hidden among the trees is an absolute jewel of a hunting lodge and several intriguing pavilions. The formal gardens are dazzling, while the carriage museum, botanical gardens, and royal porcelain factory all add their share of interest.

GETTING THERE:

Take route U-1 of the **U-Bahn** subway to Rotkreuzplatz, the present end of the line. Here you change to streetcar #12 in the direction of Amalienburg Strasse, getting off at the Schloss Nymphenburg stop.

By car, follow Arnulfstrasse from the main train station to Roman Platz, which is very close to the palace.

PRACTICALITIES:

Schloss Nymphenburg is closed on Mondays, and some of its smaller pavilions are closed from October through March. Fine weather will greatly enhance this trip. For more information contact the Munich tourist office listed in the previous chapter.

FOOD AND DRINK:

Schlosswirtschaft zur Schwaige (in the south wing of the palace, next to the Carriage Museum) The palace inn, both a restaurant and a beer garden. Phone (089) 17-44-21. $ and $$

Königlicher Hirschgarten (Hirschgartenalle 1, a half-mile southeast of the palace) Munich's largest outdoor beer garden, noted for its food. Phone (089) 17-25-91. $

SUGGESTED TOUR:

You will get a good view of the palace complex from the **streetcar stop** (1) on Notburgastrasse. Walk along the ornamental canal to the central building and purchase a combined ticket for the *Schloss*, carriage museum, and the park pavilions.

Enter the **Palace** (2) and step into the **Great Hall** *(Steinerner Saal)*, a vast room of rococo splendor. The ceiling frescoes, full of allegorical references, are well worth a detailed examination. Stroll through the gorgeously decorated north wing, noting the gallery with the paintings of Nymphenburg as it appeared in the 1720s.

For most visitors, however, the south wing is more interesting. Here you will find King Ludwig I's famous **Gallery of Beauties**—36 paintings commissioned by the king of the most beautiful women of his time. Included in the group is the notorious Lola Montez, an Irish-born "Spanish" dancer who ultimately became his undoing. At the ripe old age of 60 the king took her as his latest mistress, an act that did not sit well with the conservative Bavarians, and which was partly responsible for his forced abdication in 1848. Poor Lola was sent into deepest exile—the far-off United States, where she entertained folks from New York to California. Today she lies buried in Brooklyn.

Close to this is the bedroom in which Ludwig II, the "mad" king, was born on August 25th, 1845. You will probably be meeting up with him, or at least his creations, several times during your Bavarian adventures.

Other particularly interesting rooms nearby include the South Gallery, with its paintings of various Wittelsbach properties, and the Chinese Lacquer Room. The palace is open on Tuesdays through Sundays, from 9 a.m. to 12:30 p.m. and 1:30–5 p.m. During the winter season the hours are 10 a.m. to 12:30 p.m. and 1:30–4 p.m.

Leave the palace and walk out into the gardens. The part facing you, laid out in a formal manner, is called the **Large Parterre** (3). Statues of mythological gods adorn the paths leading to the fountain.

Follow the trail on the left to ***Amalienburg** (4), an exquisite hunting lodge in the rococo style by Cuvilliés. Its exterior is rather restrained, but once inside you will be treated to a visual feast. The most sumptuously decorated room here is the circular Hall of Mirrors. The Pheasant Room, kitchen, and bedrooms are also outstanding.

A path leads through the trees to the *Dörfchen*, a tiny group of cottages reminiscent of the *hameau* at Versailles. The nearby 18th-century pump house still works the big fountains in the parterre. Continue on to the **Badenburg** (5), an elegant bath house complete with a banquet hall and a luxurious indoor swimming pool. The trail now follows along the side of a lake to the Monopteros, a little love temple on the water's edge.

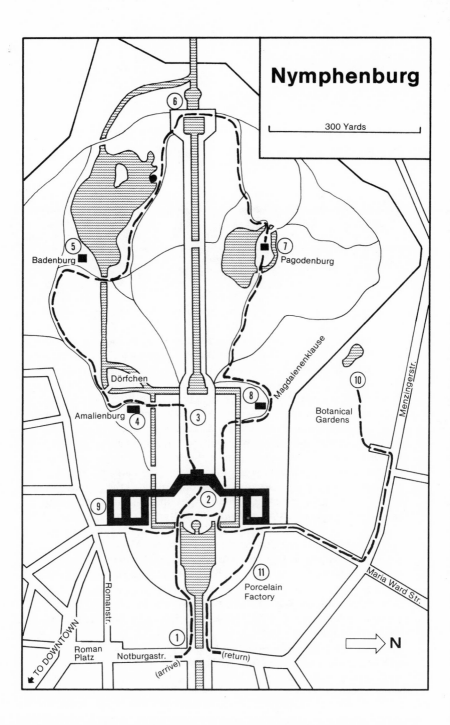

Nymphenburg

300 Yards

⑥

⑤ Badenburg

⑦ Pagodenburg

Magdalenenklause

Dörfchen

⑧

Amalienburg ④ ③

Botanical Gardens

⑩

Menzingerstr.

⑨ ②

⑪ Porcelain Factory

Maria Ward Str.

Romanstr.

TO DOWNTOWN

Roman Platz Notburgastr. ① (arrive) (return)

⟹ N

Nymphenburg Palace from the Large Parterre

The elaborate **Cascade** (6) marks the beginning of the main canal. Stroll through the woods beyond to the **Pagodenburg** (7), an octagonal tea pavilion whose upper floor is decorated in Chinese motifs.

Returning in the direction of the palace brings you to the **Magdalenenklause** (8), also called the Hermitage. A refreshing change after all the splendor, this at first seems to be in a state of ruin. Don't be deceived—it was built that way in 1725 for the private meditations of the ruler; the appearance of poverty then being very fashionable. The interior contains a strange chapel in the form of a grotto, and unadorned rooms where the ceremonies of court life could be avoided.

Continue through the ornamental gardens and exit the grounds via a passageway under the palace. To the right, in the south wing, is the **Carriage Museum** *(Marstallmuseum)* (9). Here the state coaches and sleighs of the Wittelsbachs are on display, including the utterly fantastic ones used to transport Ludwig II on his nocturnal escapades.

The **New Botanical Gardens** *(Botanischer Garten)* (10), slightly to the north of Nymphenburg on Menzinger Strasse, provide a delightful end to this trip. Various climates of the world are skillfully re-created and planted with appropriate flora in this wonderful landscape of natural beauty. It is open daily from 9 a.m. to 5 p.m., but the hothouses close between noon and 1 p.m.

On the way back to the streetcar stop (1) you may want to pause at the **Royal State Porcelain Factory** (11), where Nymphenburg porcelain is still made to traditional rococo designs and may be purchased from the factory.

Lake Starnberg

Long a popular playground for the people of Munich, Lake Starnberg is a delightful daytrip destination within sight of the Alps. Its particular attraction, beyond natural beauty, lies in the fact that it is so easy to reach. Only a half-hour ride from the city by commuter train or car, the lake has a good boat service that carries visitors onwards to lovely, secluded villages.

Royalty has been drawn to these shores for centuries. The castle at Berg, still a residence of the Wittelsbachs, was always a favorite of King Ludwig II. It was here, too, that his bizarre life ended in tragedy. The artistic collaboration between Ludwig and the composer Richard Wagner was first realized at Starnberg, with many later scenes in their strange relationship taking place nearby.

For travelers, the Lake Starnberg region offers a wonderful alternative to staying in Munich. A wide choice of accommodations, at prices often well below those in the city, is available through the local tourist office in Starnberg.

GETTING THERE:

Trains to Starnberg leave frequently from the lower level of Munich's main station. They may also be boarded at other S-Bahn stations, including those under Marienplatz or Karlsplatz. Take route S-6 in the direction of Tutzing for the half-hour ride to Starnberg. Those without railpasses should follow the ticketing instructions on page 28.

By car, Starnberg is some 16 miles southwest of Munich on the A-95 Autobahn.

PRACTICALITIES:

This trip is most pleasant on a fine, warm day in summer; and is well suited for weekend travel. The local **Tourist Information Office** *(Verkehrsamt)* in Starnberg is at Wittelsbacherstrasse 9, Phone (08151) 130-08. Bicycles may be rented at the train station during the season. The town of Starnberg has a population of about 20,000.

FOOD AND DRINK:

In Starnberg:

Seerestaurant Undosa (Seepromenade 1, on the lake) A big, lively restaurant, indoors and outdoors. Phone (08151) 80-21. $$

Tutzinger Hof (Tutzinger-Hof-Platz 7, at the north end of Hauptstr.) An old hotel restaurant noted for its Bavarian specialties. Phone (08151) 30-81. $$

Ristorante Da Roberto (in Seehof Hotel, Bahnhofsplatz 4, by the station) Italian cuisine, with an outdoor café. Phone (08151) 22-21. $$

Around the lake:

Strandhotel Schloss Berg (Seestr. 17, by the dock in Berg) A lovely, quiet hotel at the edge of the lake, with indoor and outdoor dining. Phone (08151) 501-01. $$

Dorint-Hotel Starnberger See (Assenbucherstr. 44, by the dock at Leoni) A modern lakeside hotel with two restaurants and outdoor dining. Continental and Bavarian cuisine. Phone (08151) 50-60. $$ and $$$

Café am See (Marienstr. 16, near the dock in Tutzing) A cozy little restaurant on the lake, specializing in fresh fish. Phone (08158) 74-90. X: Tues. $$

SUGGESTED TOUR:

Leave the **Starnberg train station** (1) and stroll over to the **pier**, just a few yards away. Study the posted boat schedule and decide whether to take a ride to Berg now, or see the town of Starnberg first. If you choose the latter, continue up Wittelsbacher Strasse to Kirchplatz, where the tourist office and parish church are located.

Cross Hauptstrasse and follow the map past the town hall, climbing uphill to the 16th-century **Castle** (2) around which the town developed. This is now occupied by government offices, but you can poke your head in for a look. Just beyond the *Schloss* there is a beautiful garden with fine views of the lake and the distant Alps.

Schlossbergstrasse leads over a boldly designed arch to the **St.-Josef-Kirche**, an enchanting 18th-century rococo church typical of Bavarian villages. Its interior is well worth a visit, especially for the high altar. Return to lakeside via the Günther Steig, Achheimstrasse, and Bahnhofstrasse. Turn right just before the railway to the **Heimatmuseum** (Local Folk Museum) (3). This is located in a charming early-16th-century log-built house, one of the oldest structures of its kind in Germany. Visits may be made from Tuesdays through Sundays, from 10 a.m. to noon and 2–5 p.m.

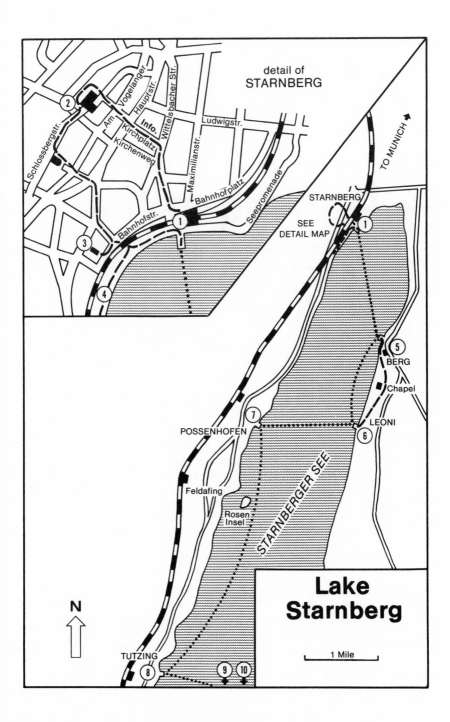

detail of
STARNBERG

Vogelanger

Hauptstr.

Schlossbergstr.

Am

Kirchplatz

Info.

Kirchenweg

Wittelsbacher Str.

Ludwigstr.

Maximilianstr.

Bahnhofplatz

Seepromenade

Bahnhofstr.

TO MUNICH

STARNBERG

SEE
DETAIL MAP

BERG

Chapel

LEONI

POSSENHOFEN

STARNBERGER SEE

Feldafing

Rosen
Insel

**Lake
Starnberg**

N

TUTZING

1 Mile

The Pier at Starnberg

From here you can take a lovely stroll along the **lakeside promenade** (4). There are several outdoor cafés and restaurants along the
way, as well as places where you can rent electric boats quite reason-
ably. This may be a more intriguing idea than the boat ride, or you
may prefer to rent a bicycle at the station to explore around the lake.

Walk back to the pier (1) and board the boat. The short round-
trip cruise *(Kurzrundfahrt)* goes to Berg and Leoni before returning to
Starnberg and takes about 45 minutes, not including stopovers. The
longer round-trip *(Rundfahrt)* covers the entire 12-mile length of the
lake, stopping at Berg, Leoni, Possenhofen, Tutzing, Ammerland,
Bernried, Ambach, and Seeshaupt; and then makes the same halts on
the way back. This takes a total of about three hours, again not count-
ing any stopovers.

A highly recommended trip is to take the boat to Berg, walk a bit
over a mile to Leoni, then either return to Starnberg or continue on
the long cruise. If you do the latter you can get off at Possenhofen or
Tutzing and catch an S-Bahn train back to Munich rather than return
to Starnberg.

Disembarking at **Berg** (5), walk up Wittelsbacher Strasse past **Berg
Castle**, a favorite residence of King Ludwig II. This is where he spent
his last captive hours after being deposed in 1886. It is still occupied

The Cross in the Water

by the family and cannot be visited. From here a path, Am Hofgarten, leads through the woods to the **Votive Chapel** erected in his honor. At the water's edge a **cross** marks the spot where the young monarch's body was found along with that of his doctor. Both drowned under highly mysterious circumstances, possibly murder but more likely a struggle to escape followed by suicide. Completely out of touch with reality, Ludwig's dream world was shattered and he had nothing more to live for.

Following the path to **Leoni** (6), you can either take a boat back to Starnberg or continue on the long cruise. Suggestions for a stop along the way include **Possenhofen** (7), where Ludwig's distant cousin, the empress Elisabeth of Austria, spent much of her time. At one point he was engaged to her younger sister Sophie, but this was hastily terminated by the king as the actual date drew near.

From here the boat passes the Roseninsel, a tiny island where Ludwig had yet another castle, and where some of his affairs took place. **Tutzing** (8), a quiet resort, is the last stop on the lake to be served by S-Bahn commuter trains. Those venturing beyond will have to return by boat. Two other interesting halts are at **Ammerland** (9), an ancient fishing village with a castle; and **Seeshaupt** (10), the southern end of the lake, practically next door to the Alps.

The Ammersee

Another lovely lake within easy commuting distance of Munich is the Ammersee. More secluded than Lake Starnberg and virtually unknown to foreign tourists, it has the added attraction of a gorgeous rococo monastery at Andechs, which brews what some consider to be Germany's finest beer. This is the perfect daytrip for anyone who loves riding boats, walking quiet trails, and drinking fabulous brew in a convivial atmosphere.

Like Starnberg, the Ammersee region has fine hotels and guest houses that offer lower prices than those in Munich—a practical alternative to staying in the city.

GETTING THERE:

Trains on the S-Bahn commuter service leave frequently from the lower level of Munich's main station, after first making underground stops at Marienplatz, Karlsplatz, and other midtown stations. Take the S-5 line all the way to the last stop, Herrsching, a journey of about 45 minutes. Those without railpasses should follow the ticketing instructions on page 28.

By car, leave Munich on the A-96 Autobahn in the direction of Landsberg to the Oberpfaffenhofen exit, then follow local roads past Wessling and Seefeld to Herrsching. The total distance is about 25 miles southwest of Munich. You can drive to Andechs instead of walking if you prefer.

PRACTICALITIES:

The Ammersee should be visited on a fine day in the summer season. This is a good weekend trip, especially on Sundays. The local **Tourist Information Office** (Verkehrsamt), phone (08152) 52-27, is near the Herrsching train station at Bahnhofplatz 2. **Bicycles** may be rented at the station from April through October. Herrsching has some 9,000 inhabitants.

FOOD AND DRINK:

Piushof (Schönbichlstr. 18, 4 blocks east of the pier in Herrsching) A quiet rustic inn with seasonal specialties. Phone (08152) 10-07. X: Mon. lunch. $$$

Alba-Seehotel (Seepromenade, just south of the dock in Herrsching) Regional specialties and classic cuisine. Phone (08151) 20-11. $$

Andechs Klosterbrauerei (in Kloster Andechs) Simple food and the monks' own beer, indoors or outdoors. $

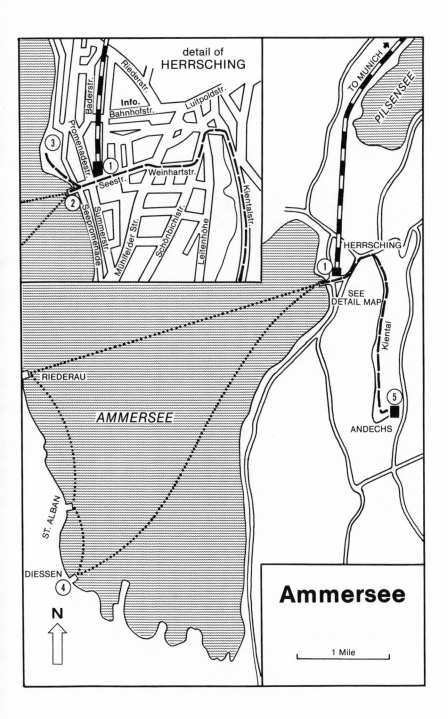

detail of
HERRSCHING

Riederstr.

Baderstr.

Luitpoldstr.

Info.
Bahnhofstr.

Promenadestr.

③

①

Seestr.

Weinhartstr.

②

Summerstr.

Seepromenade

Mühlfelder Str.

Schönbichlstr.

Leitenhöhe

Kientalstr.

TO MUNICH

PILSENSEE

HERRSCHING

①

SEE
DETAIL MAP

Kiental

⑤

ANDECHS

RIEDERAU

AMMERSEE

ST. ALBAN

DIESSEN

④

N

Ammersee

1 Mile

Kloster Andechs

SUGGESTED TOUR:

Leaving the **Herrsching train station** (1), stroll over to the **pier** (2) and check the schedule of boats to Diessen. If you have a wait before the next departure you may want to visit the **Kurpark** (3) with its picturesque little castle.

The boat ride to **Diessen** (4) takes a little over 30 minutes. Sights to see there include the sailing school and the **Stiftskirche** (Abbey Church), a masterpiece of the Bavarian rococo style.

Return to Herrsching by boat and follow the map to St. Martin's Church, where the **woodland trail** to Andechs begins as Kientalstrasse. The two-mile walk to the monastery takes you through a lovely ravine and alongside a little stream. At the end it climbs up the Holy Mountain, a place of pilgrimage for centuries. You can also get there by taking bus number 951 from the Herrsching station, or by bicycle following regular roads.

*Kloster Andechs (The Benedictine Monastery of Andechs) (5) overlooks the surrounding countryside from its lofty perch. Originally a castle dating from the 12th century, it was later rebuilt as an abbey due to the discovery of important relics in its chapel. The present church was first constructed in the 15th century. In the mid-1700s, however, it was completely redone in the rococo manner, with frescoes and stuccoes by the famous artist J. B. Zimmermann. The result is simply dazzling—one of the very best examples of that style anywhere.

From here it is only a few steps to the **beer garden**, where the second reward of your pilgrimage awaits. The golden brew of the Andechs monks is renowned all over the land. Join the queue for a one-liter stein and sit down at one of the indoor or outdoor tables for a rest before returning to Herrsching.

*Oberammergau and Linderhof

Everyone has heard of the once-a-decade Passion Play of Oberammergau. What many may not realize, however, is that this ancient woodcarvers' village is equally as attractive during the nine out of ten years when its stage is empty. People come here in all seasons to enjoy the mountains, the quaint old houses, and the magnificent palace of King Ludwig II at Linderhof.

Easy to reach, Oberammergau makes an excellent daytrip from Munich. By staying overnight or longer it can also be used as a convenient base for one-day excursions by bus or car to nearby Garmisch-Partenkirchen, the Zugspitze, Füssen, or Mittenwald.

GETTING THERE:

Trains for Garmisch-Partenkirchen leave hourly in the morning from Munich's main station. Take one of these as far as Murnau and there change to the connecting local for Oberammergau. This last segment of the trip is extremely lovely as you slowly climb the mountain. The total journey from Munich takes less than two hours. Special one-day return fares are available for those without a railpass. Service back to Munich operates until early evening.

By car, leave Munich on the A-95 Autobahn in the direction of Garmisch-Partenkirchen. Just north of that town, at Oberau, turn right on a local road leading to Oberammergau, which is about 50 miles southwest of Munich.

PRACTICALITIES:

A fine day in warm weather will make this trip more enjoyable. Schloss Linderhof is open every day, although its grotto and Moorish pavilion are closed in winter. Anyone going to Oberammergau while the Passion Play is on should expect crowds. The local **Tourist Information Office** (Verkehrsamt) is in the convention center on Eugen-Papst-Strasse. You can phone them at (08822) 10-21. **Bicycles** may be rented at the train station from April through October. Oberammergau has a **population** of about 5,200.

FOOD AND DRINK:

Wolf (Dorfstr. 1, near the Heimatmuseum) Local Bavarian dishes in a traditional setting, with game and fish specialties. Phone (08822) 69-71. $$

Wittelsbach (Dorfstr. 21, near the town center) International and Bavarian cuisine at a friendly inn. Phone (08822) 10-11. X: Tues. $$

Alte Post (Dorfstr. 19, near the town center) A Bavarian chalet-style inn with a rustic restaurant. Phone (08822) 10-91. $

There is also a restaurant and café at Schloss Linderhof.

SUGGESTED TOUR:

Upon arrival at the **Oberammergau train station** (1) you should check the posted schedule of buses to Linderhof. These may be boarded here or, more conveniently, in front of the town hall (5). Decide which bus you would like to take and how much time can be spent first in Oberammergau, allowing at least two hours to see Linderhof. Those with cars or bikes will, of course, be riding there instead.

The **Passion Play Theater** *(Spielhaus)* (2) is easily reached by following the map across the Ammer River. As the whole world knows by now, this sometimes controversial play is held once a decade, from May through September, in the years ending in zero. Every day during that period this otherwise peaceful village is invaded by thousands of visitors. Tickets to the event are available only in combination with overnight accommodation, and are usually sold out well in advance.

The play itself, depicting the story of Christ's Passion, lasts about six hours and uses the talents of some one thousand local amateur performers, many of whom have taken a few months off from their erstwhile occupation of woodcarving. It was first performed during the 17th century as a result of a vow taken by surviving villagers after deliverance from the black plague. The theater, seating about 4,000 spectators, is a marvel of ingenious design. It is open to visitors, and guided tours of its interior are offered daily from 10 a.m. to noon and 1:30–4:30 p.m.

Stroll over to the **Heimatmuseum** (3) for a look at some wonderful antique Christmas *crèches* and fine examples of the local woodcarvers' art. You may want to visit this on the way back to the station as it is open in the afternoons only, on Tuesdays through Sundays from April through October, and on Saturdays only the rest of the year.

Turn right at the square and walk down Dorfstrasse. This leads to the magnificent 18th-century **Pfarrkirche** (Parish Church) (4), well worth a visit for its marvelous rococo interior. Wandering around the

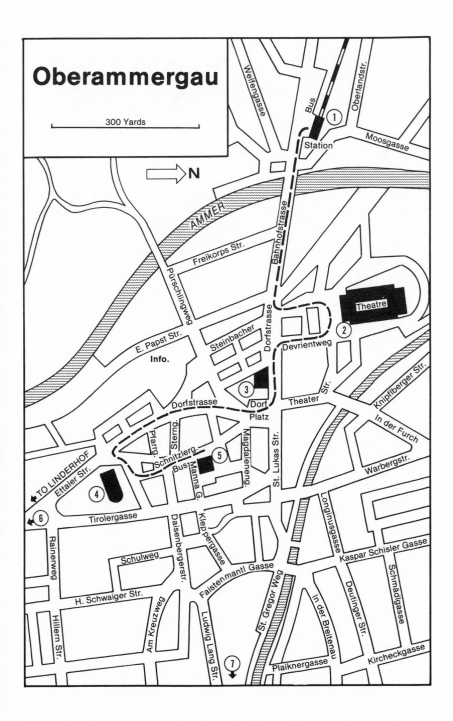

Oberammergau

300 Yards

N

Welfengasse

Bus ①

Station

Oberlandstr.

Moosgasse

AMMER

Pürschlingweg

Freikorps Str.

Bahnhofstrasse

Theatre

②

Dorfstrasse

E. Papst Str.

Info.

Steinbacher

Devrientweg

③

Dorf Platz

Theater Str.

Knipflberger Str.

Dorfstrasse

In der Furch

Warbergstr.

Pfarrg.

Sterng.

Schnitzlerg.

Bus

Manna G.

⑤

Magdaleneng.

St. Lukas Str.

TO LINDERHOF

Ettaler Str.

④

⑥

Tirolergasse

Rainenweg

Schulweg

Daisenbergerstr.

Kleppergasse

Faistenmantl Gasse

Longinusgasse

Kaspar Schisler Gasse

Schmädigasse

H. Schwaiger Str.

Am Kreuzweg

Ludwig Lang Str.

St. Gregor Weg

In der Breitenau

Deutinger Str.

Hillern Str.

Plaiknergasse

Kircheckgasse

⑦

Schloss Linderhof

nearby streets will reveal several examples of *Lüftmalerei*, the "air paintings" with which many of the houses are decorated.

The bus to Linderhof may be boarded in front of the **Rathaus** (Town Hall) (5) on Schnitzlergasse. By car or bike the distance is under ten miles. Leave town via Ettaler Strasse and bear right to Linderhof.

*Schloss Linderhof (6) is the most satisfying of "mad" Ludwig's creations, and the only one where he actually spent much time. Built between 1870 and 1879, the palace is best understood as a stage set in which a deranged mind could work out its fantasies. A incredible amount of opulence is packed within this relatively small structure.

To see the interior, as well as the grotto and Moorish pavilion, you must join one of the very frequent guided tours that begin in front of the palace. These are offered daily from April through September, from 9 a.m. to 5:30 p.m.; and again daily from October through March, from 10 a.m. to 4 p.m., but without the grotto and Moorish pavilion during that period. Some are held in English. Tickets are sold at the park entrance, opposite the bus stop. A descriptive booklet in English is also available.

When the palace tour is finished you should be sure to climb uphill to the **Grotto**, an artificial cave entered by way of a hinged boulder.

View of Oberammergau

Here the inside of the Venus mountain from Wagner's *Tannhäuser* is re-created, complete with lake, waterfall, and a cockle-shell boat in which the king was transported more deeply into his dream world.

Sometimes these illusions took other shapes, as when Ludwig decided to play the role of an Oriental potentate. For this, he erected the **Moorish Pavilion** on the path that leads back to the palace. Don't miss seeing this—the peacock throne is spectacular.

Finish your tour of Linderhof by strolling through the splendid gardens, then return to the bus stop and Oberammergau. An additional sight there, if time allows, is a cable car ride up the **Laber Mountain** for a superb view. The **lower station** (7) is about one mile from Dorf Platz by way of a path along the creek, just beyond the Wellenberg recreation center.

Garmisch-Partenkirchen

It was the Winter Olympics of 1936 that made Garmisch-Partenkirchen famous. Formerly two separate resort towns, they were merged for that event and have shared the unwieldy name ever since. Neatly split down the middle by the Partnach stream, with Garmisch to the west and Partenkirchen—once the Roman settlement of *Parthanum*—to the east, the combined entity has become Germany's leading center for winter sports. Today, most people just call it "Garmisch," as will this book.

Mountains are what Garmisch is all about. The town lies in a broad, flat valley at the foot of the highest peak in Germany, the Zugspitze, and is surrounded on all sides by towering Alps, whose bases literally run right into the village streets. Despite immense popularity, Garmisch remains remarkably unspoiled in its easygoing Bavarian manner.

By getting off to a very early start and cutting the tour short it is possible to combine this trip in the same day with one to the Zugspitze, covered in the next chapter. With its wide range of accommodations, the town also makes an excellent base for daytrips to Oberammergau, Mittenwald, or Füssen; all served by local buses.

GETTING THERE:

Trains depart Munich's main station hourly for the 90-minute trip to Garmisch-Partenkirchen, with return service until mid-evening. Reduced-price excursion tickets *(Ausflugskarte)* valid for 2 days are available.

By car, Garmisch-Partenkirchen is 55 miles south of Munich via the A-95 Autobahn.

PRACTICALITIES:

The resort is open all year round, but the Partnachklamm may be closed after a heavy snow or spring melt. Those making this walk should be prepared to get a trifle wet, and need suitable shoes. They might also want to bring along a folding umbrella and a small flashlight. The mountains can be chilly, even in summer. The local **Tourist Information Office**, phone (08821) 18-06, is at Richard-Strauss-Platz, in the center of Garmisch near the casino. Bicycles may be rented at the station. Garmisch has a population of about 27,000.

FOOD AND DRINK:

Some good restaurants are:

Reindl's Restaurant of the Partenkirchener Hof (Bahnhofstr. 15, 2 blocks east of the station) Well known for its international European cuisines. Dress up and reserve, Phone (08821) 580-25. X: mid-Nov.-mid-Dec. $$$

Mühlenstube (Hotel Obermühle, 4 blocks west of the casino) A dining room famous for its seafood. Phone (08821) 70-40. $$$

Post Hotel Partenkirchen (Ludwigstr. 49, near the Folk Museum) Traditional French and German specialties in a rusticated setting. Phone (08821) 510-67. $$$

Gasthof Fraundorfer (Ludwigstr. 15, near the Folk Museum) A rustic Bavarian inn, somewhat touristy but fun. Phone (08821) 710-71. X: Tues. $$

Clausings Post Hotel (Marienplatz 12, near the casino) Dining in a small, romantic hotel with 3 restaurants. Phone (08821) 70-90. $$

Badstubn (Klammstr. 47, in the swimming complex by the ice rink) Very popular, with an extensive menu. Phone (08821) 587-00. $

There are also several inexpensive, rustic places along the way to the Partnachklamm, and a pleasant café atop the Wank.

SUGGESTED TOUR:

Leave the **train station** (1) and follow the map along the Partnach stream to the **Olympic Ski Stadium** (2). Accommodating about 80,000 spectators, this gigantic outdoor structure was built by the Nazi regime as a showcase. Removing the swastikas did little to improve the architecture, but functionally it is still excellent and remains in use every winter. Entry is free.

Follow the road leading away from town for an easy and pleasurable walk in the woods to the dramatic Partnachklamm, one of the most memorable sights in the Bavarian Alps. In about one mile, level all the way, you will come to the tiny **Graseckbahn cable car** (3). Ride this to its upper station, near which refreshments are available.

Cross the terrace and continue along a trail with spectacular views, then descend a steep path to the upper end of the ***Partnachklamm** (4). This wildly romantic gorge, only a few feet wide but up to 263 feet deep, is filled with torrents of rushing white water. A narrow footpath with guardrails has been carved from the sheer rock sides, at times tunneling through impossible passages. You'll get a little wet, but that's a small price to pay for such a breathtaking experience. There is a modest admission charge, payable at the exit.

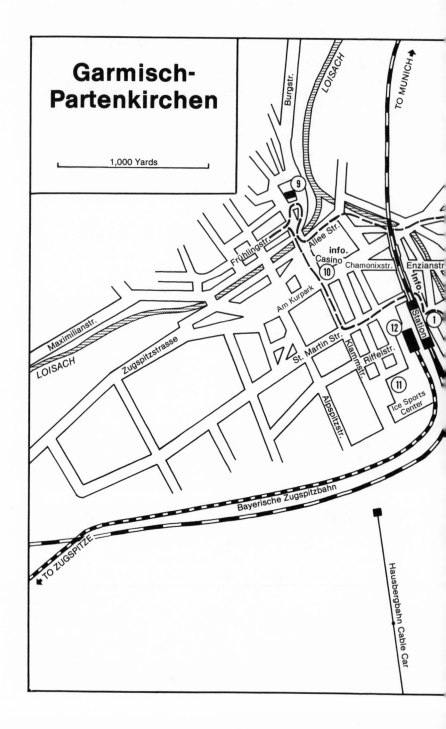

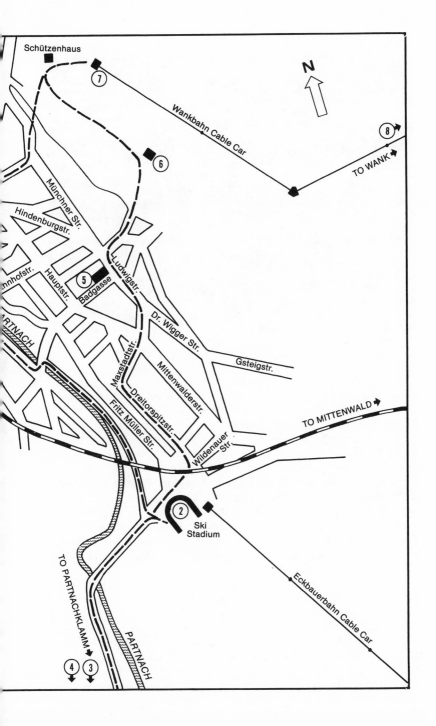

In the Partnachklamm

Leaving the gorge will put you back on the forest road to the Olympic Ski Stadium. Return there and either walk or take a bus to the **Werdenfels Folk Museum** *(Heimatmuseum)* (5) on Ludwigstrasse. This exhibition of mountain life in olden times is open on Tuesdays through Fridays, 10 a.m. to 1 p.m. and 3–6 p.m.; and on weekends from 10 a.m. to 1 p.m.

Now follow the map to the early 18th-century **Pilgrimage Church of St. Anton** (6), going past some remarkable Stations of the Cross along the hilly path. The interior of this chapel, with its frescoed oval dome and elaborate plaster work, is quite attractive and well worth the climb. On the way in you will pass a touching display of plaques, some with photographs, in memory of local sons who never returned from the last two wars.

The **Philosophenweg**, a trail with stunning views of the Alps, leads to the Schützenhaus. From there take a steep but short footpath to the lower station of the **Wankbahn cable car** (7). Board one of the small cabins for a lift up the mountain, but don't get off at the first stop. Stay on all the way to the **Wank summit** (8) for the most glorious panorama possible of the Zugspitze and the Wetterstein range towering over a toy-like Garmisch, safely nestled in its valley below. There is a sunny **outdoor café** to help you enjoy the scene even more.

View from the Wank Summit

At 5,850 feet, the summit is a center for the thrilling sport of hang gliding. This is a fast way down for some brave souls, but you will probably prefer to return on the cable car.

Leave the lower station and follow the map through Partenkirchen and into Garmisch. A path along the Partnach stream brings you to the **Kurpark**, from which it is a short stroll to the **Old Church** *(Alte Kirche)* (9). Located in a picturesque district, its origins may predate the spread of Christianity into this area. Or at least according to local tradition. Some of the mural paintings date as far back as the 13th century. The church itself was originally Romanesque, but later rebuilt in the Gothic style.

Take a look down **Frühlingstrasse**, a colorful street of quaint chalets. Straight ahead, at Zoeppritzstrasse 42, is the villa of the composer Richard Strauss, who died in Garmisch in 1949.

Along the way back to the station, you might want to stop at the **Casino** *(Spielbank)* (10) for a fling with Lady Luck, or visit the **Olympic Ice Sports Center** (11), which seats 12,000 spectators under one roof and is the largest in Europe. Close to this and adjacent to the train station is the **Zugspitz Bahnhof** (12), from which private cog-wheel trains depart for an excursion up the Zugspitze mountain by train and cable car, as described in the next chapter.

*The Zugspitze

One of the classic daytrips in Bavaria is an excursion to the top of the Zugspitze. At nearly ten thousand feet, Germany's highest peak offers a fantastic panoramic view extending across four nations. At one time only mountain climbers could enjoy this spectacle, but today an ingenious network of cable cars and a rack railway make the ascent fast, easy, and safe.

There are several possible ways up the mountain. The route suggested here is the most common and could be done in reverse if desired. If you don't like cable cars, you can go both ways by rail instead.

Germany shares its peak with Austria, which has its own cable-car system as well as a café and restaurant at the top. Be sure to bring your passport for crossing the lofty frontier.

This excursion can be combined in the same day with an abbreviated version of the Garmisch-Partenkirchen trip by getting off to a very early start, but only during the summer when the hours of sunlight are longer.

GETTING THERE:

Trains from Munich's main station leave hourly for Garmisch-Partenkirchen, a ride of about 90 minutes. From the Garmisch station walk over to the adjacent Zugspitz Bahnhof and take one of the hourly trains operated by the Bayerische Zugspitzbahn, a private company. Railpasses are not valid for this rack railway; however holders of the Eurailpass do get a discount. A bargain excursion ticket, going all the way from Munich or Augsburg to the highest peak and back, including the cable cars, is available.

By car, leave Munich on the A-95 (E-6) Autobahn and drive 55 miles south to Garmisch-Partenkirchen, parking there at the Zugspitz Bahnhof. Take the rack railway as above. It is also possible to drive to the Eibsee and pick up the trip from there.

PRACTICALITIES:

The ascent of the Zugspitze may be made all year round, but clear weather is necessary to enjoy the sights. Should the skies cloud over en route you might consider making the Garmisch-Partenkirchen or Oberammergau trip instead. Remember, however, that the weather

The Zugspitze towers above Garmisch-Partenkirchen
(Photo courtesy of Garmisch-Partenkirchen Tourist Office)

atop the Zugspitze is often clear when the valley is socked in. Ask at the Zugspitz Bahnhof if in doubt. You should bring a sweater or jacket, even in summer. The **Tourist Information Office** in Garmisch-Partenkirchen, phone (08821) 18-06, is at Richard-Strauss-Platz, in the center of Garmisch. You can phone the **Bayerische Zugspitzbahn** at (08821) 79-79-79.

FOOD AND DRINK:

Meals and drinks on the mountain are available at:

> **Sonn Alpin** (at the Zugspitzplatt) A rustic self-service restaurant with a terrace and panoramic view. $
>
> **Gipfel Cafeteria** (at the summit of the Zugspitz) A pleasant self-service restaurant with great views. $

In addition, there is a restaurant on the Austrian side of the peak, several places around the Eibsee and, of course, excellent choices in Garmisch-Partenkirchen.

SUGGESTED TOUR:

Leave the **Garmisch-Partenkirchen train station** (1) and walk over to the **Zugspitz Bahnhof**, a separate station for the privately owned rack railway going up the mountain. Purchase a round-trip ticket *(Run-*

dreise), which includes the rack railway, summit cable car, and the Eibsee cable car (unless you already have a bargain excursion ticket). Departures are hourly from 7:35 a.m. to 2:35 p.m., with some variations.

The train first travels along a relatively level route, then begins the climb to the **Eibsee** (3), a lovely lake near the foot of the mountain, reached in about 40 minutes. Those with cars can drive this far and board the train here. This is also the lower station of the Eibsee cable car, going all the way to the very top, on which you will probably be returning.

Shortly after this the train plunges into a long tunnel, winding its way like a corkscrew through the inside of the Zugspitze, and reaches the **Zugspitzplatt** (4) about 75 minutes after leaving Garmisch-Partenkirchen. At 9,340 feet above sea level, this is Germany's highest skiing area, where the fun starts in November and lasts until May. Walk out on the terrace for a ***view** from the heights, perhaps stopping at the rustic Sonn Alpin restaurant for a meal, snack, or drink.

This is still not the top of the Zugspitze. To get there, take the **Gletscherbahn** glacier cable car, which runs at least every half-hour and takes only four minutes to reach the peak.

Finally at the ***Zugspitzgipfel** (the very top) (5), stroll out onto the sunny terrace and survey the world nearly 10,000 feet below. It is possible to cross the **border** (6) to Austrian soil—or snow. Food, snacks, and drinks are available on both sides.

The return journey begins on the German side of the peak. From here take the large **Eibsee cable car** *(Seilbahn)* for the thrilling ten-minute descent directly to the Eibsee (3). Alternatively, you could return by way of the glacier cable car to the Zugspitzplatt (4) and then ride the train back, although this way is much slower.

From the Eibsee continue on by rack railway back to Garmisch-Partenkirchen, where you board the regular train to Munich. These operate until mid-evening.

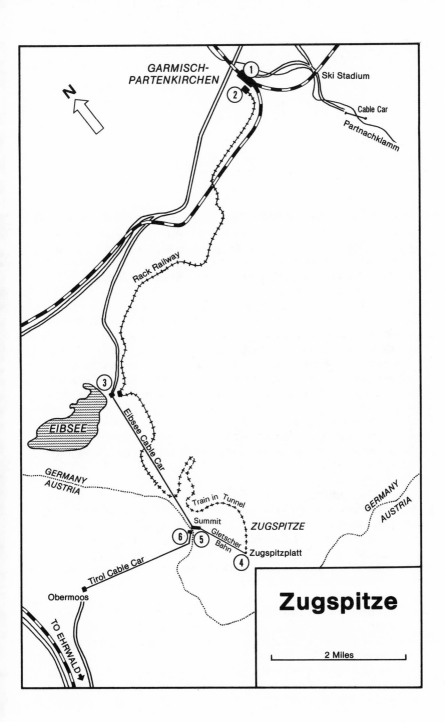

Mittenwald

If you were asked to design a stage set for an Alpine romance, you could hardly do better than to copy Mittenwald. This dreamy resort on the Austrian border has everything—a rugged mountain peak rising vertically from its own back yard, colorfully painted houses lining the peaceful streets, and a rich musical heritage as the "Village of a Thousand Violins."

The latter is Mittenwald's chief industry, next to tourism. Once a prosperous trading post on the Venice-to-Augsburg road, its economy fell to ruin as traffic moved to other passes. Then, in the 17th century, an unlikely miracle happened. A local lad named Matthias Klotz had moved to Cremona, where he learned the art of violin making from the legendary Nicolo Amati. On his return in 1684 he founded the trade that today exports Mittenwald string instruments to the entire world.

Although not as high as Garmisch's Zugspitze, a ride up the Karwendel mountain at Mittenwald is a more satisfying experience as its summit is wide open, allowing good opportunities for hiking, climbing, or just playing in the snow.

GETTING THERE:

Trains depart Munich's main station hourly for Mittenwald, a trip of less than 2 hours. Be sure to board the right car as some are dropped off en route. Return service operates until early evening.

By car, Mittenwald is 68 miles south of Munich's. Take the A-95 Autobahn to Garmisch-Partenkirchen, then continue on the B-2 road.

PRACTICALITIES:

Mittenwald is a year-round resort, but good weather is really necessary to enjoy it. You might want to bring along hiking shoes and a sweater for a romp in the snow atop the Karwendel. The local **Tourist Information Office**, phone (08823) 339-81, is in the town hall at Dammkarstrasse 3. **Bicycles** may be rented from several local firms, ask the tourist office for details. Mittenwald has a **population** of about 8,300.

Obermarkt and the Pfarrkirche
(Photo courtesy of Mittenwald Tourist Office)

FOOD AND DRINK:

Some especially good restaurants and cafés are:

Arnspitze (Innsbrucker Str. 68, 2 blocks south of the bridge) Elegant dining in Mittenwald's best restaurant. For reservations, Phone (08823) 24-25. X: Tues., Wed. lunch. $$$

Alpenrose (Obermarkt 1, near the church) Noted for its traditional Bavarian food, especially game dishes. Phone (08823) 50-55. $$

Hotel Rieger (Dekan-Karl-Platz 28, 3 blocks south of the church) A Bavarian-style inn whose restaurant has a good view of the mountains. Phone (08823) 50-71. X: Mon. $$

Hotel Post (Obermarkt 9, just south of the church) A 17th-century Bavarian inn serving local dishes in a rustic setting. Phone (08823) 10-94. $

Additionally, you can dine, snack, or drink surrounded by glorious scenery atop the Karwendel Mountain.

SUGGESTED TOUR:

Leave the **train station** (1) and follow Bahnhofstrasse to the **Rathaus** (Town Hall) (2), which houses the tourist office. From here it is a short stroll to the stunning Baroque **Pfarrkirche** (Parish Church) (3). Built in the 18th century by the famous architect Josef Schmuzer, its beautifully frescoed tower and richly decorated interior are symbols of the town's prosperity. In front of it stands a **statue** of Matthias Klotz making a violin.

A few steps down Ballenhausgasse brings you to the **Geigenbau und Heimatmuseum** (Violin-Making and Folk-Life Museum) (4). Step inside to view the process of making stringed instruments in a traditional workshop. The museum is open on Mondays through Fridays from 10–11:45 a.m. and 2–4:45 p.m.; and on weekends and holidays from 10–11:45 a.m. only. It may be closed in early spring and late fall.

Follow the map along a street called **Im Gries** to see the oldest houses in Mittenwald, among which are some outstanding examples of *Lüftmalerei,* the characteristic art of outdoor frescoes that originated during the Counter-Reformation to help proclaim the Catholic faith. Return to the church and turn right onto **Obermarkt**, the main street. This is also lined with some wonderfully frescoed structures. Walk along it to the edge of town, where it becomes Innsbrucker Strasse. Just before the first bridge a path leads off to the right.

Follow the country trail a short distance to the **Leutaschklamm** (5), a very narrow gorge filled with rushing white water. Actually in Austrian territory, the mountain ravine has a wooden gangway suspended above the torrent, which takes you to a spectacular 82-foot waterfall. The gorge may be entered during the summer season, or in winter if it is very cold. There is a tiny outdoor café at the entrance.

Return to Innsbrucker Strasse and stroll down Mühlen Weg. Cross a bridge and walk along the Isar, a river on which goods were once floated downstream to Munich. You will soon come to the lower station of the **Karwendelbahn** (6), a large cable car that transports you in 10 minutes to the heights of the Karwendel mountain.

At an altitude of 7,362 feet, the **upper station** (7) of the cable car looks nearly straight down on Mittenwald and offers fabulous views across the Bavarian, Austrian, and Italian Alps. Follow the trail leading uphill through the snow and pass the *Freistaat Bayern* sign. You are now in Austria for the second time in one day, although there is no customs post. A circular route takes you all the way to the very pinnacle *(Gipfel)* at 7,825 feet. Be careful, however. The highest section of the trail is steep and can be difficult without proper boots when the snow has become icy. This treacherous section is bypassed by a lower, easier trail. When you tire of all the sunshine, clean air, and marvelous scenery you can visit the **café** and **restaurant** adjacent to the upper cable car station for a drink or snack before returning to the valley and the train station.

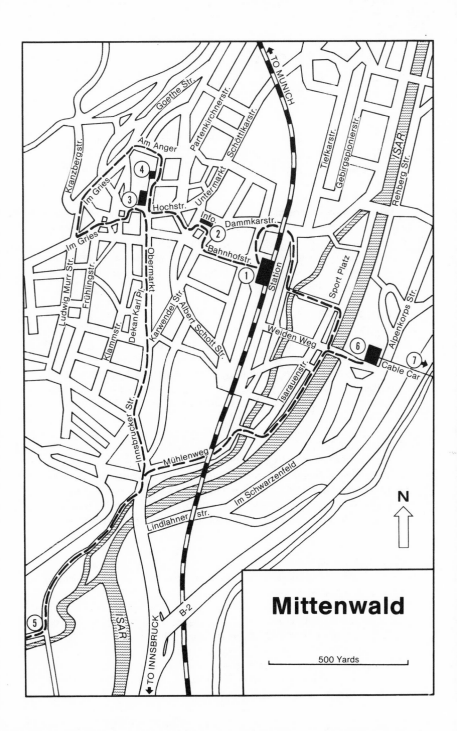

Mittenwald

500 Yards

N

TO MUNICH

TO INNSBRUCK

B-2

ISAR

Goethe Str.

Kranzbergstr.

Am Anger

Im Gries

Im Gries

Hochstr.

Partenkirchenerstr.

Schottikarstr.

Untermarkt

Info.

Dammkarstr.

Bahnhofstr.

Station

Tietkarstr.

Gebirgspionierstr.

Rehberg Str.

ISAR

Sport Platz

Alpenkorps Str.

Cable Car

Weiden Weg

Isarauenstr.

Obermarkt

Ludwig Murr Str.

Frühlingstr.

Klammstr.

Dekan Karl Pl.

Karwendel Str.

Albert Schott Str.

Innsbrucker Str.

Mühlenweg

Im Schwarzenfeld

Lindlahner str.

*Füssen and Neuschwanstein

The most instantly recognized symbol of Germany is undoubtedly Neuschwanstein, a sight that graces the covers of numerous guidebooks, brochures, and travel posters. Everything a fairytale castle should be, "mad" King Ludwig II's most spectacular creation has even served as a model for Disneyland.

While countless tourists trek through it every year, relatively few visit the neighboring castle of Hohenschwangau—in which Ludwig was actually raised—and only a small minority venture down the road to the delightful frontier town of Füssen. This trip combines all three for an exciting day filled with memorable sights, far more than you would get on a guided bus tour.

GETTING THERE:

Trains leave Munich's main station hourly for either Buchloe or Kaufbeuren, where you change to a local for Füssen. Check the schedule to determine where the change is made. Return service operates until early evening. The journey takes about 2 hours each way.

By car, leave Munich on the B-12 road, going west to Landsberg, then turn south on the B-17 to Hohenschwangau and Füssen for a total distance of 75 miles.

PRACTICALITIES:

The Royal Castles are open all year round, but are more crowded on weekends during the tourist season. There is a **Tourist Information Office** in Füssen at Kaiser-Maximilian-Platz, 3 blocks east of the station. You can phone them at (08362) 70-77. Bicycles can be rented at the station from April through October. Füssen has a population of about 16,500.

FOOD AND DRINK:

Restaurants near the Royal Castles tend to be touristy, with better values in Füssen. Some good choices are:

In Füssen:

Hirsch (Schulhausstr. 4, a block east of the tourist office) A rustic inn with a friendly restaurant. Phone (08362) 50-80. X: Jan. $$

Gasthaus zum Schwanen (Brotmarkt 4, near Kloster St. Mang) Bavarian and Swabian dishes in a cozy setting. Phone (08362) 61-74. X: Sun. eve., Mon., Nov. $

Reichenstrasse in Füssen

In Hohenschwangau:
Müller (Alpseestr. 14, near the bus stop) Country-style dining. Phone (08362) 819-90. X: Nov., Dec. $$$

Lisl und Jägerhaus (Neuschwanstein Str. 1, just south of the bus stop) Local and Continental cuisine. Phone (08362) 88-70. X: Jan. to mid-March. $$

SUGGESTED TOUR:
Leave the **Füssen train station** (1) and walk over to the bus stop across the street. Check the posted schedule of service to Hohenschwangau, also called *Königsschlösser* or Royal Castles. From this you can determine the amount of time available for exploring Füssen, allowing at least three hours for Neuschwanstein and Hohenschwangau castles.

Stroll down Bahnhofstrasse to Kaiser-Maximilian-Platz, where the tourist office is located. From here turn right on Reichenstrasse, a charming pedestrians-only street lined with outdoor cafés, which leads to **Kloster St. Mang** (2). This former Benedictine abbey was founded in the 8th century and rebuilt during the 18th. It now serves as the town hall and contains a small museum. In the courtyard is the

Chapel of St. Anne, noted for its unusual *Totentanz* (Dance of Death) painting from 1602, and the parish church with its ancient 9th-century crypt. Both are worth a visit.

Climb uphill to the **Hohes Schloss** (Castle) (3), once a residence of the bishops of Augsburg, who claimed it after Emperor Heinrich VII forfeited on a loan they had made to him. The present structure, curiously painted, dates from the 13th and 16th centuries. Long before that, in the 3rd century A.D., the Romans had a castle on the same site to protect their Via Claudia road that ran from Verona to Augsburg. The splendid Knights' Hall and other rooms may be visited daily, from 2–4 p.m.

Now follow the map to the **Lech Waterfall** (4), a very beautiful spot just yards from the Austrian border. Cross the Maxsteg footbridge over the cascade and return via Tiroler Straase. Once across the main bridge bear right onto Brotmarkt and Brunnengasse, then return to the bus stop.

Board the bus to Hohenschwangau *(Königsschlösser)*, a distance of about two miles. You could, of course, walk or drive there instead, or even rent a bike at the station. Check the posted return bus schedule upon arrival.

From the **Hohenschwangau bus stop** (5) it is a fairly steep climb via a woodland trail to Neuschwanstein Castle, with park benches provided en route. This can be avoided by taking one of the rather touristy horse-drawn carriages, or by a special bus (still requiring a little uphill trek), both of which start from a point opposite the bus stop, next to the parking lot. At the top of the climb, just below the castle, there is a restaurant and **outdoor café** where you can rest before tackling the main attraction.

*Neuschwanstein Castle (6) is pure fantasy. By comparison, King Ludwig II's other creations of Linderhof and Herrenchiemsee, although wildly extravagant, have at least some basis in reality—other kings have built lavish palaces for themselves before. For this one, however, there is no model except possibly the Wartburg in Thuringia. Ludwig was obsessed with strange notions of a transfigured past whose gods, knights, and swans form the hazy bedrock of Wagnerian opera. Completely withdrawn from the industrial world of the 19th century, this lonely monarch wrapped himself in a cloud of long-forgotten dreams, of which Neuschwanstein is simply the most spectacular manifestation.

The castle, rising from a rocky crag high above the Pöllat gorge, was designed by a theatrical scene-painter employed by the court. This was Ludwig's first creation, begun in 1869, but it remained unfinished at the time of his death 17 years later. He lived there for a total of 102 days, and it was from there that he was taken into custody after

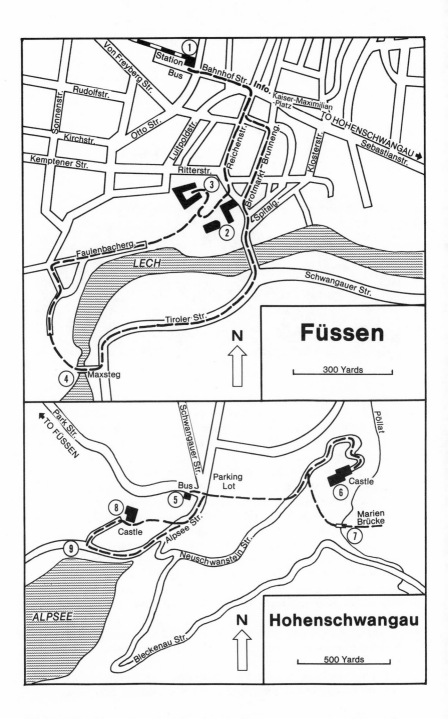

Neuschwanstein Castle from the Marienbrücke

being declared insane. The young king's life ended tragically in the waters of Lake Starnberg the very next day.

Enter the castle and join one of the very frequent guided tours, many of which are in English. Unlike the rococo fantasies of his later structures, Neuschwanstein is heavily Teutonic, with wall murals depicting those heroic sagas so dear to the hearts of Wagnerians. Tours are held from April through September, daily from 9 a.m. to 5:30 p.m.; and from October through March, daily from 10 a.m. to 4 p.m.

After the tour you may want to take a short but invigorating walk to the ***Marienbrücke** (7) for some truly splendid views.

Return to the bottom of the hill and visit **Hohenschwangau Castle** (8). Despite its excessive decoration, this *Schloss* has a homely, lived-in feel about it. Dating from the 12th century, it was heavily reconstructed by Ludwig's father, Maximilian II. The future king spent much of his youth here and was undoubtedly influenced by its dreamy, romantic atmosphere. It was here, too, that he entertained the composer Richard Wagner, who milked him for all he was worth. Tours of the castle are conducted during the same time periods as Neuschwanstein Castle, above.

From here, stroll down to the **Pindarplatz** (9) for another gorgeous view across the Alpsee, then return to the bus stop (5) and Füssen.

Lindau

Smiling, sunny Lindau, the beautiful and elegant old resort town on an island in Lake Constance, makes a delightful destination for a day-trip from Munich. Although inhabited since the 9th century and possessing many fine medieval buildings, its character is really shaped by the nearby Alps and the warm, placid lake that joins three nations together. There is just enough to see here to leave most of the day free for relaxing in the sunshine, sitting at outdoor cafés, or sailing across the shimmering waters. A day in Lindau is really a day reserved for pleasure.

Lake Constance, known to Germans as the *Bodensee,* is the third-largest lake in central Europe. It is actually a part of the Rhine, whose waters, flowing north from the Swiss Alps, are trapped in an old glacial basin before continuing their long passage to the sea. This area has been settled since prehistoric times. For centuries it formed an important link in joining the economies of northern Europe with those south of the Alps. Today the lake is a playground for the people of Germany, Austria, and Switzerland.

GETTING THERE:

Trains leave Munich's main station hourly for Lindau, a trip of about 2½ hours. Return service operates until early evening.

By car, Lindau is approximately 110 miles southwest of Munich, following the A-96 Autobahn. You are probably better off parking on the mainland and walking across the bridge.

PRACTICALITIES:

A sunny day in warm weather will make Lindau even more enjoyable, but be prepared for crowds on weekends and holidays. The local **Tourist Information Office**, phone (08382) 26-00-30, is opposite the train station. Bicycles may be rented at the station. Lindau has a population of about 25,000.

FOOD AND DRINK:

This old resort has plenty of restaurants and cafés, including:

Spielbank Restaurant (in the Casino) Elegant dining overlooking the lake, with outdoor tables in a manicured garden. Phone (08382) 52-00. X: Thurs. $$$

Helvetia (Seepromenade, near the Mangturm) A good hotel restaurant overlooking the harbor. Phone (08382) 40-02. X: Nov.-Mar. $$

Lindauer Hof (Seepromenade, between the Mangturm and the Altes Rathaus) A stately old hotel on the harbor, with an outdoor terrace. Phone (08382) 40-64. X: Jan.–Mar. $$

Zum Sünfzen (Maximilianstr. 1, 2 blocks northeast of the Altes Rathaus) Hearty regional specialties in a colorful old inn, outdoor tables on the pedestrian street. Phone (08382) 58-65. X: Feb. $$

Weinstube Frey (Maximilianstr. 15, a block west of the Altes Rathaus) A delightful 16th-century wine tavern with upstairs dining. Phone (08382) 52-78. X: Sun. $$

Bräugaststätte zum Schlechterbräu (In der Grub 28, east of the Peterskirche) A rustic place with traditional Bavarian fare, served indoors or in the beer garden. Phone (08382) 58-42. $

SUGGESTED TOUR:

Begin your walk at the **train station** (1). It was the coming of the railway in the late 19th century that radically changed the character of this former Free Imperial City. For centuries before that, Lindau was a prosperous trading center—a port from which goods were exchanged across the lake. This business died as the tracks continued on to Austria and Switzerland. But those trains provided an easy way for vacationers to reach these sunny shores, and the old warehouses were soon torn down to make way for grand hotels.

A stroll along the Seepromenade will take you past these. Stop at one of the **piers** (2) to ask about round-trip ***sightseeing cruises** (*Rundfahrt*) on the lake. A wonderful way to spend an hour or so, the cruises usually take you by Bregenz in Austria and Rorschach in Switzerland. The size of the lake is astonishing. It is easy to see why it played such an important part in the early days of aviation. Both the Zeppelins, whose home base was always in Friedrichshafen, just 12 miles away, and the Dornier flying boats were developed on these waters.

Back on land, continue along the Seepromenade to the **Mangturm**, an old lighthouse erected in the 13th century as part of the defensive fortifications. It may be climbed for a good panaroma. Beyond this lies the **Römerschanze** (3), once a separate island and now a terrace offering views across the harbor. A large statue of the Bavarian Lion proudly stands guard at the end of the quay.

Stroll back along the harbor and into Reichsplatz. The beautifully frescoed **Altes Rathaus** (Old Town Hall) (4), whose façade has both a sundial and a clock, was first built in 1422 and later modified in the Renaissance style. Once the meeting place of a 15th-century Imperial Diet, it now serves as the town library and may be visited.

Turn right, passing the Fountain of Lindavia, onto the picturesque

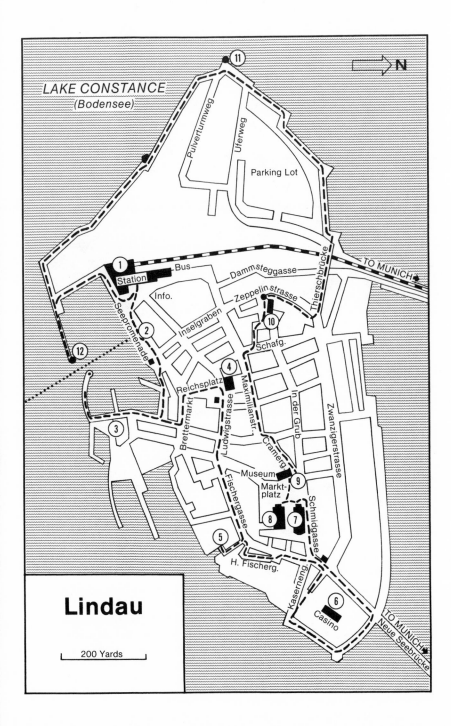

Lindau Harbor and the Mangturm

Ludwigstrasse. This leads past the ancient Stadttheater and into Fischergasse. Along here you will find a little passageway through a building between numbers 19 and 21 on the right, which winds its way around old houses to the **Gerberschanze** (5), a charming spot on the water.

Return to Fischergasse and make a right into a very narrow alleyway called Kickengässele. In a few steps you will come to Hintere Fischergasse, a relic of olden times. A left on this quaint street puts you back on Fischergasse, which continues on to the **Heidenmauer** (Heathens' Wall), the remains of a defensive bastion probably dating from Roman days. To the right are the public gardens and the **Casino** *(Spielbank)* (6), where gambling begins at 3 p.m. daily.

Stroll through the gardens and turn right on Schmidgasse. The Protestant **Stefanskirche** (St. Stephen's Church) (7) was built in 1180 and later reconstructed in the Baroque style. Next to it is the Roman Catholic **Stiftskirche** (St. Mary's Church) (8), formerly part of a convent, with its rococo interior. Both are worth seeing.

Cross the market square and visit the **Haus zum Cavazzen** (9). This grand old patrician mansion now houses the Municipal Museum *(Städtische Kunstsammlungen)*. You can easily spend an hour here looking at the old room settings, folk art, armaments, and paintings ranging from medieval to Art Nouveau *(Jugendstil)*. The museum is open on Tuesdays through Saturdays, from 9 a.m. to noon and 2–5

The Altes Rathaus

p.m.; and on Sundays and holidays from 10 a.m. to noon. It closes from November through March.

Now follow the map along Cramergasse to the pedestrians-only Maximilianstrasse, a particularly inviting main street lined with beautifully restored old houses and **sidewalk cafés**.

Continue on to the **Diebsturm** (Thieves' Tower) (10), whose turreted spire, a landmark of Lindau, evokes a vision right out of the Middle Ages. Built in 1420, this was once both a watch tower and a prison. Directly adjacent to it is the former **Peterskirche** (St. Peter's Church), reputed to be the oldest building on Lake Constance. Now a war memorial, it dates from about the year 1000 and contains what are probably the only surviving frescoes by the Swabian artist Hans Holbein the Elder.

Walk along the top of the old town walls following Zeppelinstrasse and turn left across a bridge. Follow the path by the water's edge to the **Pulverturm** (Gun Powder Tower) (11), another medieval defensive work. From here continue back to the harbor where you can go out on the breakwater to the **Neuer Leuchtturm** (New Lighthouse) (12). A climb to the top reveals a spectacular view of Lindau and the distant peaks in Austria, Liechtenstein, and Switzerland. After this it is only a few steps back to the train station.

Augsburg

Although it was founded by the Romans as far back as 15 B.C., Augsburg is really a city of the Renaissance. At that time its merchant dynasties made this one of the richest places in Europe, a magnet to which great talent was naturally attracted. Much of that heritage remains intact and surprisingly well preserved today, and can be seen in the form of magnificent architecture and some really outstanding museums. This is a city for serious travelers; those looking for history, art, and culture rather than natural splendor or foot-stomping merriment.

Because of its proximity to Munich and its location at the junction of major transportation routes, Augsburg makes an excellent alternative base for daytrips throughout Bavaria. Many of its hotels and restaurants offer exceptionally good value for money. A visit here could also be combined in the same day with one to Ulm by cutting both tours short.

GETTING THERE:

Trains to Augsburg depart Munich's main station very frequently, taking about 30 minutes for the run. Return service operates until after midnight.

By car, Augsburg is 42 miles northwest of Munich. Take the A-8 Autobahn to the Augsburg-Ost exit and park as close to Königsplatz as possible.

PRACTICALITIES:

Avoid going to Augsburg on a Monday, when most of its attractions are closed. Good weather is not essential for this trip. The local **Tourist Information Office**, phone (0821) 50-20-70, is at Bahnhofstrasse 7, 2 blocks east of the train station, with a branch on Rathausplatz by the Town Hall. Bicycles may be rented at the station. Augsburg has a population of about 264,000.

FOOD AND DRINK:

There is a fairly wide selection of restaurants and cafés in every price range. Among the best choices are:

> **Sieben Schwaben Stuben** (Bürgermeister-Fischer-Str. 12, 1 block south of St. Anne's Church) Swabian specialties in an Old World atmosphere. Phone (0821) 31-45-63. $$

Fuggerkeller (Maximilianstr. 38, a block north of the Schaezler Palace) An elegant hotel dining room in a historic mansion. Phone (0821) 51-62-60. $$

Fuggerei Stube (Jakoberstr. 26, by the Fuggerei) A popular grill restaurant. Reservations advised, Phone (0821) 308-70. X: Mon. $$

Ratskeller (in the Town Hall basement) Solid German food under a vaulted brick ceiling. X: Sun. eve., Mon. Phone (0821) 15-40-87. $

SUGGESTED TOUR:

Augsburg's main **train station** *(Hauptbahnhof)* (1) was built in 1845 and is today the oldest in any large German city. Leave it and follow Bahnhofstrasse past the tourist office to Königsplatz. Continue along Bürgermeister-Fischer-Strasse and turn right onto Maximilianstrasse. This elegant old street was once part of the *Via Claudia Augusta,* an ancient Roman road leading north from Verona. A that time Augsburg, named after the emperor Augustus, was the capital of the province of Rhaetia. Today this broad thoroughfare is part of the famous Romantic Road, a heavily promoted tourist route from Würzburg to Füssen going by way of Rothenburg and Augsburg.

The early 16th-century **Fugger House** (2) was the town residence of one of the wealthiest families on Earth. Jakob Fugger the Rich, financier of emperors and a man of incredible power, lived here until his death in 1525. Be sure to see the inner courtyards, particularly the **Damenhof** with its curiously Florentine appearance. It is accessible through the main entrance.

Now follow the map to the **Römisches Museum** (Roman Museum) (3), located in a former Dominican church. Many valuable artifacts from Augsburg's Roman era are displayed in this magnificent setting, including a superb gilded horse's head from the 2nd century A.D. The museum is open on Tuesdays through Sundays, from 10 a.m. to 5 p.m., closing at 4 p.m. from October through April.

Return to Maximilianstrasse and visit the **Schaezler Palace** (4), facing the Hercules Fountain of 1602. The building itself features a stunning rococo ballroom, once used to entertain Marie Antoinette on her way to marry Louis XVI, and now houses the city's two major art museums. The first of these, nearest the entrance, is the **German Baroque Gallery** with its important works from the 17th and 18th centuries. But the real treasures are in the **State Gallery** *(Staatsgalerie),* reached via a connecting passage through the festival hall. The well-known portrait of **Jakob Fugger the Rich* by Albrecht Dürer is here, along with many great masterpieces of the Renaissance. Both museums are open during the same times as the Roman Museum, above.

At the far end of Maximilianstrasse is the Catholic **Basilica of SS. Ulrich and Afra** (5) and, adjoining it, the smaller Protestant **Church of St. Ulrich**. Together they symbolize the spirit of the Peace of Augsburg, an agreement of 1555 that brought religious freedom to the peers of the realm, although not to their subjects. Both are worth visiting, with the Catholic church being the more interesting. St. Afra, a Swabian who died a martyr in A.D. 304 during the rule of Diocletian, is buried in its crypt along with St. Ulrich, a 10th-century Swabian bishop who saved Augsburg from the Huns.

Continue on to the **Rotes Tor** (Red Gate) (6), a fortified bastion first built in 1546. Go through the entrance on its right and into a park, passing a large open-air theater in which opera performances are given during July and August. Amble around through the park and turn left at the herb garden, then left again through a courtyard of the 17th-century Heilig-Geist-Spital to the **Handwerkermuseum** (Hand Crafts Museum) (7). This free exhibition of local handicrafts is open every day except on Saturdays, from 2–6 p.m.

Now follow the map through a former Dominican convent, exiting through a gate onto Margaretenstrasse. Continue along the Schwibbogengasse and a stream to the 15th-century **Vogel Tor** (Bird Gate) (8), opposite which are impressive sections of the medieval city wall, moats, and a watermill.

Turn left on Neuer Gang and right on Mittlerer Lech, then cross the little stream into the romantic old Lechviertel district. A right on Vorderer Lech brings you to the **Holbein House** (9), where the artist Hans Holbein the Elder, born in Augsburg in 1465, lived during the early 16th century. The original house was destroyed in 1944 but later reconstructed. Now a city art gallery for special exhibitions, it has some memorabilia on Holbein and is open at various times according to exhibits.

The route leads across the busy Oberer Graben and into what is probably the most significant sight in Augsburg. The **Fuggerei** (10) is hardly where Jakob Fugger the Rich lived. It is, however, where he shrewdly took out insurance on his soul, buying eternal salvation through an act of charity. For the unbelievably low rent of 1.72 Marks a year, poor, elderly, deserving Catholics from Augsburg can live out their days in comfort and dignity in this, the world's first public housing development. The payment, equal to one Rhenish Guilder, has remained unchanged since the Fuggerei was opened in 1519. In addition, the residents must also promise to pray every day for the souls of the Fuggers.

The Fuggerei is actually a rather attractive town-within-a-town, complete with its own walls and gates, which are closed at night for security. Although the houses appear to be quite old, most are post-

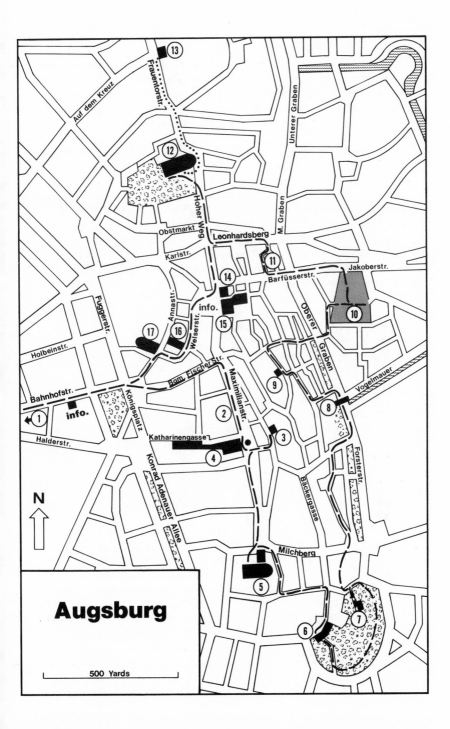

Augsburg

500 Yards

war reconstructions with modern facilities. One of the few originals to survive is now a **museum**, furnished as it was during the 17th and 18th centuries. Located at Mittleren Gasse 13, it is open from April through October, daily from 9 a.m. to 6 p.m. The house next door at number 14 is also an original, and was occupied by one Franz Mozart, the composer's great-grandfather, from 1681 to 1693.

Exit onto Jakoberstrasse and follow the map to the **Bertold Brecht House** (11) at Auf-dem-Rain 7. Born here in 1898, the famous author of the *Threepenny Opera* later moved to America before settling down after the war in East Berlin, where he died in 1956. His leftist leanings made him a pariah in Augsburg, but now that he's safely dead his house has become a tourist attraction. It's open on Tuesdays through Sundays, from 10 a.m. to 5 p.m., closing at 4 p.m. in winter.

A left on Leonhardsberg and a right on Hoher Weg leads to the ***Cathedral** *(Dom)* (12), a romantically beautiful structure begun in the 9th century and enlarged in the Gothic style during the 14th century. To the left of its main entrance, midway to the west end along the south side and protected by a gate, there is a fascinating ***bronze door** decorated with strange reliefs depicting both mythology and the Old Testament. This dates from the 11th century. Equally ancient are the **stained-glass windows of the Prophets**, said to be the oldest of their kind in the world. There are several altar paintings by Hans Holbein the Elder, and other excellent works of art.

From here you might want to make a short side trip north to visit the **Mozart House** (13) at Frauentorstrasse 30. Wolfgang Amadeus was, of course, born in Salzburg, but his father Leopold was raised here, and the house is an interesting museum of Mozart memorabilia. The family's fortunes had certainly improved since the time that Wolfgang's great-grandfather Franz lived in the Fuggerei! The house is open on Mondays, Wednesdays, Thursdays, and Fridays from 10 a.m. to noon and 2–5 p.m., closing at 4 on Fridays; and on Sundays from 10 a.m. to noon.

Continue down Hoher Weg to the **Perlachturm** (14), originally built in the 12th century as a watchtower but extended to its present height of 256 feet during the 17th century. You can climb to the top from April through September, daily from 10 a.m. to 6 p.m., for a bird's-eye view of the town and countryside. The Alps are visible when a yellow flag is flown. Hidden behind the tower is a tiny church that also dates from the 12th century.

Next to the tower is the early 17th-century **Rathaus** (Town Hall) (15), badly damaged during the last war but now so completely restored that it seems to have been built only yesterday. Perhaps after it ages a bit, it will once again be considered as one of the finest Renaissance structures in Germany. Its spectacular (and rather ostentatious)

The Perlachturm and the Rathaus

Golden Hall may be visited on weekdays from 10 a.m. to 6 p.m., provided it's not in use.

The adjacent **Rathausplatz** is a handsome open square, embellished with a 16th-century statue of the emperor Augustus. Around it are a number of inviting **outdoor cafés** and pubs, which you might be in need of by now.

Walk down Philippine-Welser-Strasse past the former residence of the Welser family at number 24. Like the Fuggers, this dynasty was incredibly rich, and at one time actually owned most of Venezuela. Unfortunately, they left little behind and have since fallen into obscurity. Their house is now occupied by the **Maximilian Museum** (16), which displays some outstanding souvenirs of Augsburg's past. It is open on Tuesdays through Sundays, from 10 a.m. to 4 p.m.

St.-Annakirche (St. Anne's Church) (17) is entered through a side door to the left in the Annahof. In 1518 Martin Luther found sanctuary in this former Carmelite monastery, which has been Protestant since the Reformation. Inside, there is a remarkable burial chapel of the Fuggers, and the famous *Portrait of Luther* by Lucas Cranach the Elder. The church is open daily from 10 a.m. to noon and 2:30–6 p.m. From here it is a relatively short walk back to the train station.

Ulm

The city of Ulm has a lot to offer today's travelers. Admittedly, not too many foreign tourists come this way, but that's their loss. For starters, Ulm's cathedral easily ranks among the greatest on Earth, and is reason enough for the journey. Then there is the medieval fishermen's quarter, oozing with quaintness; and one of the most splendid small art museums to be found anywhere. But the real attraction of this small city lies in its atmosphere, an intangible element at once both captivating and refreshing.

Ulm may seem like a part of Bavaria, but in fact it lies just within the *Land* of Baden-Württemberg, whose capital is Stuttgart. Its situation at the confluence of the Danube, Iller, and Blau rivers as well as major land routes made it an important trading center as early as the 9th century. In 1164 the growing town received its municipal charter from Frederick Barbarossa, and in 1274 became a Free Imperial City. One of the first democratic constitutions was granted to its various trade guilds in 1397. The Thirty Years War brought a decline from which Ulm did not recover until the late 19th century. It was badly devastated during World War II and later rebuilt along mostly modern lines, although much of the city's medieval heritage either survived or has since been reconstructed.

By getting off to an early start, a trip to Ulm could be combined in the same day with one to Augsburg. This would, of course, require cutting both tours short.

GETTING THERE:

Trains leave Munich's main station at least hourly for Ulm, making the journey in less than 90 minutes. Return service operates until late evening.

By car, Ulm is 86 miles northwest of Munich via the A-8 Autobahn. Get off at the Ulm-Ost exit and use a parking facility near the train station.

PRACTICALITIES:

A prerequisite for a trip to Ulm is good weather, as very little time will be spent indoors. Avoid coming on a Monday, when the art museum is closed. The local **Tourist Information Office**, phone (0731) 161-2830, is in the Stadthaus in front of the cathedral. Bicycles may be rented at the station. Ulm has a population of about 115,000, and Neu-Ulm around 50,000.

FOOD AND DRINK:

Ulm has a wide range of restaurants and cafés all over town. Some suggestions are:

> **Zur Forelle** (Fischergasse 25, near the Fischerplätzle) Contemporary international cuisine, especially seafood, in a cozy, historic old house. Reservations advised, Phone (0731) 639-24. X: Sun., holidays. $$$
>
> **Zum Pflugmerzler** (Pfluggasse 6, 3 blocks northeast of the cathedral) A small and discreetly elegant restaurant with superb cuisine. Reservations advised, phone (0731) 680-61. X: Sun., holidays. $$$
>
> **Historisches Brauhaus Drei Kannen** (Hafenbad 31/1, 3 blocks northeast of the cathedral) Local and international cooking, with a great beer garden and special brews. Phone (0731) 677-17. X: Mon. $ and $$
>
> **Zunfthaus der Schiffleute** (Fischergasse 31, near the Fischerplätzle) Swabian specialties in an original setting. $

SUGGESTED TOUR:

Leave the **train station** (1) by way of the underground passage to reach Bahnhofstrasse, where the modern building at number 20 occupies the spot where Albert Einstein was born in 1879. From here follow the pedestrians-only Hirschstrasse, a main shopping street, to Münsterplatz and the striking new Stadthaus.

Ulm Cathedral *(Münster)* (2) is the second-largest Gothic church in Germany and has the tallest steeple on the face of this Earth. It was begun in 1377 but not completed until 1890, when its spire was at last raised to pierce the heavens.

The cathedral's interior is awe-inspiring, with a ceiling nearly one hundred feet above the central nave. There is no transept, but the four aisles contribute to a feeling of immense spaciousness. Note in particular the magnificent 15th-century carving on the *choir stalls, the work of Jörg Syrlin the Elder—probably the best example of this sort of art anywhere. If you are lucky enough to come during an organ recital you will have the opportunity to experience the effect that near-perfect acoustics have on the sounds produced by 8,000 pipes. The pulpit, dating from 1500, has above it a splendid sounding board and a second pulpit for the Holy Ghost.

Before leaving the cathedral you will have to decide on whether to climb the 530-foot *tower. Bear in mind that you can always turn around if it gets to be too much. The first part is relatively easy and offers glorious views. As you approach the top, however, the staircase becomes virtually open and quite narrow—an almost terrifying experience for the faint-hearted. The reward, of course, is the magnificent panorama, which on a clear day extends all the way to the Swiss Alps.

Return from the fringes of heaven and stroll over to the **Ulmer Museum** (3). Occupying several old patrician houses, the museum specializes in the arts and crafts of Ulm and Upper Swabia from the Middle Ages to the present. The various collections, exceptionally well displayed on four floors, rival those of much larger and more famous institutions. Opening hours are from 10 a.m. to 5 p.m. on Tuesdays through Sundays, remaining open on Thursdays until 8 p.m.

In front of the museum is the exquisite **Dolphin Fountain**, dating in part from 1584. The Marktplatz is only a few steps from here. It too has a notable fountain, the **Fischkasten**, built by Syrlin in 1482. This square is dominated by the elegant 14th-century **Rathaus** (Town Hall) (4). Although badly damaged in the last war, the building has been restored to its former Late Gothic and Renaissance splendor. The astronomical clock on its east façade is fascinating.

Walk down Herdbruckerstrasse and turn right onto the bridge. To your left you can see the **Adler Bastei**, the scene of one of man's earliest attempts to fly. It was in 1811 that one Albrecht Ludwig Berblinger, the "Tailor of Ulm," tried to soar across the Danube on a giant pair of cloth wings. Poor Albrecht's hopes were dashed as he plunged into the river, wiser but wetter.

Reaching the opposite bank, you are now in **Neu Ulm**, the neighboring town that belongs to Bavaria. Turn right and go down the steps onto the **Jahnufer** (5), a waterside promenade with nice views of the old city. Now retrace your steps across the bridge. At the far end turn left and walk along the top of the ancient **city walls** (Stadtmauer), built in 1480 as a defensive bastion. These failed in 1805 when the Austrian garrison guarding Ulm surrendered to Napoleon at this spot. **Boat trips** on the Danube, lasting about an hour, are offered near here from May through October.

Ulm has its own leaning tower, the **Metzgerturm** (6), which dates from 1345. This former prison tilts over six feet out of vertical. Pass through it and turn left. Unter der Metzig leads to the **Schwörhaus** (7), from whose balcony the city's constitution is annually reaffirmed. The building itself is a reconstruction of the 1613 original, which was destroyed in 1944.

Stroll down to the picturesque **Schiefes Haus** (Crooked House) (8) on the banks of the tiny Blau stream. Leaning precariously over the water, this half-timbered dwelling from about 1500 still fulfills its original purpose. Across the cobbled square is the ancient municipal mint. You are now in the medieval **fishermen's and tanners' quarter**, a peaceful district of narrow passageways, small canals, and venerable houses.

From here you may want to follow the map along the river and

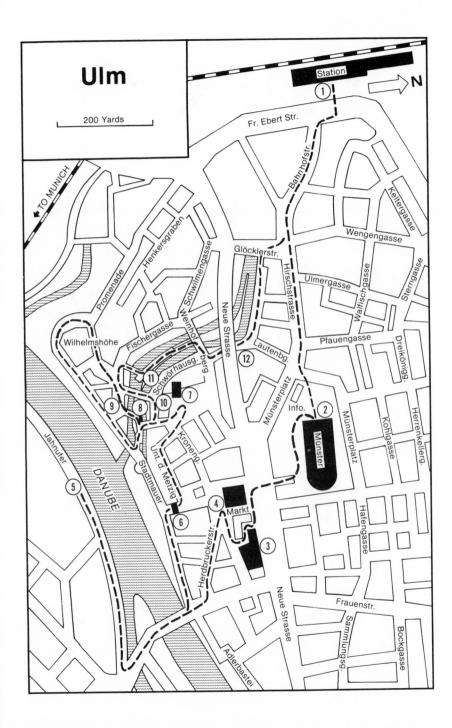

View of Ulm from the Jahnufer
(Photo courtesy of Ulm/Neu-Ulm Tourist Office)

around the Wilhelmshöhe, or save a climb and continue straight to the **Fischerplätzle** (9), which has some very appealing restaurants and cafés.

Cross the little footbridge to the right, again passing the Crooked House, and turn left onto Schwörhausgasse. Along this street you will see the **Staufenmauer** (10), a 12th-century wall. In one block again turn left, crossing a narrow stone bridge. Fischergasse leads to the right. Go along it a short way to the next bridge and cross this to **Auf der Insel** (11). This entire area is filled with a quiet Gothic charm.

When you come to the Weinhofberg bridge turn right and, once across the stream, make an immediate left onto a passage that goes under Neue Strasse. To your right is the huge **Neuer Bau** (12), a former warehouse from the 16th century. Continue along the water's edge to Glöcklerstrasse, noticing how the Blau stream is divided into two different levels before flowing down to the Danube. From here it is only a few blocks to the train station.

*Rothenburg ob-der-Tauber

Rothenburg is almost too good to be true. This once-prosperous medieval town went to sleep after the Thirty Years War and didn't wake up until centuries later, when hordes of tourists began knocking at the gates. By that time its dreamy antiquity had become a gold mine, and its citizens happily vowed to keep the town just as it was in the Middle Ages.

There was a castle at this strategic and easily defended spot high above the Tauber valley a thousand years ago. This was extended in the 12th century and around it a town developed. As the population increased the original ramparts became too confining, so that new walls—which are still completely intact—had to be built beginning in the 13th century.

During the Reformation the town turned Protestant and as a result suffered terribly in the Thirty Years War of the 17th century. Stripped of its wealth and much too poor to afford new buildings, Rothenburg sank into obscurity. Its revival began with the late-19th-century romantics, who had discovered in the midst of their rapidly industrializing nation a true miracle in the form of this long-forgotten and perfectly preserved medieval town.

The only problem with Rothenburg is that everyone knows about it. The mobs of tourists who come here in summer will thin out considerably once you get away from the town hall area, and you may even have some parts of town to yourself.

Rothenburg also makes an excellent daytrip from Frankfurt, or from smaller bases such as Würzburg, Nürnberg, or Heidelberg. The very best way to visit the town, however, is to make an overnight stop en route between Munich and Frankfurt, or vice versa.

GETTING THERE:

One well-known way to reach Rothenburg, aside from driving, is via the **Romantic Road Bus**, operated by the railroad between Munich, Würzburg, and Frankfurt. This is free to railpass holders. To use the bus you should first check the schedule and then make reservations by contacting Deutsche Touring, Am Römerhof 17, Frankfurt, phone (069) 790-3256. There are drawbacks, however. Unless you are staying overnight it will not allow enough time to see Rothenburg properly. Contrary to popular belief, it is actually possible to get there by train from either Munich or Frankfurt, or more easily from Würzburg.

Trains from Munich require a very early start and a change at Steinach. Be sure to check the schedules both ways carefully. The ride takes over three hours each way. You can also go via Würzburg, which is longer but possibly faster.

Trains from Frankfurt also call for an early start. Changes must be made at both Würzburg and Steinach. With good connections, the total trip should take about 2 $\frac{1}{2}$ hours.

By car from Munich, take the A-8 Autobahn to the Augsburg-West exit, then the B-2 north to Donauworth, and finally the B-25 road via Nördlingen and Dinkelsbühl into Rothenburg, which is 130 miles northwest of Munich. Try to park outside the walls.

By car from Frankfurt, take the A-3 Autobahn to Würzburg, then head south on the A-7 to the Rothenburg exit, which is about 115 miles southeast of Frankfurt. Again, park outside the walls.

PRACTICALITIES:

Rothenburg can be visited at any time, and is especially lovely in winter after a fresh snowfall. For your own sanity, avoid weekends and holidays during the summer. The local **Tourist Information Office**, Phone (09861) 404-92, is on the Marktplatz. **Bicycles** may be rented at the train station from April through October. Rothenburg has a **population** of about 12,000.

FOOD AND DRINK:

This popular tourist town abounds in quaint old restaurants. Among the best are:

> **Hotel Eisenhut** (Herrngasse 3, just west of the Rathaus) Exquisite dining in a lovely hotel occupying four medieval houses, with a garden terrace overlooking the valley. Phone (09861) 70-50. $$$

> **Goldener Hirsch** (Untere Schmiedgasse 16, just north of the Plönlein) The hotel's noted Blaue Terrace Restaurant offers contemporary cuisine with a view of the valley. Proper dress expected, reservations advised, phone (09861) 70-80. $$$

> **Hotel Markusturm** (Rödergasse 1, by the Markusturm) A romantic 13th-century inn noted for its game and fish dishes. Phone (09861) 20-98. $$$

The Rathaus in the Marktplatz

Ratsstube (Marktplatz 6) Regional specialties in a popular old
tavern. Phone (09861) 55-11. $$
Reichs-Küchenmeister (Kirchplatz 8, just east of St.-Jakobs
Church) An old inn famed for its game and fish. Phone
(09861) 20-46. $$
Baumeisterhaus (Obere Schmiedgasse 3, just south of the
Marktplatz) Local specialties in the courtyard or dining room
of a 16th-century patrician house. Phone (09861) 34-04. $$
Klosterstüble (Heringsbronnengasse 5, near the Franciscan
Church) A good value. Phone (09861) 67-74. $$

SUGGESTED TOUR:

Leave the **train station** (1) and follow the map to the Old Town,
which begins at the **Rödertor** (2). This 17th-century bastion leads
through the medieval walls and onto Rödergasse. Walk straight ahead
past the **Markusturm**—a surviving part of the oldest ramparts—and
into the very center of Rothenburg, the **Marktplatz**.

The imposing ***Rathaus** (Town Hall) (3) reflects the former wealth
of this small town. It consists of two adjoining structures, one in the
16th-century Renaissance style facing the market place and the other

a Gothic building completed in the 14th century, which opens onto Herrngasse. You may explore the interior by using the entrance on Marktplatz. The Imperial Hall is interesting, but the main attraction is to climb the 165-foot ***tower** for a fabulous view of medieval Rothenburg. This is reached by a difficult staircase that get progressively narrower. Be warned in advance that some minor acrobatics are required to get out on the platform. The tower is open daily from April through October, from 9:30 a.m. to 12:30 p.m. and 1–4 p.m., and on weekends from noon to 3 p.m. the rest of the year.

On the north side of the Marktplatz is the 15th-century **Ratstrinkstube**, a former tavern for the city councilors. Above this there is a **clock** with mechanical figures, which act out the story of the *Meistertrunk* at 11 a.m., noon, and 1, 2, 3, 8, 9, and 10 p.m. daily. The legend dates from the Thirty Years War, when Protestant Rothenburg was captured by the Catholic General Tilly, who ordered widespread destruction and executions. Pleas for mercy fell on deaf ears until Tilly was offered a cup of the local wine. Impressed, he agreed to spare the town if one of the councilors could drink the entire 3¼-liter bumper in one mighty draught. An ex-mayor named Nusch performed the feat, then slept for three days and nights and lived on for another 37 years before dying at the age of 80. It's a nice story. The tourist office, by the way, is in the same building.

Stroll over to the **St.-Jakob-Kirche** (St. James' Church) (4), begun in the early 14th century and consecrated in the late 15th. Its **Altar of the Twelve Apostles**, at the east end, is beautifully carved and merits a careful examination, as do the stained-glass windows. The main attraction, however, is in the west gallery, up a flight of stairs. This is the ***Altarpiece of the Holy Blood**, a major work by the renowned sculptor Tilman Riemenschneider, completed in 1504. Its depiction of the Last Supper is simply fantastic. The church is closed from noon to 2 p.m. between November and Easter.

Now follow the map to the **Klingentor** (5), a 14th-century town gate attached to the very curious fortified **Church of St. Wolfgang**. The latter dates from the late 15th century and has windows on the south side only. To the north it is a fortress, whose casemates and subterranean passages may be explored via an entrance near the High Altar.

Continue along the walls to the **Burg Tor** (Castle Gate) (6), leading into a park built on the site of the original 10th-century castle. All that remains of its 12th-century successor is the Chapel of St. Blasius, now a war memorial. There is a marvelous view from the gardens, extending across the Tauber valley and encompassing the tiny and rather odd Toppler Castle, just below, and the medieval fortified Double Bridge to the left.

Leave the gardens and walk around to the **Franciscan Church** (7),

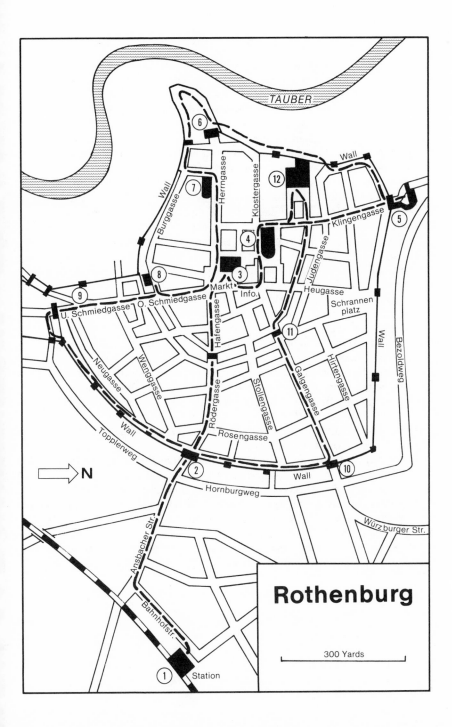

TAUBER

Wall

Burggasse

Herrngasse

Klostergasse

Wall

Klingengasse

Jüdengasse

Heugasse

Schrannen platz

Markt

Info.

U. Schmiedgasse

O. Schmiedgasse

Hafengasse

Neugasse

Wenggasse

Rodergasse

Stollengasse

Galgengasse

Hirtengasse

Wall

Bezoldweg

Topplerweg

Wall

Rosengasse

Wall

Hornburgweg

Würzburger Str.

Ansbacher Str.

Bahnhofstr.

N

Rothenburg

300 Yards

Station

the oldest in town, which dates from the 13th century. An unusual feature is the wooden screen separating the nave from the choir. It also contains some fine tombs. From here the elegant and wide Herrngasse, lined with stately homes of the gentry, leads back to the Town Hall.

Turn right on Obere Schmiedgasse, passing several beautiful patrician houses. The most notable of these is the Renaissance-style Baumeister House at number 3, with statues of the seven virtues and the seven deadly sins adorning its upper façade. In a few steps you will come to the *Kriminalmuseum (Crime Museum) (8), a large and fascinating display of medieval life and justice. The collections occupy four floors of an ancient building and every item, from the gruesome to the humorous, is thoroughly explained in both German and English. Don't miss seeing this special treat, open daily from April through October, from 9:30 a.m. to 6 p.m.; and daily from November through March, from 2–4 p.m.

The most famous spot in Rothenburg is the **Plönlein** (9), the subject of countless travel pictures. Formed by the intersection of two cobbled streets, each with a tower, and framed by half-timbered houses, this little square is almost unbearably picturesque. Continue straight ahead through Siebers Tower and turn left to the walls.

From here you can walk along the top of the **Ramparts**, remarkably unchanged since the 14th century. At the Rödertor (2) it is possible to climb out into the tower for an even better view. Stay on the walls as far as the **Galgentor** (Gallows Gate) (10), then descend and follow the map past the 12th-century **Weisser Turm** (White Tower) (11), another part of the earliest town walls.

A series of narrow streets lead to the **Reichsstadtmuseum** (Imperial City Museum) (12), located in a former Dominican convent. Here you will find the whole history of Rothenburg displayed in surviving artifacts, including the famous wine tankard used by the ex-mayor Nusch to perform his heroic feat. The museum is open daily from 10 a.m. to 5 p.m., with shorter hours from November through March. Now walk over to the nearby Marktplatz, from which you can retrace your steps back to the train station.

Würzburg

Although situated on the Main River, Würzburg really belongs to the south of Germany. This "Town of the Madonnas" is renowned for its splendid Residenz and other triumphs of the Baroque style, as well as for its delicious wines. Curiously enough, and despite its central location, Würzburg is all too often overlooked by foreign tourists as they scurry from Heidelberg to Rothenburg and Munich. That's a pity, for this lovely old town at the northern end of the famed "Romantic Road" has a lot to offer the traveler.

Würzburg dates from at least the 7th century, and its history is filled with the comings and goings of saints, kings, and emperors; including the likes of Charlemagne and Frederick Barbarossa. The noted sculptor Tilman Riemenschneider worked here most of his life, was elected mayor, and in 1525 led a peasant revolt for which he was imprisoned.

Würzburg's greatest era, however, was the 18th century. It was then that the ruling prince-bishops moved down from their fortress on the Marienberg and into the magnificent new Residenz, where they set a style of unparalleled opulence. By the early 19th century the grandeur subsided as the town became a part of Bavaria. The vast destruction of World War II led to a near-total restoration, so that the Würzburg you see today looks very much as it did in centuries past.

This trip can also be taken from Frankfurt, which is considerably closer than Munich. Würzburg makes a good alternative base for day-trips in Franconia and along the Main Valley, or as a stopover between Munich and Frankfurt.

GETTING THERE:

Trains depart **Munich's** main station about hourly for the under-2½-hour run to Würzburg. Most of these are of the ICE class. Return service operates until mid-evening.

Trains depart **Frankfurt's** main station hourly for the 75-minute ride to Würzburg. Most are of the IC or EC class. There is good return service until mid-evening.

By car from **Munich**, Würzburg lies 173 miles to the northwest. Take the A-9 Autobahn to Nürnberg, then the A-3 to Würzburg.

By car from **Frankfurt**, Würzburg is 73 miles to the southeast via the A-3 Autobahn.

PRACTICALITIES:

Würzburg may be visited in any season, but avoid coming on a Monday, when the most important sights are closed. There is a local **Tourist Information Office** in front of the train station, phone (0931) 374-36; and at the Marktplatz, phone (0931) 373-98. **Bicycles** may be rented at the station from April through October. Würzburg has a **population** of about 129,000.

FOOD AND DRINK:

The local Franconian wines, in their characteristic *Bocksbeutel* flask, are superb, as is the local beer. Some good restaurant choices are:

Hotel Rebstock (Neubaustr. 7, 4 blocks south of the Town Hall) A centuries-old palace, now a luxury hotel, with a gourmet restaurant and a wine tavern. Phone (0931) 309-30. $$ and $$$

Zur Stadt Mainz (Semmelstr. 39, 5 blocks north of the Residenz) An old inn famed for its local cuisine. Phone (0931) 531-55. X: Mon., late Dec.-late Jan. $$ and $$$

Ratskeller (Langgasse 1, in the Town Hall) A vaulted cellar restaurant with local wines and country cooking. Phone (0931) 130-21. $$

Bürgerspital Weinstuben (Theaterstr. 19, 3 blocks northwest of the Residenz) A characteristic old wine tavern with Franconian cooking. Phone (0931) 138-61. X: Tues. $$

Juliusspital (Juliuspromenade 19, 6 blocks northwest of the Residenz) An historic wine tavern with hearty local specialties and superb wine from their own vineyard. Phone (0931) 540-80. X: Wed. $$

Goldener Hahn (Marktgasse 7, by the Marktplatz) A small Gasthof with good-value Franconian fare. Phone (0931) 519-41. X: Mon. $

SUGGESTED TOUR:

Leave the **train station** (1) and pass the tourist office located just outside. From here follow the map to Würzburg's main attraction, the ***Residenz** (2). Primarily the work of the renowned architect Balthazar Neumann, this magnificent Baroque palace was built between 1720 and 1744 as a residence for the prince-bishops of Würzburg, who had previously lived in the Marienberg fortress.

Inside, the most spectacular sight is of the ***Grand Staircase.** As you approach the first landing you become aware of a dazzling ceiling depicting the four continents known at that time. This fresco, one of the largest on Earth, is regarded as the supreme achievement of the Venetian master, Giambattista Tiepolo. The **Weisser Saal** (White

The Residenz

Hall), an elegant monochromatic masterpiece of pure rococo, provides visual relief before continuing on to the **Kaiser Saal** (Imperial Hall). Again, Tiepolo outdid himself on the frescoes and, together with the architect Neumann and the sculptor Antonio Bossi, created one of the most splendid interior spaces in Germany. There are other wonderful rooms to see before leaving the palace, especially the **Garden Room** on the ground floor. The Residenz is open on Tuesdays through Sundays from 9 a.m. to 5 p.m.; and from 10 a.m. to 4 p.m. from October through March. The admission includes a guided tour.

The **Hofkirche** (Court Chapel), another part of the complex, is entered from the outside. This marvelous accomplishment by the same team is in every way equal to what you've seen in the palace proper. A gate next to this leads into the delightful **gardens**, which deserve to be explored thoroughly.

Stroll down Hofstrasse to the **Cathedral** *(Dom)* (3). Begun in the 11th century on the site of an earlier cathedral, it has been greatly modified in the years since, including some modern works installed as part of a postwar restoration. There are several fine sculptures by Tilman Riemenschneider, particularly the tombs of the prince-bishops Rudolf von Scherenberg and Lorenz von Bibra. Also noteworthy is the outstanding Schönborn Chapel, designed by Balthazar Neumann, in the north transept.

The **Neumünster Church** (4), just a few steps away, has a fine Baroque façade at its west end. Much of this church dates from the 11th and 13th centuries and was built on the burial site of the Irish monk St. Kilian, who was murdered here in 689. Again, the rich interior has several excellent sculptures by Riemenschneider. There is a small garden on the north side, called the **Lusamgärtlein**, in which the famous 13th-century minnesinger Walther von der Vogelweide is supposed to be buried.

From here follow the map to the **Marktplatz** (5). There are two remarkable structures on its north side. One of these is the **Haus zum Falken**, a former inn with a fabulous rococo façade, which now houses a tourist office. The other is the late-Gothic **Marienkapelle** (St. Mary's Chapel). Enter through its north portal and take a look at the tombstone of Konrad von Schaumberg—another great carving by Riemenschneider—and the tomb of Balthazar Neumann, the architect who brought so much splendor to Würzburg.

Walk around to the **Rathaus** (Town Hall) (6), a picturesque complex of buildings from different eras, one of which dates from the 13th century. Step inside and visit the Wenzelsaal, named for King Wenceslas, who dined here in 1397. You can do the same, but only downstairs in the Ratskeller.

As you walk around this area, you may notice that many of the old houses have small statues of the Virgin set into corner niches. This is why Würzburg is called the "Town of the Madonnas."

The **Alte Mainbrücke** (Old Bridge) (7) still carries pedestrians over the Main River, as it has since the 15th century. This medieval span is beautifully adorned with statues of saints. Stroll across it and climb up to the **Festung Marienberg** (Marienberg Fortress) (8), home to the prince-bishops from the 13th to the 18th centuries. You can spare yourself the stiff climb by taking bus number 9 instead, which runs every half-hour from April through October, from the intersection of Kaiserstrasse and Juliuspromenade. There is, of course, a great view of the town from here. Defensive fortifications of some sort have existed on this hill since about 1000 B.C., but the earliest part now remaining is the **Marienkirche** (St. Mary's Church) in the courtyard, consecrated in 706. You can tour the various sections of the fortress on Tuesdays through Sundays, from 10 a.m. to 5 p.m.; closing at 4 p.m. in winter.

Be sure to see the ***Mainfränkisches Museum** (Franconian Museum) (9), located in the former Zeughaus (Arsenal) of the fortress. A showcase for the arts and artifacts of Würzburg, it contains an entire gallery of sculptures by Tilman Riemenschneider as well as works by

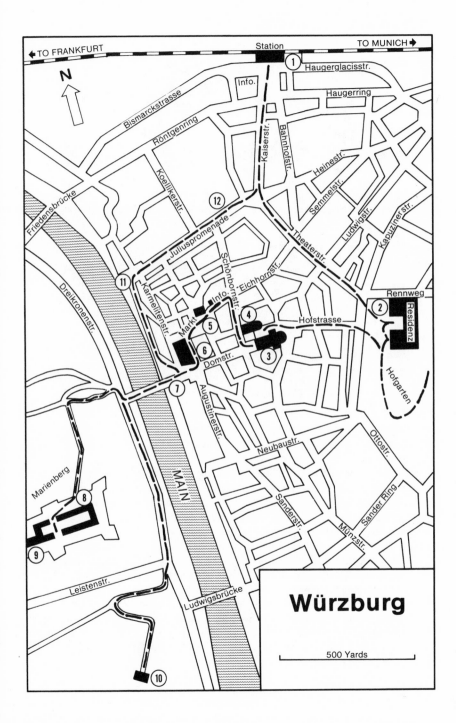

Festung Marienberg from the Alte Mainbrücke

Tiepolo and others. The displays of **wine making** are especially interesting as this hill is itself covered with vineyards.

Return to the bridge. Before crossing it, you may want to visit the **Käppele** (10), a Baroque pilgrimage church on a nearby hill. Built by Balthazar Neumann in the 18th century, it has some wonderful frescoes by Matthias Günther, and a fabulous view of both the Marienberg and Würzburg.

Recross the ancient bridge and walk along the bank of the river to the **Old Crane** (11), an 18th-century reminder that Würzburg is also a port town. There is an attractive **outdoor beer garden** overlooking the water's edge adjacent to this; just the place to relax after a hard day's sightseeing. If you'd rather sample the local wine, why not stop instead at the *Weinstuben* of the **Juliusspital** (12), an atmospheric old institution founded in 1576. While there you might ask to see the rococo apothecary and the gardens. From here it is only a short way back to the train station.

*Nürnberg

(Nuremberg)

Often regarded as the most German of German cities, Nürnberg makes a fascinating daytrip destination whose very name recalls a contradiction of images. It is at once the perfect medieval city, the toy capital of the world, the setting for Wagner's incomparable opera *"Die Meistersinger,"* and a charming center of intellect and culture. Yet, Nürnberg was the place chosen by Hitler for the infamous Nazi rallies of the '30s, and the city that lent its proud name to the despicable laws of racial purity. In retribution, it was practically leveled during World War II, and is still best known for the war-crime trials held there after the collapse of the Third Reich. Since then, the old part of town has been largely restored to its former appearance so that it at least *looks* ancient. It is commonly known in English as Nuremberg.

Not really old as medieval cities go, Nürnberg was founded about 1040 as a military stronghold by Emperor Heinrich III. With the downfall of the Imperial House of Hohenstaufen in the 13th century it became a free city, fortunately located at the junction of several important trade routes. During this period the arts flourished with such local talents as Albrecht Dürer and Hans Sachs. Prosperity came to an end with the Thirty Years War, when Nürnberg's population and wealth declined greatly. It was not until the Industrial Revolution of the 19th century that the city, by now a part of Bavaria, regained its prominent position in German affairs.

This daytrip can easily be taken from Frankfurt as well as from Munich. Nürnberg is also a good base for excursions to Würzburg, Bamberg, Bayreuth, Regensburg, or even Rothenburg.

GETTING THERE:

Trains depart **Munich's** main station at least hourly for Nürnberg, less than 100 minutes away by ICE express, or a bit longer by ordinary trains. Return service operates until mid-evening.

Trains leave **Frankfurt's** main station hourly for Nürnberg. Most of these are of the IC or EC class and take about two hours for the journey. Return trains run until mid-evening.

By Car from **Munich**, take the A-9 Autobahn 103 miles north to Nürnberg.

By car from **Frankfurt**, take the A-3 Autobahn 138 miles southeast to Nürnberg.

PRACTICALITIES:

Several of Nürnberg's best attractions are closed on Mondays. Good weather is not essential for this trip as much of the time is spent indoors. There is a local **Tourist Information Office** in the main train station, which may be phoned at (0911) 233-6132, and a branch office at Hauptmarkt 18, Phone (0911) 233-6135. Nürnberg has a **population** of about 500,000.

FOOD AND DRINK:

The local specialty is Bratwurst, those little sausages that taste better here than anywhere else. Nürnberg is also noted for its Lebkuchen cookies, excellent Franconian wines, and superb beer. Among the choice restaurants are:

Essigbrätlein (Weinmarkt 3, a block west of St. Sebaldus Church) Modern and traditional local cuisine in elegant, ancient surroundings. Dress nicely and reserve, Phone (0911) 22-51-31. $$$

Goldenes Posthorn (Glöckleinsgasse 2, across from St. Sebaldus Church) Inventive Franconian cuisine, in business since the 15th century. Phone (0911) 22-51-53. X: Sun. $$$

Nassauer Keller (Karolinenstr. 2, opposite St. Lorenz Church) Traditional cuisine in the cellar of a 13th-century house. Phone (0911) 22-59-67. $$ and $$$

Heilig Geist Spital (Spitalgasse 12, on the Pegnitz River) An authentic wine tavern, very popular with tourists for its inexpensive lunches. Phone (0911) 22-17-61. $ and $$

Bratwurst Häusle (Rathausplatz 1, across from the Old Town Hall) A boisterous, fun place for grilled sausages and sauerkraut. Phone (0911) 22-76-95. X: Sun. $

Bratwurstglöcklein (in the Handerwerkerhof by the Königstor) A rustic place for bratwurst, sauerkraut, potato salad, and beer. Phone (0911) 22-76-25. X: Sun., holidays. $

SUGGESTED TOUR:

Begin your walk at the **main train station** *(Hauptbahnhof)* (1), where the tourist office is located. From here use the underground passageway to reach the **Königstor** (2), a part of the massive old fortifications. These walls, constructed over a period of centuries, remain intact today and give Nürnberg a medieval appearance that is largely missing from other major German cities. Next to the tower is an entrance to the **Handwerkerhof**, a courtyard of small shops where present-day craftsmen carry on in the medieval tradition. You may want to return here later.

Stroll along Königstrasse to the **St.-Lorenz-Kirche** (St. Lawrence's

The Heilig Geist Spital

Church) (3). Built between the 13th and 15th centuries, this is the city's largest house of worship. It contains some remarkable works of art, including the 16th-century *Annunciation* by Veit Stoss that hangs suspended in the choir. Other pieces to look for are the tabernacle by Adam Kraft, to the left of the high altar, and the wonderful stained-glass windows in the choir.

Opposite the front of the church is the tower-like **Nassauer Haus**, parts of which date from the early 13th century. It is reputed to be the oldest dwelling in town, and now houses a delightful restaurant. Continue along Königstrasse, here reserved for pedestrians, to the Museum Bridge. To your right is one of those wonderful scenes so typical of Nürnberg. The **Heilig-Geist-Spital** (4), a 14th-century almshouse spanning the Pegnitz River, still serves its original purpose and also contains a very popular *Weinstube* and restaurant.

You are now only steps from the **Hauptmarkt** (main market place) (5), an open area usually filled with farmers' stalls. The traditional *Christkindlmarkt* is held here each December for the sale of toys and ornaments. Facing the east side of the square is the 14th-century **Frauenkirche** (Church of Our Lady), which provides a free spectacle every day at noon in the form of mechanical figures acting out the story of the Golden Bull of 1356. Step inside to see the famous Tucher altarpiece from 1440.

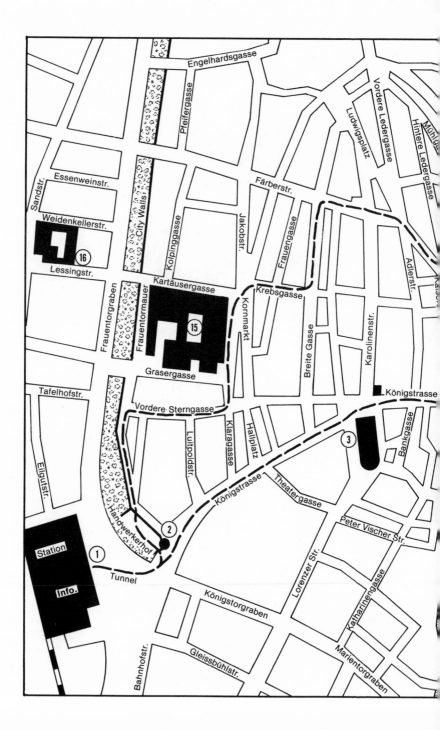

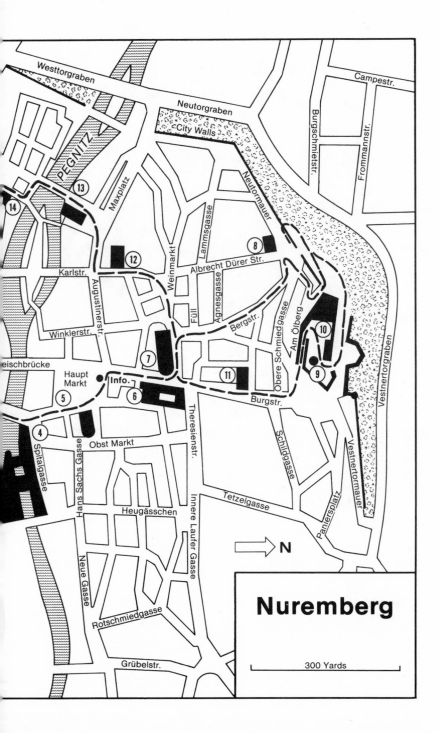

Detail of the Schöner Brunnen

One of the best-known sights in Nürnberg is the ***Schöner Brunnen** (Beautiful Fountain) in the northwest corner of the square. Dating from the 14th century, it is decorated with 40 sculpted figures arranged in four tiers, and surrounded by a 16th-century wrought-iron grille. Now walk up to the **Altes Rathaus** (Old Town Hall) (6), where you can take a gruesome tour through the 14th-century dungeons and visit the torture chamber. The cells are open from April through September, on Mondays through Fridays from 10 a.m. to 4 p.m.; and on weekends from 10 a.m. to 1 p.m.

St.-Sebaldus-Kirche (St. Sebald's Church) (7) was begun in 1225, making the transition from the Romanesque to the Gothic style. On the outside of its choir, facing the Old Town Hall, is the magnificent Schreyer-Landauer tomb of 1492 by Adam Kraft. Enter through the west portal and visit the ***Shrine of St. Sebaldus**, a wonderful 16th-century bronze sculpture containing the silver coffin of Nürnberg's patron saint. There are several other exceptional works of art, including a sunburst Madonna on a north aisle pillar, a Crucifixion group by Veit Stoss near the main altar and, in the south aisle, a stone sculpture by Adam Kraft of Christ bearing the Cross.

A climb up Bergstrasse leads to the ***Albrecht Dürer House** (8), where the great artist lived from 1509 until his death in 1528. The first three floors are open as a museum, and give a good impression of the surroundings in which he lived and worked. Of particular interest is

The Square by the Dürer House

the original kitchen, a replica of his printing press, and copies of his works. The house is open daily except on Mondays, from 10 a.m. to 5 p.m. On weekdays during the winter season it opens at 1 p.m., and is open on Wednesday evenings all year round. The picturesque square next to this has some attractive **outdoor cafés**.

Follow the map uphill and through a garden to an opening in the town wall, from which you will have a marvelous **view** of the square. Return through the garden and stroll past the **Fünfeckiger Turm** (Pentagonal Tower), which dates from 1040 and is regarded as the oldest structure in Nürnberg. Adjoining this are the Imperial Stables, used as a youth hostel. You are now within the precincts of ***Nürnberg Castle**, a residence of all acknowledged German kings and emperors from 1050 to 1571. Continue on to the 13th-century **Sinwellturm** (9), a massive round tower that may be climbed for the best possible panoramic view of the city. Close to this is the **Tiefer Brunnen** (Deep Well), a source of water since the earliest days. It, too, may be visited.

The major part of the castle, the **Kaiserburg** (10), was begun in the 12th century, although most of what you see today dates from the 15th and 16th centuries. There are frequent guided tours through its Gothic interior visiting, among other rooms, the interesting 12th-century **chapel**, a double-deck affair where emperors worshipped above the heads of lesser folk. The castle is open daily from 9 a.m. to noon and 12:45–5 p.m.; closing at 4 p.m. in winter.

Walk down and turn right on Burgstrasse. This leads to the **Fembo Haus** (11), an excellent museum of life in old Nürnberg, located in a well-preserved Renaissance mansion. Be sure to see the large model of the Old City on the fourth floor. The museum is open on Tuesdays through Sundays from 10 a.m. to 5 p.m., remaining open on Wednesdays until 9 p.m.; with shorter hours in winter.

The route again passes St. Sebald's Church, then follows Weinmarkt and Karlstrasse to the ***Spielzeug Museum** (Toy Museum) (12). A wealth of delightful playthings from all over the world is on display, ranging from simple dolls to elaborate model railway setups. Toys have been a major Nürnberg industry for centuries, making a visit here especially appropriate. The museum is open on Tuesdays through Sundays, from 10 a.m. to 5 p.m.; closing at 9 p.m. on Wednesdays.

Continue on to the **Maxbrücke** (13), a bridge with stunning views up and down the Pegnitz River. The large half-timbered structure to your left, the Weinstadel, was built in 1446 as a home for lepers. Later used for wine storage, it is now a residence for university students. Adjacent to this is the Wasserturm, a part of the older 14th-century fortifications. From here the Pegnitz is spanned by a covered wooden footbridge called the **Henkersteg**, or hangman's bridge, to whose solitary dwelling it led. To the right, the view of the medieval walls arched over the river is equally engaging.

Follow the map past the 15th-century **Unschlitthaus** (14), a former granary, and through a more modern part of town to the formidable **Germanisches National Museum** (Germanic National Museum) (15). Dedicated to the many aspects of German art and culture from prehistoric times to the 20th century, this vast treasure house requires several hours to see properly. It is open on Tuesdays through Sundays, from 10 a.m. to 5 p.m.; staying open until 9 p.m. on Wednesdays.

Railfans and kids, as well as some otherwise normal people, will really enjoy a visit to the **Verkehrsmuseum** (Transportation Museum) (16) just beyond the walls on Lessingstrasse. Its collection of old trains features the *Adler,* the first locomotive to operate in Germany, and "mad" King Ludwig II's incredible private cars. Three floors of exhibits are almost entirely devoted to railroading, with a special treat being the huge model train layout *(Modellbahn),* which runs hourly on the half-hour. There is an inexpensive cafeteria with local dishes and drinks served in a 19th-century machine shop setting. The museum is open daily from 9:30 a.m. to 5 p.m., except on holidays.

From here it is only a short walk back to the station.

Bamberg

Of all the medieval cities in Germany, Bamberg stands out as perhaps the one least touched by the ravages of war. Well over a thousand years of history enrich this ancient ecclesiastical and commercial center in Upper Franconia. It is a place filled with picturesque corners, charming waterfront houses and narrow, winding streets, as well as magnificent churches whose spires cap the seven hills on which it is built.

Although this area has been settled since the late Stone Age, the earliest documented reference to *Castrum Babenberg*, as it was then called, dates from A.D. 902. Bamberg was well established as a center of learning before the 12th century. Despite occupation by the Swedes during the Thirty Years War, the town was spared the destruction of the Reformation and remained true to the Catholic faith. It was not until 1802 that it was secularized and made a part of Bavaria. Industrialization began in the late 19th century, but this took place at the eastern end of town, well away from its ancient core. Bamberg survived World War II virtually unscathed, and today offers visitors a chance to experience a city whose fabric has remained intact for centuries.

This trip can be made from Frankfurt as well as from Munich, or from other bases such as Nürnberg or Würzburg.

GETTING THERE:

Trains leave **Munich's** main station about hourly for the 3-hour trip to Bamberg, which may require a change at Nürnberg. Return connections run until mid-evening.

Trains depart **Frankfurt's** main station hourly for Würzburg, where you change for Bamberg. The total trip takes under 3 hours. Return service operates until mid-evening.

By car from **Munich**, take the A-9 Autobahn to Nürnberg, then the A-73 to Bamberg. Bamberg is 143 miles northwest of Munich.

By car from **Frankfurt**, it is 130 miles east to Bamberg. Take the A-3 Autobahn past Würzburg, then head north on the B-505.

PRACTICALITIES:

Bamberg is compact and can be comfortably explored in any season. Some of its sights are closed on Mondays and holidays. The local **Tourist Information Office**, phone (0951) 87-11-61, is at Geyerswörthstrasse 16, 3 blocks southeast of the Altes Rathaus. Bicycles may be rented at the train station. Bamberg has a population of about 70,000.

FOOD AND DRINK:

The most famous specialty of Bamberg is its unique *Rauchbier* (smoked beer), an acquired taste definitely worth trying. Its regular beers are superb, and its citizens probably quaff more of the suds than any other people on Earth. Some recommended restaurants are:

Weinhaus Messerschmitt (Langestr. 41, 3 blocks northeast of the E.T.A. Hoffmann House) A romantic medieval inn run by the same family since 1832. Excellent dining room. For reservations phone (0951) 278-66. $$$

Gasthof Weierich (Lugbank 5, 3 blocks southwest of the Altes Rathaus) Franconian cuisine at a small, rustic inn. Phone (0951) 540-04. $$

Würzburger Weinstuben (Zinkenwörth 6, near Schillerplatz, a block northwest of the E.T.A. Hoffmann House) An old half-timbered inn with Franconian specialties. Phone (0951) 226-67. X: Tues. eve., Wed., late Aug. to mid-Sept. $$

Brauereigaststätte Schlenkerla (Dominikerstr. 6, 2 blocks west of the Altes Rathaus) *The* place for Rauchbier, a rustic old beer hall with a boisterous crowd and hearty food. Phone (0951) 560-60. X: Tues. $

Wilde Rose (Kesslerstr. 7, a block east of the Grüner Markt) A small inn with excellent meals for the price. Phone (0951) 283-17. X: Sun. eve. $

SUGGESTED TOUR:

Leave the **train station** (1) and follow the map to the Kettenbrücke, a bridge spanning the Regnitz. You will probably see barge traffic on the river, as Bamberg is a major inland port. Cross the bridge and continue on Hauptwachstrasse.

Walk straight ahead past Maximiliansplatz, with its "new" town hall and market place, and into the delightful **Grüner Markt** (2). This large open square, dominated by the Baroque St. Martin's Church and the 17th-century Neptune Fountain, is reserved for pedestrians.

Obstmarkt leads to the Untere Brücke, a bridge over the left arm of the Regnitz. In the center of this stands the ***Altes Rathaus** (3), easily the most remarkable old town hall in Germany. Its extraordinary position in the middle of the river was determined by the local politics of the Middle Ages. At that time it had to administer both the ecclesiastical and civic halves of the city without showing preference for either, hence the truly mid-stream stance. Originally built in the 15th century, it was heavily reconstructed in the rococo style during the 18th. Looking downstream, you will have a good view of the colorful fishermen's houses along the Regnitz, an area known as **Klein-Venedig** (Little Venice).

The Altes Rathaus

After crossing the river, make the first left and then another left onto the Obere Brücke, which goes through the old town hall, allowing a more detailed examination. Return to the left bank and stroll to a small footbridge from which you will have the best possible view of the Altes Rathaus and the 17th-century half-timbered building curiously attached to it.

On the other side make a right at Geyerswörth Castle, built in 1585 as the town residence of the prince-bishop. Continue along to the next bridge and turn right. Midway across this you can stroll out on Untere Mühlbrücke for a wonderful view.

Now follow the map through the Old Town to Domplatz, one of the most attractive public squares in Germany. The ***Cathedral** *(Dom)* (4), first consecrated in 1012 by Emperor Heinrich II, was rebuilt in its present form during the 13th century after two fires destroyed the original structure. It contains the only tomb of a pope in Germany, that of Clement II, who died in 1047 and is buried in the west chancel. The cathedral is exceptionally rich in works of art, the most renowned of which is the ***Bamberger Rider**, a 13th-century equestrian statue of a king by an unknown sculptor. Just to the right of this is the elaborate

*Sarcophagus of Emperor Heinrich II and his wife **Kunigunda**, carved in 1513 by Tilman Riemenschneider. Another masterpiece, on the west wall of the south transept, is the **Maria Altar** by Veit Stoss. The **Diocesan Museum**, adjacent to the cathedral, contains many more treasures, including the imperial cloak of Heinrich II and the robes of Pope Clement II.

Walk across the square to the **Neue Residenz** (New Residence) (5), a massive Baroque structure erected between 1697 and 1703 for the very wealthy Prince-Bishop Franz von Schönborn. Step inside for a look at the magnificent **Kaisersaal** (Emperor's Room) and the luxurious apartments of the prince-bishops. There is also a splendid art gallery with pictures ranging from the Middle Ages to the 18th century. The Neue Residenz is open daily except on some holidays, from 9 a.m. to noon and 1:30–5 p.m. It closes an hour earlier in the winter season. While there, be sure to get out into the **Rose Garden** for a superb view of the town.

The 16th-century gabled **Ratstube**, across the square, is now the home of the **Historisches Museum** (Bamberg History Museum). Although small, it has several fascinating exhibits well worth seeing, and is open from May through October, on Tuesdays through Sundays, from 9 a.m. to 5 p.m.; and for special exhibitions the rest of the year.

Next to this is the Reiche Tor, a richly ornamented gate leading into the **Alte Hofhaltung** (Old Imperial Court) (6), one of the most enchanting sights in Bamberg. The grandiose, quiet inner courtyard is surrounded by half-timbered buildings and the remains of the old Diet Hall, which was used as the seat of local government for over 500 years after 1085.

A gate at the rear of the courtyard opens into Domstrasse. From here follow the map to **St. Michael's Church** (7), part of a former Benedictine abbey originally founded in the 11th century. Inside, there are several interesting things to see, particularly the **tomb** of St. Otto behind the high altar. Crawling through the hole in this is, according to local tradition, a sure cure for lumbago. The ceiling is also unusual, featuring paintings of over 600 different medicinal herbs. As you leave the church, turn right and amble out to the terrace, which offers a wonderful view of the surrounding countryside.

The same monastic complex also houses the **Fränkisches Brauereimuseum** (Franconian Brewery Museum), where the local art of making great beer is explored. This is particularly appropriate in a town whose *average* citizen consumes some 330 liters of beer a year, the world's record. The museum is open on Thursdays through Sundays from 1–4 p.m.

The route back to the Old Town takes you by the 14th-century **Obere Pfarrkirche** (Upper Parish Church) (8), considered by many to be

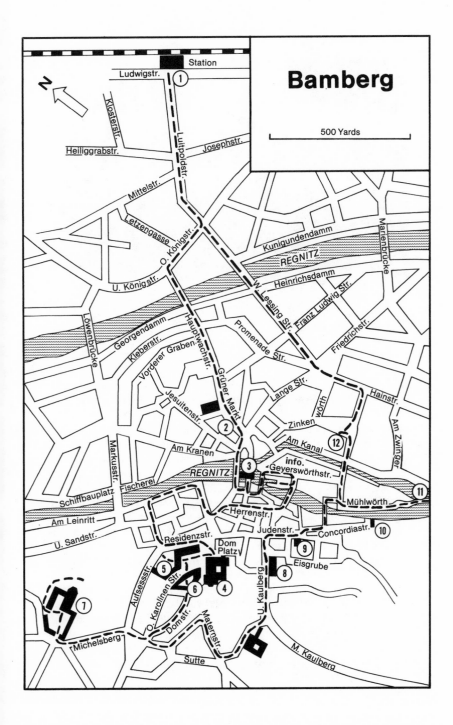

The Alte Hothaltung

Bamberg's finest Gothic structure. Turn right on Judenstrasse and take a look at the **Böttinger House** (9), one of the finest examples of a private mansion in the Baroque style. Built in 1713, it was the winter residence of the court privy councilor Böttinger, who thought of himself as the supreme ruler of Bamberg—although Prince-Bishop von Schönborn entertained similar notions. Böttinger also had another mansion, this one for summer use, just a stone's throw away on the Regnitz.

Walk along the narrow Concordiastrasse for a block, then turn left and cross the tiny footbridge. In this area there are several old mills that have been converted into homes. An alleyway on the other side leads to the Mühlwörth, with an interesting view of Böttinger's other palace, the **Concordia House** (10) on the water's edge. Continue on past the locks of the former **Ludwig Canal** (11) for a short distance, then return and cross the Nonnenbrücke. Along the water, to the left, you can see two interesting old cranes.

The very narrow **E.T.A. Hoffmann House** (12) on Schillerplatz was the home of that great romantic writer from 1809 to 1813. It was his stories that formed the basis for Offenbach's opera *The Tales of Hoffmann*. The house may be visited from May through October, on Tuesdays through Fridays from 4–6 p.m., and on weekends from 10 a.m. to noon. Now follow the map back to the train station.

Bayreuth

For admirers of Wagnerian opera, a daytrip to Bayreuth is a delightful pilgrimage—perhaps the highlight on their entire visit to Germany. Others may find this to be a day largely wasted in the boondocks of Franconia. How much joy you get out of this trip is determined by your musical tastes, and only you can know the answer to that.

There was a town here long before Wagner was ever born, of course. During the 18th century this was a minor cultural oasis under the influence of Princess Wilhelmina, the very talented sister of Frederick the Great, king of Prussia. An ineptitude for diplomacy led to her being married to the exceedingly dull Margrave of Bayreuth, a fate she made bearable by creating what few treasures the town has to offer aside from those associated with the composer.

The annual Bayreuth Festival, which had its premiere on August 13th, 1876, has since turned this provincial Bavarian town into a world-class mecca for music lovers. Organized by Richard Wagner for the express purpose of performing his own operas in his own theater, it helped revolutionize the status of composers from glorified servants of the nobility to entrepreneurs. More than that, it began the entire concept of annual music festivals, now held all over the world.

Bayreuth is a bit difficult to reach from Munich, but dedicated fans will find it well worth the effort. It may also be visited from other Franconian bases, such as Nürnberg.

GETTING THERE:

Trains leave Munich's main station between about 6 and 7:30 a.m. for Nürnberg, where you connect to a local for Bayreuth. The entire journey takes about 3 hours. Return trains (and buses) operate until mid-evening, again changing at Nürnberg.

By car, Bayreuth is 142 miles north of Munich on the A-9 Autobahn.

PRACTICALITIES:

Unless you really love crowds, you should avoid coming during festival time, which lasts from late July until late August. Most of the sights are closed on Mondays. The local **Tourist Information Office**, phone (0921) 885–88, is at Luitpoldplatz 9, a few blocks south of the train station. Bicycles may be rented at the station. Bayreuth has a population of about 72,000.

Haus Wahnfried

FOOD AND DRINK:

Some good places for lunch are:

Königshof (Bahnhofstr. 23, by the station) Elegant dining in a
grand old hotel. Phone (0921) 240-94. $$$

Weihenstephan (Bahnhofstr. 5, south of the station) A favorite
for Franconian dishes, with indoor and outdoor dining.
Phone (0921) 822-88. X: Fri. $$

Brauereischänke am Markt (Maximilianstr. 56, west of the Altes
Schloss) Traditional German food, both indoors or in the
beer garden. Phone (0921) 649-19. $

Braunbierhaus (Kanzleistr. 15, in the Old Town just south of
Maximilianstr.) Local specialties and beers at Bayreuth's oldest eatery, in business since the Middle Ages. $

SUGGESTED TOUR:

Leave the **train station** (1) and walk down Bahnhofstrasse to the
tourist office on Luitpoldplatz. Across the square is the 17th-century
Altes Schloss (Old Palace) (2), home of the ruling margraves until
1754. Destroyed in 1945, it was later rebuilt and now houses government offices. Amble through its courtyard and visit the **Schlosskirche**

Bust of Wagner near the Festspielhaus

(Palace Church), which contains the tombs of Margrave Friedrich and his wife Wilhelmina. From here you can take an interesting stroll through the oldest part of town, perhaps stopping at the 15th-century **Stadtkirche** (Town Church) on Kirchplatz before continuing on to the first major attraction.

Richard Wagner built **Haus Wahnfried** (3) in 1873 as his first, and last, permanent home. Born in Leipzig in 1813, he had always been a wanderer, fleeing both creditors and the police until his strange relationship with the mentally unbalanced King Ludwig II began in 1864. This solved his persistent money problems—he had always lived lavishly on a precarious income—but the composer's political manipulations and loose morals quickly gained him enemies, and he was forced into exile. Eventually, Wagner's ego required that he have his very own opera house, where his works would not be contaminated by those of other composers. Thus the move to Bayreuth, a place so remote and yet within the confines of Ludwig's Bavaria that his adoring public would have to come to *him*.

Haus Wahnfried remained in the possession of Wagner's descendants until 1973, when it was deeded to the town. It has since been restored and is now open as a fascinating museum of the composer's life; one that explores his creative genius without overlooking the blemishes. Visitors may relax in the drawing room and listen to recorded concerts of the operas. Allow plenty of time for this small but intriguing museum, which is open daily except on certain holidays, from 9 a.m. to 5 p.m.

Wagner, who died in 1883, lies buried along with his wife Cosima in a simple **grave** at the rear of the house. Continue past this and wander around the lovely Hofgarten to the **Neues Schloss** (New Palace) (4). Begun in 1753, this late rococo structure reflects the refined tastes of Princess Wilhelmina, who lived here until her death in 1758. Its many charming rooms, filled with period furniture, may be seen on guided tours given frequently every day except Mondays, from 10–11:30 a.m. and 1:30–4:30 p.m., with shorter hours in winter.

Now follow Ludwigstrasse to Wilhelmina's great masterpiece, the ***Markgräfliches Opernhaus** (Margrave's Opera House) (5), otherwise known as the Old Opera. First opened in 1748, it is an absolutely delightful jewel, right up there in the same class with Munich's Cuvilliés Theater. Frequent guided tours are given daily, except on Mondays or during performances. Richard Wagner was originally attracted to Bayreuth by the thought of using this elegant theater for his festival. Alas, its stage proved much too small for both Siegfried *and* the dragon, let alone all those Valkyries. In the end, of course, he built his own opera house, which you should visit next.

Return to the train station and take the route on the map to Wagner's **Festspielhaus** (Festival Theater) (6), the most famous sight in Bayreuth. Set atop a small hill overlooking the town, this curiously nondescript structure was begun in 1872. Wagner was hardly able to raise the money for a cornerstone, to say nothing of an entire opera house, so in the end he had to appeal once again to Ludwig. The king, somewhat peeved at the choice of Bayreuth and by now short of cash as a result of his lavish castles, came up with just enough for this unadorned building. Plans to add an elaborate façade at a later date never materialized.

Inside, however, it is a marvel of technical ingenuity. The acoustics, achieved at the expense of audience comfort, are world-renowned. Singers can be heard above the roar of the orchestra, which is buried in a deep pit. The huge and highly mechanized stage was decades ahead of its time, as was the lighting. Guided tours are held on Tuesdays through Sundays, from 10–11:30 a.m. and 1:30–3 p.m., but only in the mornings from October through March. There are no tours when the theater is in use. Tickets for performances are invariably sold out long in advance. From here it is an easy downhill walk back to the train station.

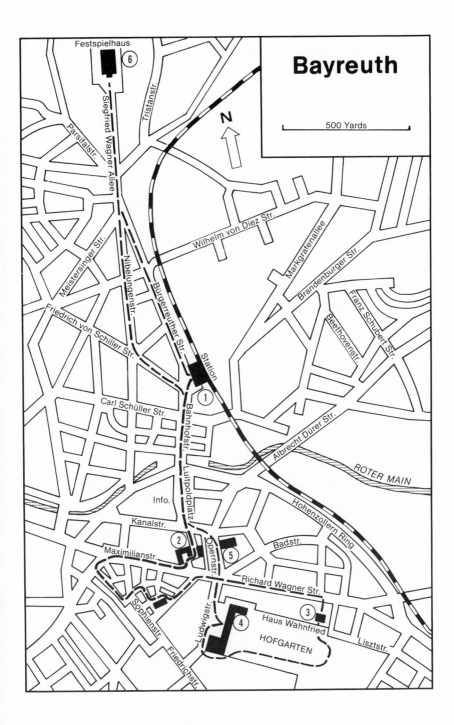

Regensburg

Nearly two thousand years of history have left their mark on unspoiled Regensburg, one of the most ancient cities in Germany. Its location in eastern Bavaria puts it well off the usual tourist circuit, but those who do come this way are in for a real treat.

Way back in A.D. 179 the Roman emperor Marcus Aurelius established a stronghold at the northernmost point of the Danube and called it *Castra Regina*. This was the real founding of the town, although the Celts had a settlement known as *Radasbona* on the site as early as 500 B.C.

In the centuries that followed the collapse of the Roman Empire, Regensburg continued to prosper, first as a bishopric and later as a residence of the Carolingian rulers. It was the capital of Bavaria until the 13th century, when it became a Free Imperial City. By the 16th century, however, its period of greatness declined as other cities such as Augsburg and Nürnberg eclipsed it in trade.

From the end of the Thirty Years War until 1806 the city regained some of its prominence as the seat of Germany's first real parliament, the Permanent Imperial Diet, but this was lost when the Holy Roman Empire of the German Nation ceased to exist. After that, Regensburg became a backwater place that slept through the Industrial Revolution and was largely untouched by World War II. Although prosperity has now returned in the form of modern industries, its center is extremely well preserved and offers tourists a remarkable variety of sights, some dating as far back as the Roman era.

GETTING THERE:

Trains leave Munich's main station several times in the morning for Regensburg, a ride of about 1½ hours. Return service operates until mid-evening.

By car, Regensburg is 75 miles northeast of Munich via the A-9 and A-93 Autobahns.

PRACTICALITIES:

Regensburg may be visited at any time, remembering that the major museum is closed on Mondays and some holidays. The local **Tourist Information Office**, Phone (0941) 507-4410, is in the Altes Rathaus. **Bicycles** may be rented at the train station. Regensburg has a **population** of about 137,000.

The Steinere Brücke and the Cathedral
(Photo courtesy of Regensburg Tourist Office)

FOOD AND DRINK:

Some good choices are:

Kaiserhof am Dom (Kramgasse 10, directly west of the cathedral) Excellent German cuisine in the restaurant of an old hotel. Phone (0941) 58-53-50. $$

Ratskeller (Rathausplatz 1, just east of the Altes Rathaus) Traditional German and International dishes in a vaulted cellar or outdoor courtyard. Phone (0941) 517-77. X: Sun. eve., Mon. $$

Historische Wurstküche (Thundorferstr. 3, on the Danube just east of the bridge) One of Europe's oldest eating establishments offers sausage, sauerkraut, and beer; a not-to-be-missed experience. Phone (0941) 590-98. $

Hofbrauhaus (Rathausplatz, opposite the Altes Rathaus) A more sedate outpost of the Munich original. Phone (0941) 512-80. X: Sun. $

SUGGESTED TOUR:

Leave the **train station** (1) and walk down Maximilianstrasse to the **Alter Kornmarkt** (2), which continues to serve as a market place. On its western side stand two very old structures joined by an archway. One of these is the **Römerturm** (Roman Tower), mainly dating from the Carolingian period but partially of Roman construction. To the left of it is the **Herzogshof** (Ducal Court), built around 1200 as a palace for the local dukes.

Stroll under the archway and visit **St. Peter's Cathedral** *(Dom)* (3), often considered to be the finest Gothic structure in Bavaria. It was begun in 1275 and completed in the 16th century, although the steeples were not added until the 1860s. The western façade is graced with an unusual triangular porch. Go inside and look at the 14th-century **stained-glass windows,** then at the famous statues of the * **Regensburger Angel** and the **Madonna** on the two western pillars of the transepts.

There is a **treasury** *(Domschatzmuseum)* containing some splendid works in gold along with medieval vestments just off the north aisle. Guided tours are offered of the **cloisters**, which largely predate the cathedral, visiting the 10th-century **Chapel of St. Stephan** and the very lovely Romanesque **Allerheiligenkapelle** (All Saints' Chapel). If you happen to be in the cathedral at the right time, you may be treated to a concert by its renowned boys' choir, called the **Domspatzen**.

Amble through the Domgarten to the **Niedermünster** (4), a parish church where excavations have revealed parts of structures from the Roman *Castra Regina*. Continue on to the **Porta Praetoria** (5), the 2nd-century north gate of the original Roman fortifications. Some segments of this, incorporated into a later structure, are remarkably well preserved.

The Danube is only a block away. You may be interested in taking one of the **boat rides** offered along the quay, or in having a marvelous lunch at the **Historische Wurstküche** (6), one of the oldest places to eat in Germany. No one seems to know just how long it has been serving those delicious and inexpensive sausages, but legend has it that the restaurant began as a kitchen for workers building the bridge—and that was in the 12th century! A more recent event is commemorated by a **highwater mark** on the kitchen wall dated March 27, 1988, when the whole place was nearly swept away by floods.

Walk around the ancient salt warehouse and through the **Brückturm** gateway to the ***Steinerne Brücke** (Stone Bridge) (7), a triumph of medieval engineering skills. Although constructed between 1135 and 1146, it still carries vehicular traffic and is indeed the oldest stone bridge in the country.

Cross the bridge for a wonderful view, then return and follow the map past the Fischmarkt. Nearby, at number 5 Keplerstrasse, is the **Kepler-Gedächtnishaus**, home of the famous astronomer Johannes Kepler, who died in 1630. Now a museum of his life, it may be seen on guided tours conducted on Tuesdays through Sundays.

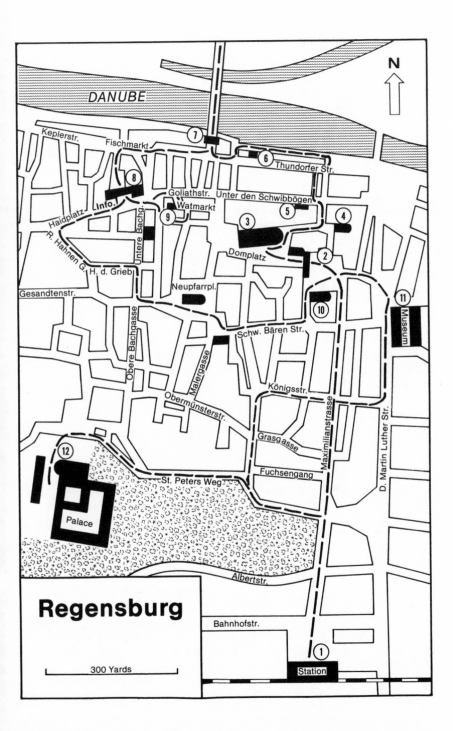

N

DANUBE

Keplerstr.

Fischmarkt

⑦

⑥ Thundorfer Str.

⑧

Info.

Goliathstr. Unter den Schwibbögen

Watmarkt ⑤

Haidplatz

R. Hahnen G. H. d. Grieb

⑨

③ ④

②

Gesandtenstr.

Domplatz

Obere Bachgasse

Untere Bachg.

Neupfarrpl.

⑩

⑪ Museum

Schw. Bären Str.

Malergasse

Königsstr.

Obermünsterstr.

Maximilianstrasse

D. Martin Luther Str.

Grasgasse

⑫

St. Peters Weg

Fuchsengang

Palace

Albertstr.

Regensburg

Bahnhofstr.

300 Yards

①

Station

An alleyway leads to the *Altes Rathaus (Old Town Hall) (8), which houses the tourist office. Most of this imposing complex of structures dates from the 14th through the 16th centuries. Guided tours are conducted through its **Reichssaal** (Imperial Hall)—where the Permanent Imperial Diet met on and off between 1663 and 1806—and the sinister **torture chamber**, preserved in all its original hideousness. These are offered from April through October, on Mondays through Saturdays, from 9:30 a.m. to 4 p.m., and on Sundays from 10 a.m. to noon; and from November through March on Mondays through Saturdays from 9:30–11:30 a.m. and 2–4 p.m., and on Sundays from 10 a.m. to noon.

From here you can stroll through the adjacent Kohlenmarkt for a look at two 13th-century **patrician towers** (9), built in the style of the Italian nobility and unique to Regensburg among cities north of the Alps. These are the **Baumburgerturm** in the Watmarkt and the **Goldener Turm** on Wahlenstrasse. Return to Kohlenmarkt and follow Neue-Waag-Gasse to Haidplatz, a colorful old square with several historic structures.

Continue on Rote-Hahn-Gasse and Hinter-der-Grieb, a delightful medieval lane with more patrician tower-houses. The map shows a route through interesting old streets, going past the 16th-century **Neupfarrkirche**, which was built on the site of a former synagogue after the Jews were expelled from town in 1519. Just beyond this is the Romanesque **Church of St. Cassian**, documented as long ago as 885, and remodeled in the rococo style during the 18th century.

Schwarze-Bären-Strasse and Kapellengasse lead to the **Alte Kapelle**(Old Chapel) (10). More than a thousand years old, it too was given a sumptuous rococo interior during the 18th century, and is very well worth a visit.

Cross the Alter Kornmarkt and walk over to the **Stadtmuseum** (Municipal Museum) (11), housed in a former 13th-century monastery. Allow plenty of time for this as it explores two millenia of history in over a hundred rooms. You don't have to see it all, of course, but once inside you will probably be so intrigued by the Roman relics, Renaissance art, period room settings, and other treasures that time will just seem to fly by. The one item that should not be missed is the foundation plaque of *Castra Regina,* which clearly establishes Regensburg's beginning in A.D. 179. The museum is open on Tuesdays through Saturdays, from 10 a.m. to 4 p.m., and on Sundays from 10 a.m. to 1 p.m.

On the way back to the train station you may want to make an interesting side trip to **St. Emmeram's Church** and the adjacent **Schloss Thurn-und-Taxis** palace (12). The church, one of the oldest in Germany, was built over a long period of time beginning in the 8th century. During the 18th century it was magnificently redecorated in

At the Historische Wurstküche
(Photo courtesy of Regensburg Tourist Office)

the Baroque style by the famous Asam Brothers of Munich. There is some wonderful art inside, as well as three very ancient crypts.

The palace adjoining this is still occupied by the Thurn-und-Taxis family, who got rich running Europe's first postal service. Its lavish interior may be seen on guided tours given several times daily except on Saturdays. There is also a large coach museum. From here it is a short walk to the station.

The Chiemsee

The enchanting Chiemsee, Bavaria's largest lake, lies just north of the Alps within easy reach of Munich. It was on an island in these idyllic waters that Ludwig II, the unbalanced "Dream King," built a Teutonic version of Versailles as his final castle. He was not the first to appreciate the lonely beauty of this spot, however. As far back as 782 a Benedictine convent was founded on a neighboring island; its 15th-century replacement remains there to this day, as does an old fishing community that is fast becoming a modest resort. Between the nearby town of Prien and the ferry dock a 19th-century narrow-gauge steam train shuttles enthusiastic visitors out for a day of fun, sun, and exploration.

GETTING THERE:

Trains depart Munich's main station several times in the morning for the one-hour ride to Prien, the starting point of this trip. Return service operates until mid-evening.

By car, the Chiemsee is 60 miles southeast of Munich via the A-8 Autobahn. Use the Bernau exit and follow signs for Prien, parking at the ferry dock.

PRACTICALITIES:

The best time to visit the Chiemsee is between late May and late September, when boats are frequent and the steam train operates. The castle is open daily all year round, except for a few major holidays. Some boats operate during the off-season. Good weather will greatly enhance this trip. The local **Tourist Information Office**, phone (08051) 690-50, is near the train station in Prien. **Bicycles** may be rented at the Prien station from April through October.

FOOD AND DRINK:

Some choice restaurants and cafés are:

At Stock-Hafen:

Reinhart (Seestr. 117, near the pier) Rustic country charm. Phone (08051) 69-40. $$

Herrenchiemsee Palace

Seehotel Feldhütter (Seestr. 101, near the pier) Has an outdoor beer garden. Phone (08051) 43-21. $$

König Ludwig Stuben (Seestr. 95, right by the ferry pier) An outdoor beer garden with food. Phone (08051) 48-02. $

On Herreninsel:

Schlosshotel Herrenchiemsee (by the Altes Schloss) Noted for its fish dishes, also has outdoor tables and a café. Phone (08051) 15-09. $$

On Fraueninsel:

Zur Linde (near the pier) A gasthof from the 14th century. Phone (08054) 316. $$

Inselwirt (near the convent) Specializes in lake fish. Phone (08054) 630. $$

Kloster Café (next to the convent) A full restaurant and café. Phone (08054) 77-65. $

SUGGESTED TOUR:

Begin at the **Prien Train Station** (1). From there you can get to the ferry pier *(Stock-Hafen)* by either the 19th-century ***Chiemsee Bahn** steam train departing from the adjacent station, or by bus, depending on which is running at the moment. Just follow the crowds—they're going to the same place. A combination round-trip ticket for the steam train or bus plus the ferry rides is available. If you decide to walk, or are driving, just follow Seestrasse for about one mile.

Ferries for the two islands depart from the **Stock-Hafen Pier** (2), and are timed to meet the arrival of trains and buses. Boat tickets are also sold there.

The **Chiemsee** (pronounced *keem-zay*) covers an area of over 31 square miles and has three islands; one of which, Krautinsel, is uninhabited. Of the other two, Herreninsel (Men's Island) has had a monastery since the Middle Ages, and Fraueninsel (Ladies' Island) a nunnery since 782. According to legend, Krautinsel (Vegetable Island) was the spot where the monks and nuns got together, at least to grow veggies.

The boat ride to **Herreninsel** takes only 15 minutes. Upon arrival at its **landing stage** (3), walk uphill to the 17th-century **Altes Schloss** (4), once the home of Augustinian canons. There is an attractive **outdoor café** and restaurant in its precincts. From here a path leads through the woods, opening suddenly to reveal the palace in all its splendor.

King Ludwig II of Bavaria was just about the strangest monarch ever to rule a European country. Born centuries too late, he lived in a sheltered dreamworld of his own making. In the end, events swept him aside and he died tragically at the age of 40. The legacy he left behind, from the operas of Richard Wagner to the fantastic castles dotting the Bavarian landscape, has, however, greatly enriched all of Western civilization.

Rising before you, the ***Palace of Herrenchiemsee** (5) was Ludwig's final paean to an age that vanished long before he was born. Ludwig purchased the island, a religious center until 1803, as the site for his Teutonic Versailles. Louis XIV of France had long been his idol, and he made two visits to Paris to study the palace of the "Sun King." The similarity between the two buildings, while striking, is only superficial—most of the interior decoration at Herrenchiemsee is distinctly German. Construction began in 1878 and continued until 1885, when funds gave out. Ludwig occupied the unfinished *Schloss* on only one occasion, and then for only 10 days. This was in the fall of 1885. Less than a year later he was deposed, and afterwards found drowned in Lake Starnberg.

The interior of the palace is simply incredible. To see it you will have to join one of the very frequent guided tours, some of which are in English. An illustrated booklet describing the entire palace is available at the entrance, where there is also a small **museum** devoted to Ludwig's life. Visits may be made daily from April through September, 9 a.m. to 5 p.m.; and from October through March, 10 a.m. to 4 p.m.

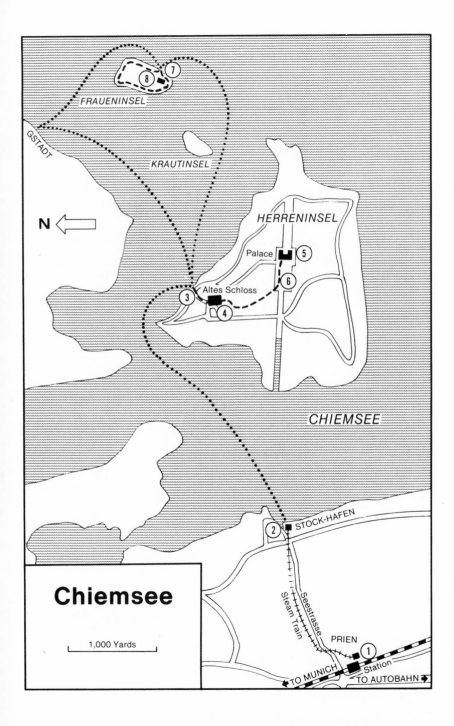

N

FRAUENINSEL

KRAUTINSEL

HERRENINSEL

Palace

Altes Schloss

GSTADT

CHIEMSEE

STOCK-HAFEN

PRIEN

Steam Train

Seestrasse

Station

TO MUNICH

TO AUTOBAHN

Chiemsee

1,000 Yards

View from Fraueninsel

Leaving the palace, walk straight ahead to the **Latona Fountain** (6), which erupts into jets of water at frequent intervals. From here stroll back to the landing stage and board the next boat for Fraueninsel. Ask to make sure that you are on the right boat, as some go to other points on the lake.

Arriving at the **Fraueninsel landing stage** (7), recheck the posted schedule to determine just how much time can be spent there. Turn left and walk around the Benedictine nunnery, founded in 782 and rebuilt several times. Its **Abbey Church** (8), dating from the 13th and 15th centuries and combining Romanesque, Gothic, and Baroque elements, is very well worth a visit.

Besides the convent, Fraueninsel is essentially a fishing village, albeit one that is rapidly being taken over by vacationers. A circular stroll around its perimeter reveals an oasis of quiet beauty with a panorama of mountains to the south, a perfect spot to relax at one of the **outdoor cafés** before returning to Stock-Hafen, Prien, and Munich.

If you have time left in Prien, you might want to visit the town's **Folk Museum** (*Heimatmuseum*) in an old farmhouse at Friedhofweg 2, about three blocks west of the train station. It's open on Tuesdays through Fridays from 10 a.m. to noon and 3–5 p.m., and on Saturdays from 10 a.m. to noon, with shorter times in winter.

Bad Reichenhall

Bad Reichenhall makes an interesting change of pace if you've already sampled Bavaria's more famous alpine resorts. In many ways the most elegant spa of the entire *Freistaat,* it still retains much of the atmosphere of an Edwardian watering place. Germans flock there by the thousands to relax in beautiful surroundings and take the curative treatments for a wide variety of ailments, real or imagined. Casual tourists will be more attracted to its mountains, the marvelous old salt works, the fashionable life style, or even the gambling casino.

It was the presence of salt in the nearby mountains that brought prosperity to Reichenhall as early as Celtic times. The local springs contain saline concentrations ranging up to 24%, the highest in Europe. These were exploited by the Romans, who shipped the salt throughout their empire. In the Middle Ages the trade continued to flourish and was largely responsible for the settlement of Munich during the 12th century. For the past hundred years, however, the springs have been used primarily for curative purposes.

GETTING THERE:

Trains leave Munich's main station between around 7 and 9 a.m. for the $2\frac{1}{4}$-hour trip to Bad Reichenhall. A change at Freilassing may be necessary; otherwise be sure to get on a car marked for Berchtesgaden as through trains split en route. Return service operates until early evening.

By car, Bad Reichenhall is 85 miles southeast of Munich via the A-8 Autobahn.

PRACTICALITIES:

Bad Reichenhall is a year-round resort, but daytrippers will find it more attractive in summer. The salt works are open daily from April through October. The local **Tourist Information Office**, Phone (08651) 30-03, is at Wittelsbacher Strasse 15, just north of the Kurgarten. **Bicycles** may be rented at the station from April through October. Bad Reichenhall has a **population** of about 18,500.

FOOD AND DRINK:

Kurhotel Luisenbad (Ludwigstr. 33, a block south of the Kurgarten) Inventive cuisine at a famous old spa. Phone (08651) 60-40. X: Nov. to mid-Dec. $$$

Hotel Axelmannstein (Salzburgerstr. 4, by the Kurgarten) The expensive Park Restaurant features International cuisine,

Along Ludwigstrasse

while the popular Axel-Stüberl sticks to modified Bavarian dishes. Phone (08651) 77-70. $$ and $$$

Brauerei Bürgerbräu (Waaggasse 2, just west of the Rathaus) Good food at a simple inn. Phone (08651) 60-89. $

Hansi (Rinckstr. 3, a block northeast of the Kurgarten) Vegetarian and other healthy dishes featured. Phone (08651) 983-10. X: Mon., Dec. $

SUGGESTED TOUR:

Leaving the **train station** (1), walk along Bahnhofstrasse to the **Kurgarten** (2), a delightful park containing the **Casino**, music pavilion, drinking hall, and other features. The most unusual of these is the **Gradierwerk**, a strange structure near the entrance in which salt water is filtered through walls of twigs to create a healthier air for breathing while briskly walking through. Try it.

Continue along the pedestrians-only Salzburger Strasse and Ludwigstrasse to **Rathaus Platz** (3), a market square in front of the beautifully frescoed old town hall.

The major sight in Bad Reichenhall is the ***Alte Saline** (Old Salt Works) (4), just a few steps away. Built in 1834 by King Ludwig I, it has some utterly fantastic 19th-century machinery for pumping the salt water up from the springs below. Unlike nearby Berchtesgaden (and Hallein in Austria), where salt deposits are removed by flooding the sink works with clear water, the brine here comes directly from the

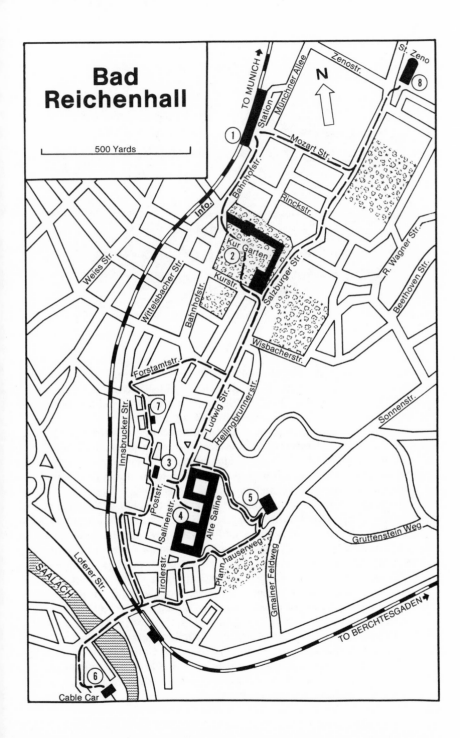

The Rathaus Platz

earth in natural form. **Conducted tours** through the tunnels and caves are given daily from April through October, 10–11:30 a.m. and 2–4 p.m. During the remainder of the year they are usually held on Tuesday and Thursday afternoons only, from 2–4 p.m.

Follow the map uphill to **Schloss Gruttenstein** (5), a 13th- to 17th-century castle that offers great views of the town and surrounding mountains. Although it is now used for private housing, you can enter the courtyard and look around. Another path leads down to Obere Lindenplatz in the old part of town.

Cross the bridge over the Saalach River and turn left to the lower station of the **Predigtstuhl Bahn** (6). This cable car takes you in 10 minutes to the top of the highest mountain in the vicinity for a marvelous panorama across the Alps. There is a **café** near the summit, and several **trails** that can be walked.

Return to the town and stroll down Poststrasse to the **Heimatmuseum** (7). Open from 2–6 p.m., Tuesdays through Fridays, it has an interesting collection of local crafts and artifacts reflecting the region's long history.

Now follow the map to the **Church of St. Zeno** (8). Originally built in the 12th century, it was reconstructed in the Gothic style in 1520 and later given Baroque features. The carved altarpiece, containing some splendid 16th-century sculpture, is particularly attractive. From here it is only a few blocks back to the station.

Berchtesgaden

Berchtesgaden is one of the most popular resorts in Germany, and with good reason. Few places in the country offer such spectacular mountain scenery, and none have anything that equals the sublime beauty of its lake, the Königssee. Then there is the town itself, whose old castle and fascinating salt mines are certainly worth more than a detour. But, ironically, to many people the area is known only for its association with Adolf Hitler and his gang, who held court there during the short span of the Third Reich. That dreadful era is long since over, and Berchtesgaden has survived with all of its natural splendors intact.

The only problem with a daytrip to Berchtesgaden is that it requires some hard choices—you can't possibly see everything in the time available. The best solution, of course, is to stay overnight or longer, remembering that the town makes an excellent base for excursions to Bad Reichenhall, the Chiemsee, or even Salzburg in Austria.

GETTING THERE:

Trains depart Munich's main station around 7 and 9 a.m. for the nearly 3-hour trip to Berchtesgaden. A change at Freilassing may be necessary; otherwise be sure to get on the right car as through trains split en route. Return service operates until early evening.

By car, Berchtesgaden is 96 miles southeast of Munich via the A-8 Autobahn to the Bad Reichenhall exit, then the B-20 road.

PRACTICALITIES:

The period between mid-May and mid-October is the best time to visit Berchtesgaden. Good weather will make the trip much more enjoyable, but you should still bring along a sweater or jacket if you visit the salt mines or the Eagle's Nest. Be sure to check the opening times of each attraction before making your plans. The local **Tourist Information Office** (*Kurdirektion*), phone (08652) 96-70, is just across the bridge from the train station. **Bicycles** may be rented at the station from April through October. Berchtesgaden has a permanent **population** of about 8,200.

FOOD AND DRINK:

In town:

Hotel Vier Jahreszeiten (Maximilianstr. 20, north of the train station) A traditional hotel dining room with a broad choice of specialties. Phone (08652) 50-26. $$

Post (Maximilianstr. 2, near the Kurgarten) A small hotel with a beer garden and a good restaurant. Phone (08652) 50-67. $$

The Königssee area has several tourist restaurants between the bus stop, the lake, and the Malerwinkel.

On the Obersalzberg:

Kehlsteinhaus (in the Eagle's Nest) Food and drink in a mountain aerie overlooking the world. Phone (08652) 29-62. $$

Zum Türken (near the Obersalzberg-Hintereck parking lot) A famous little inn on the Obersalzberg plateau. Phone (08652) 24-28. X: Nov., Dec. $

SUGGESTED TOUR:

The three do-it-yourself tours described here all begin at the centrally located train station (1). You will only have time to do two of these in one single day.

THE TOWN:

Leave the **train station** (1) and follow the map uphill to the **Kurgarten** (2), a delightful little park with lovely views. Continue on through a colorful pedestrians-only area, passing the old market place, and walk under a passageway into the **Schlossplatz** (3). This picturesque square is lined on its western side with 16th-century arcades.

The **Stiftskirche** (Abbey Church), on the eastern side, dates from 1122 and is well worth a visit for its fine works of art. Directly adjacent to it is the **Schloss** (Castle), originally built as an Augustinian monastery. In 1803 this was secularized and afterwards used as a summer residence for Bavaria's ruling family, the Wittelsbachs. One of their descendants, Crown Prince Rupprecht, who had a tenuous (very tenuous) claim to the British throne through his maternal Stuart ancestors, lived here until his death in 1955. Its marvelous interiors are now open to the public, and its sumptuous collection of art and furnishings are shown on **guided tours** lasting about an hour. These are given daily, except on Saturdays and major holidays, from 10 a.m. to 1 p.m. and 2–5 p.m. From October until Easter it is also closed on Sundays.

A highlight of any trip to Berchtesgaden is a tour through the ***Salzbergwerk** (Salt Mines) (4), which can be reached on foot via Bräuhausstrasse and Bergwerkstrasse. In operation since 1517, the mines were the original source of wealth for the priory, and are still in active use today. Visitors are loaned traditional miners' clothes for protection

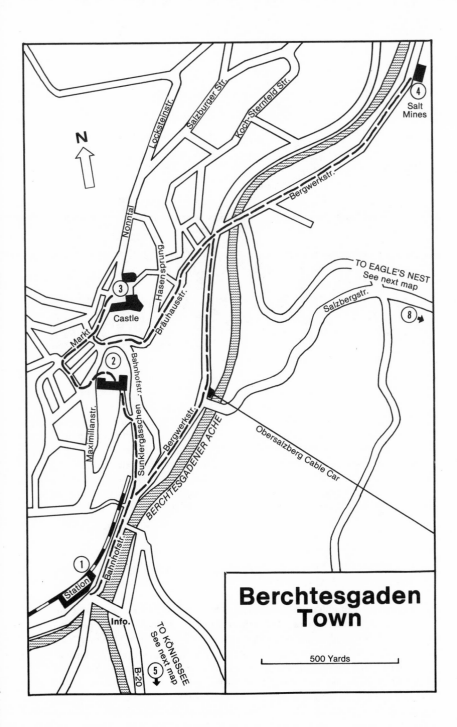

N

Locksteinstr.

Salzburger Str.

Koch-Sternfeld Str.

④ Salt Mines

Bergwerkstr.

Nonntal

Hasensprung

③ Castle

Bräuhausstr.

TO EAGLE'S NEST
See next map

Salzbergstr.

⑧ →

Markt

② Bahnhofstr.

Maximilianstr.

Sunklergässchen

Bergwerkstr.

BERCHTESGADENER ACHE

Obersalzberg Cable Car

① Station

Bahnhofstr.

Info.

TO KÖNIGSSEE
See next map

⑤ ↓

B-20

Berchtesgaden
Town

500 Yards

The Schlossplatz

against the cold and damp environment; then loaded aboard a motor-ized cart for the dark, eerie, half-mile-long journey into the bowels of the earth. Different parts of the subterranean excavations are reached via exciting **downhill slides** and a **boat ride** across an underground lake. About 90 minutes later you will return to the outer world on another little tram. This fascinating tour is operated daily from May through mid-October, 8:30 a.m. to 5 p.m.; and during the rest of the year daily except on Sundays and holidays, from 12:30–3:30 p.m. From here it is a little over a mile back to the station.

*KÖNIGSSEE:

Buses to the Königssee leave frequently from the front of the **train station** (1). Those with cars or bikes will, of course, ride the two-and-a-half-mile distance, while the more ambitious can walk along a foot-path following the stream.

Many people consider the ***Königssee** (5) to be the most en-chanting lake in Germany, if not in all of Europe. It can be explored on one of the silent electric boat tours or by walking out to the Maler-winkel. Ideally, you should do both. From the bus stop or parking lot it is only a short stroll to the village, which is rather touristy but well hidden from the main part of the lake.

A path from here leads to the left and follows the lake's contours to

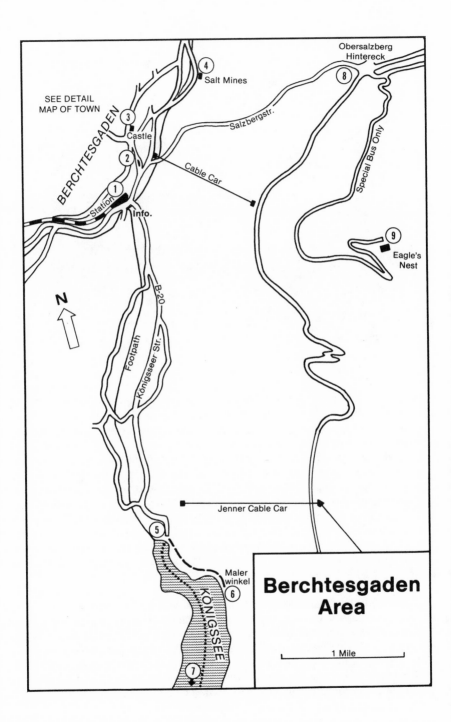

The Königssee from Malerwinkel

the ***Malerwinkel** (Painters' Corner) (6), a tranquil spot of astonishing beauty. About one-half mile from the village, it is the end of the trail—beyond which the mountains plunge vertically into the dark and mysterious waters.

Boats leave frequently from the village for the two-hour round-trip ride to St. Bartholomä and beyond. Those making the longer trip should get off at the end and take a ten-minute walk to the Obersee, once a part of the Königssee that was cut off by an avalanche eight centuries ago. The **Chapel of St. Bartholomä** (7), at the foot of the Watzmann, Germany's second-highest peak, is a scene right out of a fairy tale. When you've had your fill of natural splendor, return to the village and take the bus back to the Berchtesgaden station.

EAGLE'S NEST:

A visit to Hitler's alpine aerie begins by taking a bus to Obersalzberg-Hintereck, or by driving there—a distance of two and a half steep miles. Buses (marked Kehlstein) leave at about half-hour intervals until 4 p.m. from the front of the post office next to the **train station** (1), or you might consider a guided tour in English departing from the tourist office. There is also a **cable car** from the Bergwerkstrasse in Berchtesgaden, but this involves a walk of about a mile and a half

The Eagle's Nest

from its upper station to Obersalzberg-Hintereck.

Adolf Hitler lived on the **Obersalzberg plateau** (8) on and off from 1923 until 1933, when he began construction there on his permanent home, the Berghof. Other Nazi leaders followed suit, and by World War II the area was a highly developed complex of party and military buildings linked by underground tunnels. For obvious reasons, nearly all of this was demolished after the war.

One famous structure that does remain, however, is Hitler's hideaway, the **Kehlsteinhaus**, often called the **Eagle's Nest** (9). Located on a rocky crag high above the compound, it can only be reached by a special bus that departs frequently from the Obersalzberg-Hintereck parking lot. Other vehicles are not allowed to use the steep and dangerous road. Upon arrival you should make return reservations, then enter a tunnel and take the elevator at its end up through the rocks to the Eagle's Nest.

Seldom used by the *Führer,* this retreat was allowed to survive and is now a restaurant and café. Stroll out to the crest beyond for a fabulous view of the Alps. The Eagle's Nest can be visited daily between late May and early October, but is closed the rest of the year because of weather. From here retrace your route back to the Berchtesgaden train station.

The Wendelstein

Towering at some 6,000 feet, the Wendelstein may not be the highest peak in the Bavarian Alps, but it does provide the focus for a very enjoyable daytrip. *Münchners* have been reveling in the view from its summit ever since Germany's first alpine rack railway was built there in 1912. A cable car down its other side has since been added, making possible an exciting circular tour. Add to this the charming small resort of Bayrischzell and you have the makings of a fun-filled day in the mountains.

GETTING THERE:

Trains leave Munich's main station around 8:30 and 10:30 a.m. for the 90-minute ride direct to Bayrischzell. Those making the full circular trip will be returning via Brannenburg, from which trains to Munich run until early evening. Some of these require a change at Rosenheim. If you decide against making the full circuit you can return from Osterhofen as late as early evening. Be sure to check the schedules carefully.

By car, Bayrischzell is 48 miles southeast of Munich. Take the A-8 Autobahn to the Irschenberg exit and head south on local roads past Schliersee to Bayrischzell. It is not very practical to make the full circular tour by car, although there is limited bus service from Brannenburg back to Osterhofen.

PRACTICALITIES:

Good weather is absolutely essential for this trip as it involves a few miles of pleasant country walking, except for those who are driving. The cable car and rack railway operate all year round. Bayrischzell has a local **Tourist Information Office** *(Kuramt)*, phone (08023) 648, at Kirchplatz 2. **Bicycles** may be rented at the train station from April through October. The permanent **population** of Bayrischzell is about 1,600.

Outdoor Café in Bayrischzell

FOOD AND DRINK:

Zur Post (Schulstr. 3 in Bayrischzell) An alpine hotel noted for its cooking. Phone (08023) 226. X: Tues., mid-Oct. to mid-Dec. $$

Hotel Wendelstein (Ursprungstr. 1 in Bayrischzell) An inn with good-value meals in a beer garden. Phone (08023) 610. X: Nov., Dec. $ and $$

Deutsches Haus (Schlierseer Str. 16 in Bayrischzell) An attractive alpine inn with indoor/outdoor dining. Phone (08023) 201. X: mid-Nov. to mid-Dec. $

Bergrestaurant (at the top of the cable car) Meals, snacks or drinks with a view, indoors or out. $

SUGGESTED TOUR:

Begin at the **Bayrischzell train station** (1). Tourist information is available at the *Kur* office near the church to the left. You might want to pick up a large-scale map *(Wanderkarte)* of the area before setting out. The pretty village is small enough to explore in a half-hour or so, and has a good selection of restaurants and cafés.

From Bayrischzell you can walk along a lovely trail (sign-posted as Route K5) just north of the railway line to the cable car station in **Osterhofen** (2), a distance of just under two miles. It is also possible to

Atop the Wendelstein

get there by train, bus, taxi, car, or bike.

Those making the circular tour should purchase a combination ticket for the cable car and rack railway to Brannenburg. If you would rather return to Munich from Osterhofen you can get a round-trip cable car ticket *(Berg und Talfahrt)* instead. Board the cable car *(Seilbahn)* for the six-minute ride to the top.

From the **upper station** (3) you can stroll out on a terrace for a fabulous view of the Alps and the Chiemsee far below. Food and drinks with a view are offered at the Bergrestaurant. There is an attractive **chapel** nearby, the highest in Germany, which dates from 1718. Just below this is the entrance to the 600-foot-long **cave** *(Höhle)*, giving you a chance to explore the insides of the mountain. **Trails** lead in several directions, the most interesting of which climbs to the solar observatory at the **summit** (6,035 feet above sea level). Be sure to visit the Geo-Park.

The **rack railway** *(Zahnradbahn)* to Brannenburg leaves from a station nearby. Those making the circular trip should board it for the delightful half-hour descent to the **valley station** (4). From here it is possible to get one of the infrequent buses back to Osterhofen, or walk a little less than two miles to the **Brannenburg train station** (5) and take a train from there to Munich. Some of these require a change at Rosenheim.

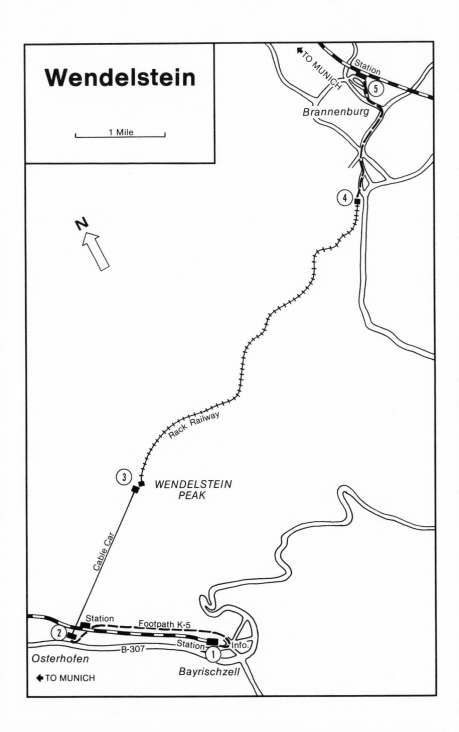

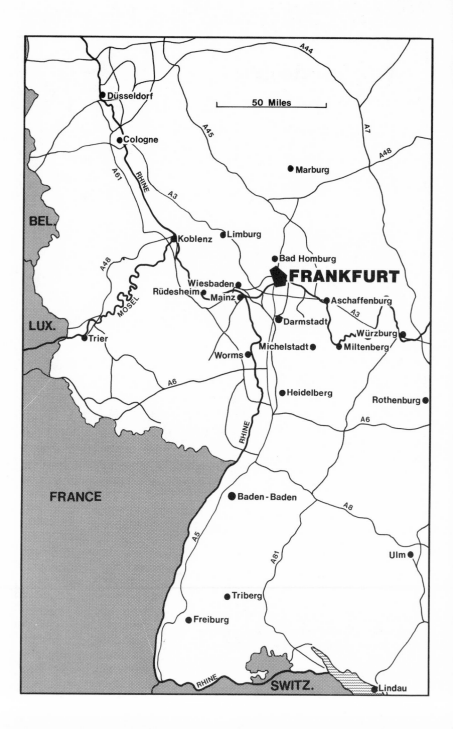

Section III

THE RHINELAND

If Bavaria is the very soul of Germany, then the Rhineland must be its heart. This large and loosely defined area offers travelers a tremendously wide variety of destinations. Such diverse experiences as a village in the Black Forest, the greatest Roman ruins north of the Alps, glittering cities and quiet university towns, elegant spas, river cruises, and wine tasting all lie within easy daytrip range of its center.

The hub of the Rhineland is Frankfurt—for many tourists the starting point of their Teutonic adventures. This is where most overseas flights to Germany terminate, and a place from which rail lines and highways reach out in all directions. Before embarking on any trips, however, you may want to devote a day to exploring the city itself by taking the walking tour described in the next chapter.

While all of the excursions outlined in this section can be made from Frankfurt, for some you may prefer alternative bases such as Mainz, Wiesbaden, Koblenz, Cologne, Darmstadt, or Heidelberg. These options are mentioned in the text whenever they are practical. Mainz and Wiesbaden are especially useful when all of the hotels in Frankfurt are booked solid, as sometimes happens.

Four of the daytrips described in the previous section on Bavaria can also be taken from Frankfurt; namely Rothenburg, Würzburg, Nürnberg, and Bamberg. Details concerning transportation from Frankfurt are given for each.

Frankfurt

Thousands of travelers pass through Frankfurt's international airport every day, most of them en route to somewhere else. For many, this bustling metropolis on the Main is just the beginning—or the end—of their journey, not a destination in itself. The city has an undeserved reputation of being cold and impersonal, and of offering little in the way of tourist interest. True, Frankfurt is hardly picturesque, nor does it project the style of a Munich or a Düsseldorf. But it does have a tremendous vitality, a sheer creative drive that makes a visit here essential to understanding what modern Germany is all about.

Frankfurt-am-Main, to use its complete name, has been a trading place since prehistoric times, a fact made inevitable by its location at a point where the Main River could be forded. The Romans had a fort there until they were driven out by a succession of tribes. Around A.D. 500, this was captured by the Franks, after which it became known as the Franks' Ford.

The growing town assumed real importance as early as the 8th century, when Charlemagne held court there. Between 1562 and 1806 Frankfurt was the coronation city of the Holy Roman emperors. The long tradition of trade fairs dates from the early 13th century, and was responsible for the rise of the banking interests that dominate the city's life today.

Nearly bombed out of existence during World War II, Frankfurt was hastily rebuilt in the modern mold, its skyline dotted with high-rise office towers. In recent years a determined effort has been made to restore what little remains of the past, and the sterility of its new architecture is gradually being relieved by attractive pedestrian zones.

Frankfurt is the hub of a vast transportation network, making it the ideal base for daytrips into central Germany. Those who prefer a less hectic atmosphere, but would still like to take advantage of its unrivaled travel facilities, should consider staying in the easily-reached suburbs, such as Bad Homburg; or in other nearby cities including Mainz, Wiesbaden, and Darmstadt. If you come without confirmed hotel reservations during a major trade fair, you may have to do this whether you want to or not. The tourist offices in the nearby towns will help you to find suitable accommodations.

GETTING THERE:

Trains from all over Germany and Europe arrive at Frankfurt's 19th-century **Hauptbahnhof** (main train station), one of the largest and old-

152

est in the nation. S-Bahn commuter trains, including those from the airport, usually (but not always) use the underground level, while expresses and other trains terminate at the street level.

By car, Frankfurt is at the center of a network of Autobahns fanning out in all directions. To find the city center, just follow the *Stadtmitte* signs.

By air, flights from all around the world arrive at continental Europe's busiest airport, **Flughafen Frankfurt**, always known to old hands as Rhein-Main. S-Bahn commuter trains depart from the lower level of the terminal building at 10-minute intervals for the 11-minute ride to Frankfurt's Hauptbahnhof station. About half of these continue on to the Hauptwache and Konstablerwache underground stations. Many InterCity and EuroCity trains stop at the airport station as well, as do the excellent **Lufthansa Airport Express** luxury trains to Bonn, Cologne, and Düsseldorf; and now also to Stuttgart.

GETTING AROUND:

While the suggested walking tour is rather short, you might want to use public transportation at some point. The system consists of subways, buses, and streetcars. A map and instructions are available at tourist information offices or information windows of Frankfurt Transit *(FVV)*.

Frankfurt, like Munich and Hamburg, has *two* subway systems; the **U-Bahn** which remains underground, and the **S-Bahn** which surfaces once beyond the main station and continues on as a suburban commuter rail network. Railpasses may be used on the S-Bahn, *but very definitely not on the U-Bahn, streetcars, or buses.* Just before boarding these (or the S-Bahn if you have no pass) it is necessary to buy a ticket from one of the automatic vending machines, labeled *Fahrscheine*, located in subway stations or by streetcar or bus stops. These are valid for any combination of modes going in a direct route to your destination. The time of purchase is stamped on the ticket, and the fares automatically increased during rush hours. Failure to have a valid ticket could result in a fine.

The system is divided into fare zones, as shown on the maps, but most of your travels will probably be within the basic inner-city zone. Note that fares are different for adults *(Erwachsene)* and children four through 14 years of age *(Kinder)*, as indicated by pictograms on the vending machines. Those using the S-Bahn should beware of boarding first-class cars with an ordinary ticket. If all this sounds confusing, you can purchase a one- or three-day ticket, allowing unlimited rides in the inner zone for that period, at one of the ticket windows or from the machines.

PRACTICALITIES:

Frankfurt may be explored in any season. The walk can be completed in about two hours, not including time spent visiting museums or sights. Most of the museums are closed on Mondays. The local **Tourist Information Office** (Verkehrsamt), phone (069) 212-8849, is in the main train station opposite track 23. There is a branch at Römerberg 27, by the old Town Hall, phone (069) 212-8708. Frankfurt has a population of about 660,000.

FOOD AND DRINK:

Although dining well in Frankfurt can be hideously expensive, it's not necessary to live on frankfurters alone to avoid bankruptcy. Some good choices, mostly in a more moderate range, are:

Restaurant Français (in Hotel Frankfurter Hof, Am Kaiserpl. 17, 2 blocks southwest of the Goethe Haus) Traditional French cuisine in luxurious surroundings. Proper dress expected, for reservations phone (069) 215-02. X: Sat. lunch. $$$

Tse-Yang (Kaiserstr. 67, 2 blocks east of the train station) Regarded as the best Chinese restaurant in Frankfurt. Phone (069) 23-25-41. $$$

Mövenpick (Opernpl. 2, by the Alte Oper) A variety of reliably good restaurants and cafés in one popular establishment. Phone (069) 206-80. $$ and $$$

Börsenkeller (Schillerstr. 11, a block north of the Hauptwache) Long favored by stockbrokers for its substantial cuisine. Phone (069) 28-11-15. X: Sun. $$

Frankfurter Stubb (in Hotel Frankfurter Hof, Am Kaiserpl. 17, 2 blocks southwest of the Goethe Haus) Traditional local specialties in an atmospheric wine cellar. For reservations phone (069) 215-02. X: Sun., holidays. $$

Café Hauptwache (An der Hauptwache) A café and restaurant in an historic landmark building. Outdoor terrace in summer. $ and $$

Steineres Haus (Braubachstr. 35, 2 blocks northwest of the cathedral) Traditional local dishes in simple surroundings. Phone (069) 28-34-91. $

Zum Gemalten Haus (Schweizerstr. 67, in Sachsenhausen, a block south of the Untermain bridge) A very popular, rustic old apple-wine place with traditional Frankfurt cooking. Phone (069) 61-45-59. X: Mon., Tues. $

SUGGESTED TOUR:

For the convenience of those staying out of town, the walk begins at the 19th-century **Hauptbahnhof** (main train station) (1), one of the

An der Hauptwache

largest in Germany. You may want to spend a few minutes soaking up the atmosphere of this busy old terminal.

Cross the square in front of the station via an underground passage, which contains a variety of shops as well as U- and S-Bahn stations. From here follow Kaiserstrasse through a somewhat seedy "eros" zone until you come to a park. To your right is a modern theater complex, used for operas and plays. Turn left and continue along Gallusanlage and Taunusanlage—the line of the old medieval town walls—to the **Alte Oper** (Old Opera House) (2). Built in 1880 in the Italian Renaissance style, it was destroyed by bombs in 1944 and later restored as a very elegant concert hall.

To the right begins what is officially known as the Grosse Bockenheimer Strasse, but called the **Fressgass** (Feeding Street) by nearly everyone as it is lined with tempting restaurants, cafés, and food shops. Walk down it, perhaps stopping for a bite, and turn left on Börsenstrasse to the 19th-century **Börse** (Stock Exchange), the nerve center of Frankfurt's financial life. Its visitors' gallery is open to individual travelers on Mondays through Fridays, from 10:30 a.m. to 1:30

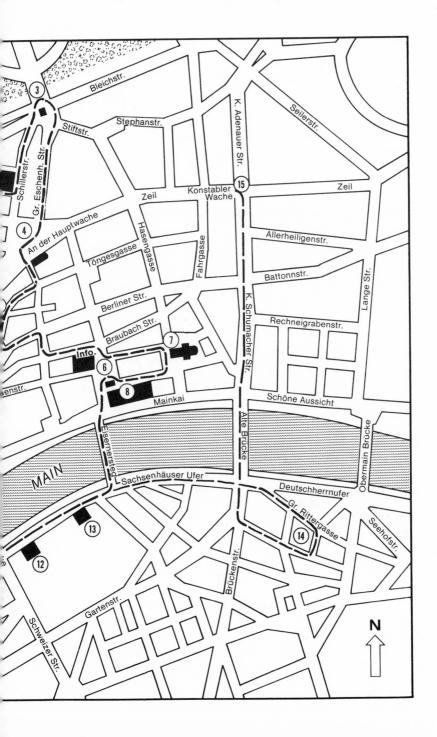

p.m.; passport or other ID required. Modern computers have replaced much of the floor action, but a visit is still worthwhile.

Stroll through the adjacent Börsenplatz and make a left on Schillerstrasse to the **Eschenheimer Turm** (3), a handsome 15th-century defensive gate and the last surviving remnant of the city's medieval fortifications. It certainly makes a surprising (and welcome!) sight amid all of the office towers.

Now take Grosse Eschenheimer Strasse to **An der Hauptwache** (4)—the very heart of modern Frankfurt. Beneath this huge open square lies a sprawling shopping center with both U- and S-Bahn stations. The 18th-century Hauptwache building in the center was once a guard house, but since 1904 has served as a perenially popular **café.** On the south side is the **Katharinenkirche** (St. Catherine's Church), where the first Protestant sermon in Frankfurt was preached in 1522, and where the great poet Goethe was both baptized and confirmed. First built in the 14th century, it was reconstructed in 1681 and again in 1954. The very beautiful interior is noted for its contemporary **stained-glass windows.**

Continue on to the ***Goethe Haus** (5), where Frankfurt's favorite son, Johann Wolfgang von Goethe, was born in 1749, and where he spent his childhood and adolescence. Whether you are a fan of Goethe or not, you will certainly enjoy a visit here if only to see how a well-to-do family lived in those times. The house was almost totally destroyed during World War II, but has since been lovingly reconstructed using as much of the original material as could be reclaimed from the rubble. An adjoining building houses a small **museum** devoted to the life of Germany's greatest literary genius. Both the house and the museum are open on Mondays through Saturdays, from 9 a.m. to 6 p.m.; and on Sundays from 10 a.m. to 1 p.m. From October through March it closes at 4 p.m. on weekdays. Don't miss seeing this.

A short stroll leads to the **Römerberg** (6), a large and heavily restored old square lined with gabled buildings. The 15th-century **Römer**, Frankfurt's historic town hall, has an Imperial Hall *(Kaisersaal)* that you can see, although its sole attraction consists of some 52 large but rather mediocre paintings of all the Holy Roman emperors from Charlemagne on. While in the square, be sure to visit the tiny **Nikolaikirche** (Church of St. Nicholas) on the south side. Originally built in the 13th century, it is noted for its restrained interior, and for its tower that vaguely resembles a minaret.

Follow Markt past the **Historische Garten**, an excavated site in the very oldest part of Frankfurt; where Roman, Carolignian, and medieval remains form a small park. Opposite this is the **Cathedral** *(Dom)* (7), built between the 13th and 15th centuries. Since 1356 all elections of German emperors were held here, and from 1562 until the dissolu-

The Eiserner Steg and Skyline

tion of the Holy Roman Empire in 1806 it was also the site of all imperial coronations. There are several splendid works of art inside, including some fine 14th-century choir stalls and medieval altars. In complete contrast, and just one block to the north, stands the stunning new **Museum of Modern Art**, an ingenious solution to an awkward site.

From here on, it is one museum after another until you reach Alt Sachsenhausen—a destination that doesn't come to life until late afternoon. Naturally, you won't want to see them all, but the following descriptions should help you select.

Return to the Römerberg. At its very southern end stands the **Historical Museum** (8), located in a complex of buildings dating from the 12th century to the present. One of these, the **Saalhofkapelle**, was the chapel of the emperor Barbarossa, and is the oldest surviving structure in Frankfurt. The exhibitions, following a suggested itinerary, cover a vast variety of subjects including everyday life, wars, industry, transportation, politics, and just about everything that ever happened in the city. You could easily spend an entire afternoon here, although a fast visit can be made in an hour or so. The museum is open daily except on Mondays, from 10 a.m. to 5 p.m., remaining open until 8 p.m. on Wednesdays.

Now walk around the corner to the Main River, where **sightseeing boats** depart at regular intervals. Cross the **Eiserner Steg**, an old iron footbridge dating from 1868, to the suburb of Sachsenhausen, which offers a broad choice of museums along its Schaumainkai. Nearly all of these are open on Tuesdays through Sundays, 10 a.m. to 5 p.m., and until 8 p.m. on Wednesdays.

The **Liebieghaus** (9) is Frankfurt's museum of sculpture. Housed in a former baronial mansion, the collection covers virtually the entire scope of the plastic arts, from ancient Egyptian through the Renaissance and Baroque periods.

From here it is only a block to the ***Städelsches Kunstinstitut** (Städel Art Institute and Municipal Gallery) (10), which ranks as one of Europe's major art museums. Just about any painter you can think of is represented in this sweeping survey, from the Flemish Primitives to Picasso. The Städel is a must-see for any art lover.

The history of communications is thoroughly explored in the **Bundespost Museum** (11), a fascinating place to visit if you have an interest in postal matters, buses, radios, telephones, and the like. To the left of it is the **Deutsches Architekturmuseum** (Museum of German Architecture), installed in a gutted period mansion. Its displays are mostly of architectural drawings, models, and photographs. Nearly adjacent to this stands the **Deutsches Filmmuseum**, a new museum devoted to German cinema and the film industry in general, with collections ranging from equipment to promotional material. Outstanding flicks can be seen in the museum's own theater.

Changing exhibitions concerning the customs of primitive people are featured in the **Museum für Völkerkunde** (Museum of Ethnology) (12). Just beyond is the **Museum für Kunsthandwerk** (Applied Arts Museum) (13), housed in a 19th-century mansion and its modern annex. Its superb collection of beautiful furniture from the Middle Ages to the present day is absolutely delightful, as are the displays of porcelains, glassware, books, carpets, and so on.

By this time you are probably ready to sit down at a café for some liquid refreshment. Luck is on your side, since it is only a short stroll to **Alt Sachsenhausen** (14). The narrow pedestrians-only streets there are lined with colorful places to eat and drink, many of them featuring the apple wine *(Ebbelwei)* peculiar to Frankfurt. Be sure to poke into some of the hidden courtyards—this is where the more interesting establishments lurk. *Prosit!*

The easiest way back to central Frankfurt is via the Alte Brücke and Schumacher Strasse. This leads to the **Konstabler Wache** (15), where there are both U- and S-Bahn stations, and around which are a variety of the city's leading shops and department stores.

Mainz

The two-thousand-year-old city of Mainz is forever linked with one of the most significant achievements in western civilization. It was here, during the 15th century, that Johannes Gutenberg invented a method for producing movable type—a crucial event making possible the widespread dissemination of knowledge through printing. Naturally proud of its native son, the city has honored him with the marvelous World Museum of Printing, well worth the trip in itself.

Mainz has several other attractions, including a splendid 10th-century cathedral that ranks among the largest and most ancient in Germany. Heavily bombed during World War II, some parts of the Old Town were beautifully restored, while in another section contemporary architects were given a free hand in creating bold new structures.

By getting off to an early start and cutting short the walking tour it is possible to combine this trip in the same day with one to Wiesbaden, Worms, or Darmstadt—all of which are easily reached by train. With its excellent transportation facilities, Mainz makes a good alternative base for exploring the Rhineland. It is very close to the Frankfurt airport.

GETTING THERE:

Trains to Mainz on the S-Bahn service (route S-14, marked for Wiesbaden) leave Frankfurt's Konstablerwache, Hauptwache, Taunusanlage, main station (lower level), and airport station at frequent intervals. The journey takes about 45 minutes. Be sure to get off at the Mainz main station (*Hauptbahnhof*), not at Süd or Nord. See ticketing instructions for the Frankfurt trip.

There are also a few regular express trains departing from Frankfurt's main station (street level), making the trip in less time. S-Bahn (*FVV*) tickets are not valid on these. Return service operates until late evening.

By car, Mainz is 24 miles southwest of Frankfurt. Take the A-66 Autobahn to the Wiesbaden-Erbenheim exit and head south on the B-455, crossing the Rhine to downtown Mainz.

PRACTICALITIES:

Mainz may be visited in any season, although it is more appealing in warm weather. All of the museums are closed on Mondays. The local **Tourist Information Office**, phone (06131) 28-62-10, is at Bahnhofstrasse 15, near the train station. Mainz has a **population** of about 190,000.

FOOD AND DRINK:

Some good restaurant choices are:

Rheingrill (in the Hilton Hotel at Rheinstr. 68, next to Rheingoldhalle) Contemporary cuisine overlooking the river. Proper dress expected, for reservations phone (06131) 24-51-29. $$$

Rats und Zunftstuben Heilig Geist (Rentengasse 2, behind the Gutenberg Museum) Contemporary German cuisine in a medieval setting. Very popular. Phone (06131) 22-57-57. X: Sun. $$

Weinhaus Kartäuser Hof (Kartäuserstr. 14, 4 blocks south of the cathedral) Traditional meals at the oldest restaurant in town. Phone (06131) 22-29-56. $$

Eisgrub-Bräu (Weissliliengasse 1a, 5 blocks south of the cathedral) A brewery and restaurant with local specialties. $

SUGGESTED TOUR:

Begin your walk at the **main train station** *(Hauptbahnhof)* (1), following the map to the pedestrians-only **Markt** (Market Place). This attractive large square really comes to life on Tuesday, Friday, and Saturday mornings when the farmers are in town. In its center stands a magnificent Renaissance **fountain** dating from 1526.

The huge six-towered ***Cathedral** *(Dom)* (2), begun in 975, completely dominates the scene. Built over several centuries, it has a mixture of styles ranging from Romanesque to late Baroque. Enter through the thousand-year-old bronze doors on the north portal and explore the interior. There is a **choir** at each end, an arrangement common in the Rhineland. Both of these have **crypts**, the eastern one being particularly interesting for its modern golden reliquary containing bits of the 22 saints of Mainz. The cathedral is noted for its fine **tombs** of the archbishops, dating from the 13th to the 18th centuries.

A doorway along the south aisle leads through the **cloister** to the ***Diocesan Museum**, where an extraordinary collection of medieval religious art is on display. You won't regret spending enough time for a careful examination of these treasures. The museum is open on Mondays through Fridays from 10 a.m. to 4 p.m., and on Saturdays from 10 a.m. to 2 p.m.

Leave the cathedral and circle around its eastern end, going by way of Grebenstrasse to the **Leichof**. From this lovely square you will have the best possible view of the church. Now stroll down Augustinerstrasse, a charming narrow street leading through the heart of the romantic old *Altstadt* part of town. The **Ignazkirche** (Church of St. Ignatius) (3), a few steps from its lower end, has a remarkable outdoor Crucifixion statue of the 16th century. On the hill behind this stands

The Cathedral and the Farmers' Market

the lovingly restored 13th-century **Stephanskirche**, noted for its modern stained-glass windows by Marc Chagall.

Return to Holzstrasse and turn right to the majestic 14th-century **Holzturm** (Wooden Tower) (4), one of the few remaining relics of the former town fortifications. Continue straight ahead until you come to the Rhine, then make a left along its quay past the KD Line pier (see chapter on Rhine Cruise).

A left here will lead you up steps to the strikingly modern **Rathaus** (Town Hall) (5), completed in 1973. Opposite this is the equally contemporary **Rheingoldhalle** where concerts are frequently held. An elevated platform, complete with outdoor café, joins these together and spans busy Rheinstrasse next to the 13th-century **Eisenturm** (Iron Tower), another medieval town gate.

Follow the map through a sleek new shopping district to the ***World Museum of Printing** (6), also known as the **Gutenberg Museum**. Exhibitions covering the entire scope of written communications throughout the ages are displayed on four floors of this modern structure. The museum's main treasure is its original ***Gutenberg Bible** of 1452–55, kept in a vault that you can enter. More fascinating than that, though, is the re-creation of Gutenberg's **printing shop** where demonstrations of old techniques are given. Other areas are devoted to the development of alphabets, the history of paper, bookbinding, and even computerized typesetting. The museum is open on Tuesdays through Saturdays, 10 a.m. to 6 p.m.; and on Sundays and holidays from 10 a.m. to 1 p.m.

Now return to the market place and walk down Schusterstrasse, circling around the ruins of **St. Christoph's Church**. From here a series of back streets leads to Deutschhaus Platz, fronted by the state parliament *(Landtag)* of Rhineland-Palatinate *(Rheinland-Pfalz)*, of which Mainz is the capital. In the square you will see an exact copy of the **Jupiter Column**, erected in A.D. 67 by the Romans. The original is in the Landesmuseum, below.

The **Römisch-Germanisches Zentralmuseum** (Roman-Germanic Museum) (7), located in the former Electoral Palace of the 17th and 18th centuries, is just across the street. Archaeological finds from the Stone Age to the Carolingian period can be seen here every day except Mondays, from 10 a.m. to 6 p.m.

Stroll down the Grosse Bleiche to the **Landesmuseum** (Provincial Museum) (8), where the history of Mainz and the Rhineland from prehistoric times to the present is on display. The museum is open daily from 10 a.m. to 5 p.m., except on Mondays and holidays, closing at 4 on Fridays. From here it's a short walk back to the train station.

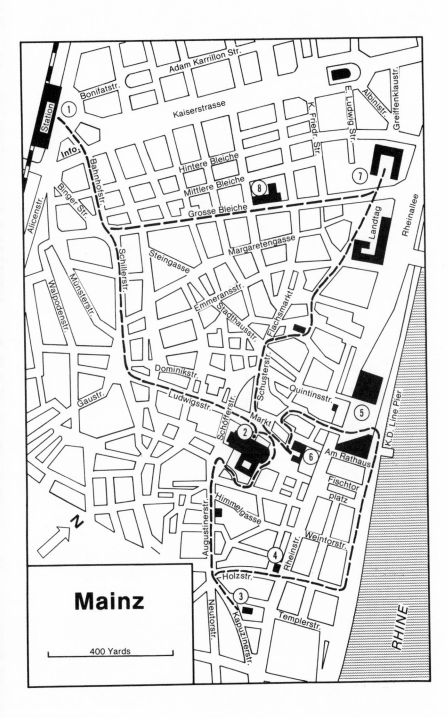

Station

Info.

Bonifatstr.

Adam Karrillon Str.

Kaiserstrasse

Alicenstr.

Binger Str.

Bahnhofstr.

Münsterstr.

Walpodenstr.

Schillerstr.

Steingasse

Hintere Bleiche

Mittlere Bleiche

Grosse Bleiche

K. Fried. Str.

E. Ludwig Str.

Albinistr.

Greiffenklaustr.

Margaretengasse

Landtag

Rheinallee

Emmeranstr.

Stadthausstr.

Flachsmarkt

Gaustr.

Dominikstr.

Ludwigsstr.

Schöfferstr.

Markt

Schusterstr.

Quintinsstr.

K.D. Line Pier

Augustinerstr.

Himmelgasse

Am Rathaus

Fischtor platz

Rheinstr.

Weintorstr.

Holzstr.

Neutorstr.

Kapuzinerstr.

Templerstr.

RHINE

N

Mainz

400 Yards

Wiesbaden

Kur und Kultur set the style in fashionable Wiesbaden, that elegant spa where the *belle époque* lingers on. Ever since the time of the Romans, who called it *Aquae Mattiacorum,* the wealthy and powerful have been flocking here to partake of its healing waters and sophisticated aura. This is the kind of place where people still dress up at night—for the casino, the opera, the many splendid restaurants. But if all this seems a little rich for your blood, it needn't be. Wiesbaden is also a fairly large city, the state capital of Hesse, a center for conventions and business meetings and, above all, a green town of manicured parks and gardens. A daytrip here needn't cost very much, and offers a chance to enjoy yet another facet of German life.

It is possible to combine this trip in the same day with one to nearby Mainz. With its superb hotel and transportation facilities, Wiesbaden also makes an excellent alternative base for exploring the Rhineland, especially since it is so close to the Frankfurt airport.

GETTING THERE:

Trains to Wiesbaden on the S-Bahn service depart frequently from Frankfurt's Konstablerwache, Hauptwache, Taunusanlage, and main station (lower level). The S-1 line goes direct and takes about 45 minutes, while the S-14 line goes via the airport and Mainz, taking about one hour. Those without railpasses should note the ticketing instructions under the Frankfurt trip. Get off at Wiesbaden's main station, the very end of the line.

It is also possible to take a regular express train from Frankfurt's main station (street level). These take about 30 minutes for the trip, and are a nice option for railpass holders. S-Bahn *(FVV)* tickets are not valid on the expresses. Return trains run until late evening.

By car, Wiesbaden is 24 miles west of Frankfurt via the A-66 Autobahn. Get off at the Erbenheim exit and follow Berliner Strasse and Gustav Stresemann Ring into town.

PRACTICALITIES:

Wiesbaden may be visited at any time, although warm weather makes it considerably more attractive. The local **Tourist Information**

The Kurhaus

Office *(Verkehrsbüro)*, Phone (0611) 172-9780, is at Rheinstrasse 15 at the corner of Wilhelmstrasse. There is a branch in the train station. Wiesbaden has a **population** of about 270,000.

FOOD AND DRINK:

There are many good restaurants and cafés along the walking route. Some choices are:

Käfer's Bistro (in the Kurhaus) A lively, Parisian bistro-style restaurant that's open for lunch. Phone (0611) 53-62-00. $$$

Nassauer Hof Bistro (Kaiser-Friedrich-Platz 3, a block west of the Kurhaus) Elegant indoor and outdoor dining, lunch or dinner. Phone (0611) 13-36-66. $$$

Rathskeller (in the basement of the New City Hall) Regional cuisine and fresh-brewed beer. $$

Dortmunder (Langgasse 34, 3 blocks southwest of the Kochbrunnen) An old-fashioned brewery restaurant. Phone (0611) 30-20-96. $

SUGGESTED TOUR:

Begin your walk at the **main train station** (1). Cross the square via an underground passageway and walk through the park to Friedrich-Ebert Allee. The **Städtische Museum** (City Museum) (2) has a fine collection of art ranging from Old Masters through the 20th century, as well as some lovely antique furniture. It is open daily except on Mondays, from 10 a.m. to 4 p.m. Just opposite this is the modern Rhein-Main Halle, used for exhibitions and conventions.

Continue along the elegant Wilhelmstrasse, passing the tourist office, and enter another park. Following the path around its pond will take you to the **Staatstheater** (State Theater), a 19th-century neo-classical opera house with a contemporary addition. Now stroll into the **Kurpark** (3), a quiet oasis of dream-like beauty. Inviting paths lead beyond a small lake to secluded spots among the old shade trees. Outdoor concerts are given here during the summer, as well as other entertainments.

Leave the park and walk around to the **Kurhaus** (4), a rather ponderous neo-classical structure of 1907 that houses the **Spielbank** (gambling casino), a concert hall, restaurants, and bars. Its superb tree-lined approach is bordered on the south by the Theater Colonnade. On the north side is the elegant early-19th-century Kurhaus Colonnade, now used for exhibitions and special events.

Follow the map to the **Kochbrunnen** (5). Set in an open square, this is the most famous of Wiesbaden's 26 hot saline springs. From here it is possible to make a side trip of about one mile to the base of the **Neroberg** (6), off the map but not too far to walk. You can also get there by bus number 8. An amusing 19th-century **rack railway** *(Neroberg Bahn),* said to be the oldest in Germany, ascends the gentle hill during the summer season for a magnificent view of the town. Near the top is the gorgeous **Russische Kapelle**, a Russian Orthodox church erected in 1855 as a tomb for the Russian wife of Duke Adolf of Nassau.

Return to the Kochbrunnen and stroll down Langgasse to the **Römertor** (7), an old town gate. Parts of this are believed to date from the late Roman period. Continue along the pedestrians-only Langgasse and turn left into Marktstrasse. The Market Fountain, dating from 1537 and topped by a golden lion, stands in front of the former **Ducal Palace** *(Schloss)* (8), now the state parliament of *Land* Hesse.

Opposite this is the Renaissance-style **Altes Rathaus** (Old Town Hall) of 1609. Cross the square to the 19th-century **New City Hall** (9) and the splendid neo-Gothic Market Church, then walk through the market place. From here, follow the map through some pleasant neighborhoods back to the train station.

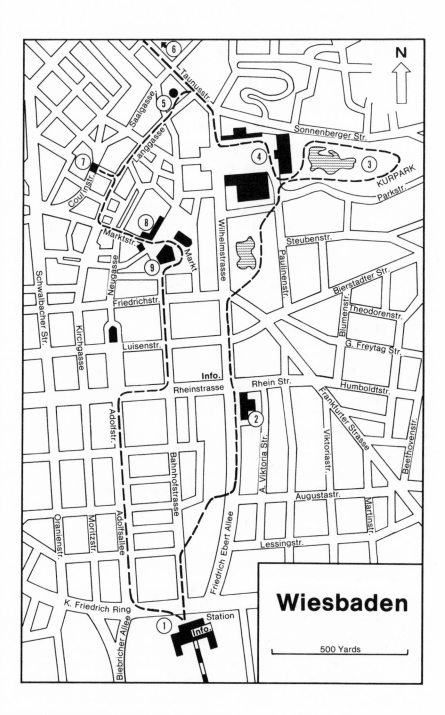

N

⑥
Taunusstr.
Saalgasse
Langgasse
Sonnenberger Str.
⑤
④
③
KURPARK
⑦
Courirstr.
Parkstr.
Steubenstr.
⑧
Marktstr.
Wilhelmstrasse
Neugasse
Markt
⑨
Paulinenstr.
Bierstadter Str.
Friedrichstr.
Blumenstr.
Theodorenstr.
Schwalbacher Str.
Kirchgasse
Luisenstr.
G. Freytag Str.
Info.
Rheinstrasse
Rhein Str.
Humboldtstr.
②
Adolfstr.
A. Viktoria Str.
Viktoriastr.
Frankfurter Strasse
Beethovenstr.
Bahnhofstrasse
Augustastr.
Martinstr.
Oranienstr.
Moritzstr.
Adolfsallee
Friedrich Ebert Allee
Lessingstr.
K. Friedrich Ring
Station
①
Info.

Wiesbaden

Biebricher Allee

500 Yards

*Rhine Cruise

For many visitors to Germany, the number-one attraction is a romantic cruise down the Rhine, steaming through its spectacular gorge past vineyards, castles, and the legendary Loreley. All of these sights are in the magnificent stretch between Rüdesheim and Koblenz, a part of the river that not only offers the best scenery but also the most frequent boat service.

Politically and economically, the Rhine is probably the greatest river on Earth. For over two thousand years this watery main street of Europe has carried the trade of many nations along its 820-mile length from the Alps to the North Sea. It has been a border between opposing civilizations since the time of Julius Caesar. Legends inspired by its mysterious beauty have produced a treasure of art, literature, and music—especially in the stretch covered by this daytrip.

There are many possibilities for a cruise on the Rhine. The one described here is particularly good for travelers staying in Frankfurt. Those starting out from Mainz or Wiesbaden may prefer to board a boat there, while people making Koblenz or Cologne their base can do the trip in reverse, remembering that boats going in that direction are much slower due to the heavy current.

Most of the steamer service on this part of the Rhine is operated by the KD Line, which accepts Eurailpasses and German Railpasses on all boats except the much-too-speedy hydrofoils.

This trip can be combined in the same day with one to Koblenz by getting off to an early start. Alternatively, it is possible to start in Koblenz and go the other way by boat, winding up in Rüdesheim for an evening of wine drinking before taking a late train back to Frankfurt (or wherever).

GETTING THERE:

Trains to Rüdesheim leave Frankfurt's main station frequently, most likely requiring a change at Wiesbaden. The entire trip takes about one hour. Return service from Koblenz operates until late evening, and may require a change at Mainz.

By car, Rüdesheim is 45 miles west of Frankfurt. Take the A-66 Autobahn past Wiesbaden to Eltville, then the B-42 road. Those driving will, of course, have to return to Rüdesheim by train to pick up their car.

PRACTICALITIES:

The KD Line operates Rhine boat cruises from the beginning of April until the end of October, with more frequent sailing during the peak summer period. Good weather will greatly enhance this trip. If possible, try to leave Frankfurt as early as 7 a.m. to make the best connections. **Information** about boat cruises is available at all train stations, or you can call the KD line in Frankfurt at (069) 28-57-28, or their main office in Cologne at (0221) 258-3011. Tourist information offices in Frankfurt, Mainz, Wiesbaden, Rüdesheim, Bingen, and Koblenz are listed in the sections dealing with those towns in this book.

FOOD AND DRINK:

Meals and drinks are available aboard the boats at moderate prices. There is a wide selection of restaurants and cafés in both Rüdesheim and Koblenz, which are listed in the next two chapters.

SUGGESTED TOUR:

Travelers staying in **Mainz** (1) may prefer to board the boat there. The KD Line pier is located near the town hall, as shown on the map for the Mainz trip. Alternatively, they could take a local train to Bingen (4) and pick up the cruise at that point (see the map on page 173).

Those making Wiesbaden their base have the option of getting on the boat at the KD Line pier in **Wiesbaden-Biebrich** (2), easily reached by bus or taxi. It is also quite simple to get to Rüdesheim from Wiesbaden by train or bus.

For travelers staying in the Frankfurt area, the best starting point for a Rhine cruise is **Rüdesheim** (3). A map and description of that town can be found in the next chapter. The KD Line pier is located a few blocks east of the train station, near the tourist office. Several other companies also offer shorter Rhine cruises from here. Board the boat, which now crosses the river to the noted wine-shipping town of **Bingen** (4), also described in the next chapter.

As you sail down the Rhine you will make numerous stops and pass many famous sights. To identify these, refer to the large **kilometer marking signs** on the banks of the river, which correspond to the 3-digit numbers on the map.

High atop a hill overlooking the river rises the colossal **Niederwald Monument**, described in the next chapter. The cruise now enters a long and fantastically beautiful stretch of the Rhine, beginning at the Binger Loch. You will soon pass the **Mäuseturm**, a small tower on a mid-stream island. Legend has it that a hated archbishop of Mainz was eaten alive here by mice during the Middle Ages. Directly opposite this, to the right, are the ruins of **Burg Ehrenfels**, a 13th-century fortress destroyed by the French in 1689.

Die Pfalz and Vineyards

The boat now stops at the romantic village of **Assmannshausen** (5), referred to in the next chapter. Across from this are three well-known castles; the first, to the left, being **Rheinstein**, built by robber barons in the 13th century. When Charlemagne's empire fell apart in the 9th century, the feudal lords who took over small bits of land set up castles to extort tolls from passing boats. In time these multiplied until just about every strategic location on the Rhine had a fortification. The next one, less than a half-mile to the right and overlooking the village of Trechtingshausen, is the 11th-century castle of **Reichenstein**. Beyond this is **Sooneck Castle**, dating from 1010. As is the case with many Rhine castles, these three were heavily restored during the wave of romanticism that swept 19th-century Germany.

The picturesque old wine town of **Bacharach** (6), whose name derives from that of the ancient god Bacchus, is an important stop for all boats. Its quaint streets are not visible from the river, however, as a medieval ring wall still blocks the view. A mile and a half downstream, ***Die Pfalz** (7) rises as a strange apparition in midstream. If ever there was a good place to put a toll booth, this is it. Built in the 14th century and as forbidding today as ever, the castle is absolutely irresistible to photographers.

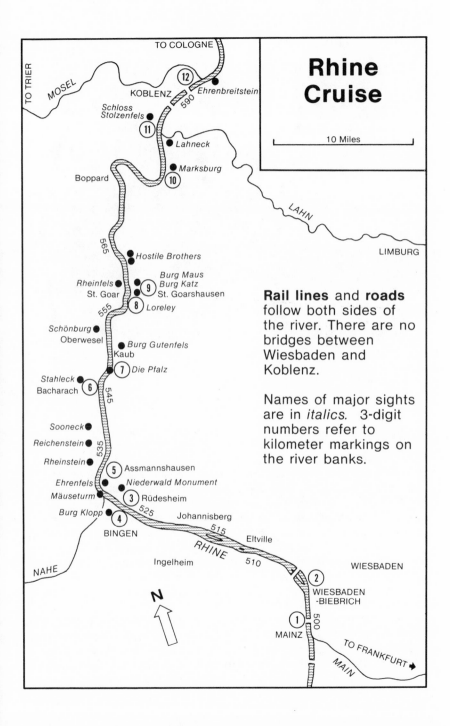

The Loreley

By this time, all of the German passengers will have gathered on the starboard side of the boat. They know what's coming next. When you hear them sing *"Ich weiss nicht was soll es bedeuten—,"* you are opposite the ***Loreley** (8), a steep legend-haunted rock that occupies a peculiar place in the Teutonic psyche. It is said that in ancient times a lovely maiden sat at the top and lured boatmen to their deaths in the turbulent waters below. It is also reputed to be the hiding place of the Nibelung's golden treasure, immortalized in Wagner's opera *Das Rheingold.* One very real property of the narrow passage is its seven-fold echo, which some of the passengers might try to exploit.

St. Goarshausen (9) is the next stop on the right bank. It is possible to get off here and return on one of the fairly frequent trains back to Rüdesheim, Wiesbaden, or Frankfurt. Above the town rises the 14th-century Burg Katz, and to the left a rival castle of the same age, Burg Maus. Over on the left bank, the impressive 13th-century ruins of **Rheinfels Castle**—once the most powerful on the Rhine—stand guard over St. Goar. Overlooking Kamp are the twin castles of the **Hostile Brothers**, who in legend fought over the love of a fair maiden. **Boppard**, a stop for all boats, was founded by the Romans about A.D. 370. Parts of their fortifications still exist.

View of Boppard

The best-preserved fortress along the Rhine gorge is **Marksburg** (10), just above the little town of Braubach, which dates from the 12th century. In all of the battles that ravaged this area, Marksburg was never humbled. It withstood both the Thirty Years War and the French occupation, and it was not until 1945 that it sustained any damage from conflict. Restoration has since been completed.

Opposite the confluence of the Lahn River is the impossibly romantic palace of **Schloss Stolzenfels** (11), originally from the 13th century but heavily rebuilt in 1836 as a dreamy 19th-century vision of the Age of Chivalry. The kaiser lived there, and it suited his taste.

The end of your cruise is now in sight as the boat approaches **Koblenz** (12). Time permitting, this is a golden opportunity to explore a wonderful old town before heading for the train station. A map and walking tour will be found in the chapter beginning on page 182.

Rüdesheim

Wine lovers will rejoice in a trip to Rüdesheim, Germany's favorite wine village. The vintages have been flowing there for some two thousand years, ever since the Romans settled the area and began growing grapes. You can have a wonderful time sampling the result—some of Germany's (and the world's) best white wines—or in just exploring this delightful town and its surroundings. Whatever you do, you won't be alone. Rüdesheim is *very* popular with tourists from all over the globe, but you'll be seeing a whole lot more than most of them on this do-it-yourself daytrip.

The suggested tour begins in the neighboring village of Assmannshausen and includes a ride across the Rhine to Bingen. If these don't interest you, it is entirely possible to spend the whole day in Rüdesheim and not get bored. Tipsy perhaps, but not bored.

GETTING THERE:

Trains depart Frankfurt's main station for Rüdesheim and Assmanshausen several times each morning, some from the main level and some from the lower S-Bahn level. In addition, there are trains and buses from Wiesbaden, which is easily reached by S-Bahn commuter trains. The direct trip takes about one hour. Return service operates until mid-evening. Be sure to check the schedules carefully, especially to determine whether the train you want also stops in Assmannshausen. If not, it is only a short distance by bus or taxi from Rüdesheim.

By car, leave Frankfurt on the A-66 Autobahn and stay on it past Wiesbaden to Eltville. From there take the B-42 road into Rüdesheim, which is about 45 miles west of Frankfurt.

PRACTICALITIES:

This trip should be taken between April and the end of October, when all of the attractions are open. The two museums are closed on Mondays as well as during the off-season. Good weather is essential. The **Tourist Information Office** for Rüdesheim, phone (06722) 29-62, is at Rheinstrasse 16, near the KD Line pier. In Bingen, they are at Rheinkai 21, phone (06721) 184-205. **Bicycles** may be rented at the Rüdesheim train station from April through October.

FOOD AND DRINK:

There is an extremely wide selection of places to eat and drink in the Rüdesheim area. A few are:

In Assmannshausen:

> **Krone** (Rheinuferstr. 10, near the train station) An old inn over-looking the Rhine; classic German cuisine. Phone (06722) 40-30. X: Jan., Feb. $$$

> **Altes Haus** (Lorcherstr. 5, a block northwest of the chair lift lower station) An historic 16th-century inn with good food. Phone (06722) 20-51. X: Tues. & Thurs. lunch. $$

> **Lamm** (Rheinuferstr. 6, 4 blocks north of the train station) Good meals at fair prices. Phone (06722) 20-55. X: Dec. to Feb. $

Near the Niederwald Monument:

> **Jagdschloss Niederwald** (near the top of the chair lift) A ducal hunting lodge featuring traditional wild game and other dishes. Phone (06722) 10-04. X: Jan. to mid-Feb. $$$

In Rüdesheim:

> **Traube-Aumüller** (Rheinstr. 6, near the Brömserburg Castle) A good choice in a touristy location. Phone (06722) 30-38. X: mid-Nov. to mid-March. $$

> **Zum Bären** (Schmidtstr. 24, a block east of the market place) Good-value international and regional cooking. Phone (06722) 10-91. $

In addition, there are many attractive wine taverns with food on and around the Drosselgasse.

SUGGESTED TOUR:

Those making the complete tour should begin at the **train station** in **Assmannshausen** (1). Follow the map through this romantic old village, whose existence was first documented in 1108. Oddly enough, it is the home of Germany's best *red* wines. The narrow streets lead past several half-timbered houses and an interesting late-Gothic church to the **chair lift** *(Seilbahn)* (2). Purchase a combination ticket to Rüdesheim and be seated for a comfortable ride to the Niederwald. Along the way you will have superb high-level views across the Rhine Valley.

Getting off at the top, walk around past the **Jagdschloss** (3), a former hunting lodge of the dukes of Nassau. It is now a very attractive castle-hotel and restaurant complete with another panoramic vista. From here take a leisurely stroll of about one-half mile or so along a forest road to the **Niederwald Denkmal** (4), one of the most colossal monuments in Germany. A late-19th-century expression of overblown nationalism, its heroic figure of *Germania* symbolizes the

The Drosselgasse

unification of Germany achieved in 1871 and is still deeply revered by the German people—although to foreign eyes it may seem somewhat amusing. The enormous bronze relief depicting military heroes surrounding Kaiser Wilhelm I and Bismarck, incidentally, faces France. There is a fabulous view across the Rhine.

Take the nearby **cable car** *(Seilbahn)* down across the vineyards to its **lower station** (5) in Rüdesheim. Make a right on Oberstrasse to the **Brömserhof** (6), an aristocratic residence dating from 1542. The interior now features a curious exhibition known as **Siegfried's Mechanical Music Cabinet**, a collection of antique self-playing musical instruments. This is open daily from mid-March through mid-November, from 10 a.m. to 10 p.m.

Rüdesheim is world-famous for the **Drosselgasse**, a narrow lane that is usually jam-packed with hundreds of thirsty visitors. You may want to return here later to relax in one of its many colorful wine taverns. Until then, however, there are several other worthwhile sights.

Continue to the bottom and turn left on Rheinstrasse, passing the tourist office. The **Marktplatz** (Market Place) has an interesting 14th-century parish church. At the eastern end of the Rheinstrasse is the **Alderturm** (Eagle's Tower) (7), built in the 15th century as part of the medieval defense fortifications.

Return along the bank of the Rhine to the ***Brömserburg** (8), an ancient castle built on late-Roman foundations between the 11th and

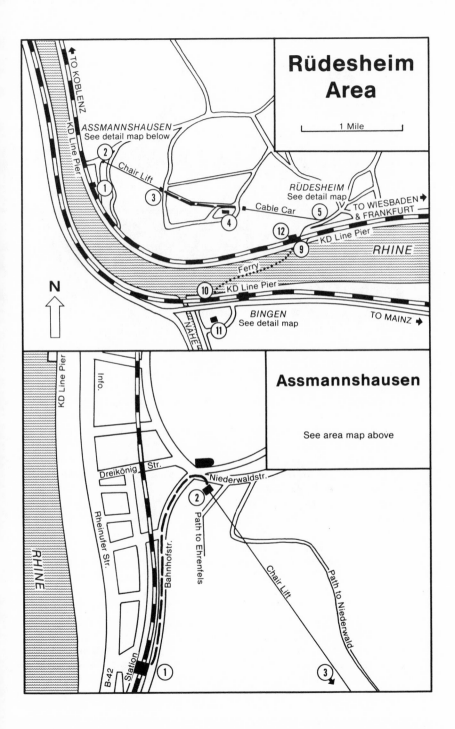

The Brömserburg

14th centuries. Formerly a refuge for the archbishops of Mainz, this formidable structure now houses the outstanding ***Rheingau Wine Museum**, a must-see for any visitor to Rüdesheim. Displays here cover the entire scope of wine-making—and drinking—down through the ages. The museum is open from March through mid-November, daily from 9 a.m. to 6 p.m.

A short stroll along the river brings you to the **passenger ferry dock** *(Personenfähre)* (9). From here you can take a quick boat ride to Bingen, just across the Rhine.

Leave the **Bingen ferry landing** (10) and follow the map past the tourist office up to **Burg Klopp** (11), a heavily rebuilt castle whose origins probably date from the Roman era. There is an exceptionally good view of the Rhine Valley from here, but the main attraction is the **Binger Heimat Museum** (Bingen Folk Museum). Step inside to see some remarkable exhibits dating from prehistoric times until the Frankish period. Probably the most interesting of these is the collection of 2nd-century Roman doctor's instruments. The museum is open from May through October, on Tuesdays through Sundays, from 9 a.m. to noon and 2–5 p.m.

Return to the ferry dock and Rüdesheim. The **train station** (12) is just across from the dock, but you will most likely want to enjoy a bit of wine sampling along the Drosselgasse before heading back to Frankfurt.

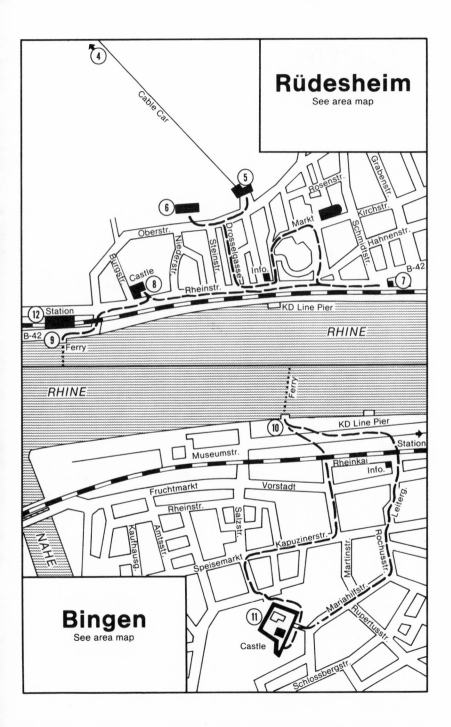

Koblenz

Relatively unknown to foreign tourists, Koblenz has long been a favorite destination for Germans. It was founded in 9 B.C. by the Romans as a stronghold guarding the confluence of the Rhine and Mosel rivers. For many centuries after that the town was a residence of the archbishops of Trier, and during the early 19th century actually became a part of France for a while. Although heavily bombed in World War II, Koblenz has been completely restored and today is a very charming and graceful medium-size city offering several delightful attractions.

A trip to Koblenz may be combined in the same day with a Rhine cruise—for which it makes a superb ending—or with Limburg, easily reached by train. With excellent rail and highway connections, it is also a fine base for travelers exploring the Rhine, Mosel, or Lahn regions.

GETTING THERE:

Trains, usually of the IC class, leave Frankfurt's main station at least hourly for the 80-minute ride to Koblenz. Return service operates until late evening.

By car, Koblenz is 76 miles northwest of Frankfurt. Take the A-66 Autobahn to Wiesbaden, then cross the Rhine on the A-643 to Mainz. From there take the A-60 to Bingen and the A-61 into Koblenz. A slower but more scenic route is to follow either side of the Rhine from Wiesbaden or Mainz.

PRACTICALITIES:

Visits to Koblenz should be made on a fine, warm day as nearly all of the attractions are out of doors. The fortress is open daily from about Easter through October, while the Middle Rhine Museum is closed on Mondays. The local **Tourist Information Office** (*Fremdenverkehrsamt*), phone (0261) 313-04, is directly across the street from the train station. Koblenz has a **population** of about 107,000.

The Schängelbrunnen

FOOD AND DRINK:

Ratsstuben (Am Plan 9, near the Liebfrauenkirche) Indoor and outdoor dining overlooking a colorful square. Phone (0261) 388-34. X: Tues. $$

Weindorf (in the Wine Village) Four taverns in a reconstructed wine village mix food with the pleasures of wine tasting. X: Nov. $$

Café and Restaurant at Ehrenbreitstein Castle Pleasant indoor and outdoor tables right in the fortress complex. $$

Altes Brauhaus (Braugasse 4, a block east of the Liebfrauen- kirche) Typical German dishes served with their own beer. Phone (0261) 150-01. X: Sun. $

SUGGESTED TOUR:

Those arriving by boat should start at the Deutsches Eck (7) and work backwards to the Rathaus (2), then stroll down Rheinstrasse to the ferry landing and continue on to Ehrenbreitstein (8), the Schloss (9), and the Weindorf (10).

Assuming that you came by train, leave the **station** (1) and follow the map to the **Rathaus** (Town Hall) (2) in Jesuitenplatz. Formerly a Jesuit college, the magnificent 17th-century structure is built around a courtyard adorned with the amusing **Schängelbrunnen**, a modern fountain with the figure of a naughty boy who spits water at unwary bystanders. Beware.

A few steps away, reached via Braugasse, is the **Liebfrauenkirche** (Church of Our Lady) (3). Of Romanesque origin, it was rebuilt in the 13th century, and has a remarkably lovely interior with fine Renaissance tombs. Now stroll through **Am Plan**, a large open square lined with attractive **outdoor cafés**, and go via Marktstrasse and Münzplatz to the 14th-century **Balduin Bridge** spanning the Mosel River. Three of its original 14 arches were destroyed by a bomb in 1945, and were replaced with a short modern section.

At the foot of this stands the handsome **Alte Burg** (Old Castle) (4), first erected during the 13th century but later extended in the Renaissance and Baroque styles. It now houses the municipal library. Turn right and enter Florinsmarkt, a delightful square fronted by the 12th-century **Florinkirche** (Church of St. Florin), built on Roman foundations.

The **Mittelrhein Museum** (Middle Rhine Museum) (5), a few yards to the left, occupies the early-15th-century Altes Kaufhaus. Step inside for a look at some superb art by regional painters, as well as antique furniture and artifacts. It is open on Tuesdays through Sundays from 10 a.m. until 5 p.m., remaining open until 8 p.m. on Wednesdays.

A short walk along the Mosel River leads to the ***St.-Kastor-Kirche** (Church of St. Castor) (6), first consecrated in 836 and renovated about 1200. It was here that Charlemagne's vast empire was divided up among his three grandsons in 843. The interesting interior features several art treasures including a particularly venerated Madonna painting. Surrounding the church are some very lovely **gardens**, offering extensive views across the two rivers from its upper terrace. Next to this stands the **Deutschherrenhaus**, the only remaining structure of a complex belonging to the Teutonic Order of Knights, who first established themselves on German soil here in 1216.

The most famous sight in Koblenz is the **Deutsches Eck** (German Corner) (7), a spit of land at the confluence of the two great rivers. An enormous 46-foot-high equestian statue of Kaiser Wilhelm I stood here since 1897, perched atop a 72-foot-high pedestal, but in 1945 this was destroyed and for nearly fifty years the base remained unadorned. Then, in late 1993, a duplicate was erected in its place amid great controversy. Whatever you think of the statue's artistic merits, the sweeping panoramic ***view** from the top of its base will reward the effort of climbing it.

Walk down to the **ferry landing** *(Fähre)* for a short ride across the Rhine to Ehrenbreitstein. On the other side turn left along the water, then right under the railway tracks and follow the signs for the **chairlift** *(Sesselift)*. You will first go through a short tunnel, then ride in an open chair to the citadel 400 feet above the Rhine.

The ***Festung Ehrenbreitstein** (8) ranks second only to Gibraltar as

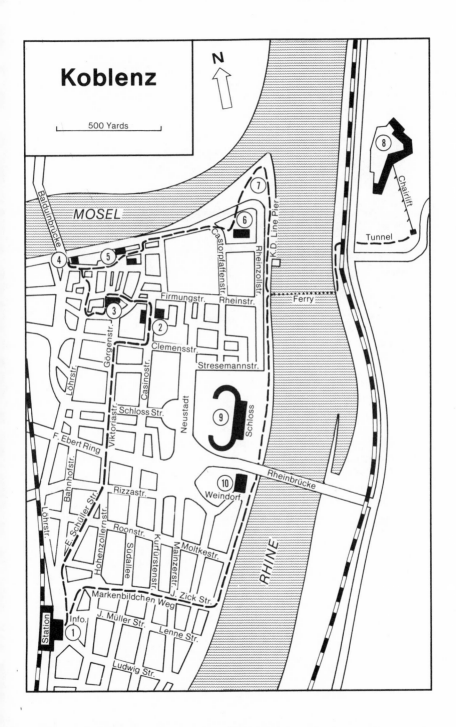

Koblenz

500 Yards

N

MOSEL

Baldninbrücke

RHINE

Station

Info.

Löhrstr.

Löhrstr.

Bahnhofstr.

E. Schüller Str.

Hohenzollernstr.

F. Ebert Ring

Görgenstr.

Viktoriastr.

Casinostr.

Schloss Str.

Neustadt

Clemensstr.

Firmungstr.

Rheinstr.

Stresemannstr.

Castorpfaffenstr.

Rheinzollstr.

K.D. Line Pier

Ferry

Schloss

Rheinbrücke

Weindorf

Rizzastr.

Roonstr.

Südallee

Kurfürstenstr.

Mainzerstr.

J. Zick Str.

Moltkestr.

Markenbildchen Weg

J. Müller Str.

Lenne Str.

Ludwig Str.

Tunnel

Chairlift

1
2
3
4
5
6
7
8
9
10

The St. Kastor Kirche

the largest stronghold in Europe. First built in the 10th century, it was destroyed by the French in 1801 and later rebuilt by the Prussians during the early 19th century. Take the time to thoroughly explore its many passageways and hidden corners before succumbing to temptation and sitting down at the **outdoor café** in its main courtyard. Needless to say, the ***view** down the Rhine Valley is spectacular. You may want to visit one or more of the three museums in the complex, mostly concerned with local history. The fortress is open daily from about Easter through October, from 9 a.m. to 5 p.m.

Return via the ferry to Koblenz and turn right along the Rheinanlagen, a very attractive river promenade. You will soon pass the **Kurfürstliches Schloss** (Electors' Palace) (9) of 1786, now used for offices. Continue on to the **Weindorf** (Wine Village) (10). Built in 1925 as part of a wine fair, this compound of half-timbered houses is a joyful spot for imbibing—and a perfect place to end the day. From here it is only a short walk to the train station.

*Trier

The greatest collection of Roman remains to be found anywhere north of the Alps is in Trier, which bills itself as Germany's oldest town. According to an ancient legend, this was founded around 2000 B.C. by Trebeta, son of Semiramis, the queen of Assyria. Historians say otherwise, although archaeological digs do reveal some trace of human habitation dating from that era. What is actually documented is that the town, then called *August Treverorum,* was established in 16 B.C. by the Roman emperor Augustus near the site of an earlier Celtic settlement.

Whatever its true age, Trier is certainly a fascinating place. Several of its Roman structures remain in use today, along with well-preserved buildings from just about every era since. For centuries this city was among the most important in Europe; at one time second only to Rome. Those days have long since ended, and Trier is now a relatively minor provincial place. Although it is quite some distance from Frankfurt, its attractions are so compelling that a journey is more than worthwhile.

GETTING THERE:

Trains of the IC class depart Frankfurt's main station at least hourly for Koblenz, where you change to a regular train to Trier. The total journey takes under three hours, and follows an exceptionally beautiful route along the Rhine and Mosel rivers. Return service operates until mid-evening.

By car, leave Frankfurt on the A-66 Autobahn, then take the A-3 north past Limburg and head west on the A-48 to the Trier exit. The total distance is about 150 miles.

PRACTICALITIES:

Trier can be visited in any season, but note that some attractions are closed on Mondays from November through March, and every day during December. A few museums close early on Sundays, and all day on some holidays. The local **Tourist Information Office**, phone (0651) 97-80-80, is next to the Porta Nigra. Bicycles may be rented at the train station. Trier has a population of about 100,000.

Porta Nigra
(Photo courtesy of Trier Tourist Office)

FOOD AND DRINK:

Trier is heavily touristed, so it has plenty of restaurants and cafés. Some choices are:

Palais Kesselstatt (Liebfrauenstr. 10, across from the Liebfrauenkirche) An elegant wine restaurant in a baroque setting, with light cuisine and garden dining available. Phone (0651) 402-04. X: Sun., Mon., Feb. $$$

Brunnenhof (in the Simeonstift next to the Porta Nigra) Typical German food in an 11th-century cloister. Phone (0651) 485-84. $$

Zum Domstein (Hauptmarkt 5) Popular for its local specialties, with a superb selection of wines. Phone (0651) 744-90. $$

Ratskeller zur Steipe (Hauptmarkt 14) In a cellar under the councillors' banqueting hall, also has outdoor tables. Phone (0651) 750-52. X: Mon. $

Museum Café (in the Rhineland Museum) A pleasant, modern place for light meals. Opens into the gardens. $

SUGGESTED TOUR:

Leave the **main train station** *(Hauptbahnhof)* (1) and walk down Bahnhofstrasse and Theodor-Heuss-Allee to the ancient ***Porta Nigra** (2), the very symbol of Trier and one of the finest Roman relics anywhere. Built towards the end of the 2nd century A.D. as a massive fortified gate, it was converted into a church about 1040 and restored to its original appearance by Napoleon after 1804, when Trier was a part of France. No mortar was used in its construction; instead, the stone blocks are joined by iron clamps. The name, meaning black gate, derives from its present color—the result of centuries of pollution. Stroll through the inner courtyard, where unsuspecting enemies could be trapped from all sides. An exploration of its bulky interior can be made any day from 9 a.m. to 6 p.m., closing earlier in winter. A joint ticket covering all of the Roman sites is available.

Adjoining this is the **Simeonstift**, a former priests' residence from the 11th century that now houses the tourist office, a restaurant, and the **Städtisches Museum**. The latter is devoted primarily to the history of Trier from prehistoric to modern times.

Walk down Simeonstrasse past the very unusual **Dreikönigenhaus** at number 19, a nobleman's town residence dating from 1230. Note the strange location of its original entrance—at an upper level where it could only be reached by a retractable ladder, a safety feature in those days of unrest.

Continue on to the ***Hauptmarkt** (3). The stone cross in its center was erected in 958 as a symbol of the town's right to hold a market. Near this stands a lovely 16th-century fountain, while the entire busy scene is dominated by the Gothic **Church of St. Gangolf**. One particularly outstanding building is the **Steipe**, a colorful 15th-century banqueting hall that houses the Ratskeller. It was rebuilt after total destruction in World War II.

Now turn down Sternstrasse to the ***Cathedral** *(Dom)* (4), a powerful fortress-like structure dating in part from Roman times. Over the centuries this was enlarged and rebuilt several times, the most visible changes having occurred during the 12th century. Its interior is an engaging mixture of Romanesque, Gothic, and Baroque styles. Don't miss the **Treasury** *(Domschatzmuseum)* to the right of the high altar, which is open on Mondays through Saturdays from 10 a.m. to noon and 2–5 p.m., and on Sundays and holidays from 2–5 p.m., closing at 4 in winter. Among its treasures are the 10th-century Altar of St. Andrew, one of the great masterpieces of the Ottonian period. The precious Holy Robe, supposedly worn by Christ at His trial, is only shown on very rare occasions.

Stroll through the cloisters, then visit the adjacent **Liebfrauenkirche** (Church of Our Lady) (5). One of the earliest Gothic churches in Germany, it was built in the form of a Greek cross during the 13th century, and is noted for its elegant interior.

Closeby, on Windstrasse, is the **Bischöfliches Museum** (6). On display here are some fascinating 4th-century ceiling paintings from the palace of the Roman emperor Constantine, discovered under the cathedral in 1945. There are also several medieval statues and other pieces of ancient religious art. The museum is open on Mondays through Saturdays, from 9 a.m. to 1 p.m. and 2–5 p.m.; and on Sundays and holidays from 1–5 p.m.

The enormous **Palastaula** (7), not far away, is the only surviving part of Constantine's great imperial palace. Once the throne room of the emperor, this colossal structure from about A.D. 310 now sees service as a Protestant church. Take a look inside, then walk around to the adjoining **Palace of the Electors**, an 18th-century rococo building presently used for government offices.

Paths through the palace gardens lead to the **Rheinisches Landesmuseum** (Rhineland Museum) (8), probably the best collection of Roman antiquities in Germany. Allow plenty of time to take it all in, from gold coins to mosaics to huge monuments. The displays also feature archaeological finds dating from prehistory as well as a rich selection of medieval art. There is an attractive **museum café** facing the gardens, a fine place for a light lunch. The museum is open on Mondays through Fridays, from 9:30 a.m. to 4 p.m.; on Saturdays from 9 a.m. to 2 p.m.; and on Sundays and holidays from 9 a.m. to 1 p.m., but closes on some holidays.

From here you may want to make a short side trip to the **Amphitheater** (9), the oldest Roman structure in Trier. Over 20,000 spectators once jammed its terraces to watch the gladiators fight, a form of spectacle that continued into the Christian era. Be sure to climb down into the cellars under the arena, and to examine the side chambers that served as cages. Much of the stone work was exploited as a quarry during the Middle Ages, but enough remains to imagine yourself back in the 1st century A.D., when it was built. The Amphitheater is open during the same times as the Porta Nigra (2), but is closed in December.

A stroll down Olewiger Strasse brings you to the ***Kaiserthermen** (Imperial Baths) (10). Not much of this extraordinary 4th-century structure remains above ground, but the maze of passageways below is fantastic and well worth exploring. The baths were established by the emperor Constantine and were among the largest in the entire Roman empire. Strangely enough, they were never completed nor used for their intended purpose. The ruins are open during the same times as the Porta Nigra (2).

If you're still bursting with energy you might want to walk down to the Mosel river to see a few more sights, otherwise you can save some steps by following the map back into town via Neustrasse and Brückenstrasse.

The long route takes you first to the 2nd-century **Barbarathermen**

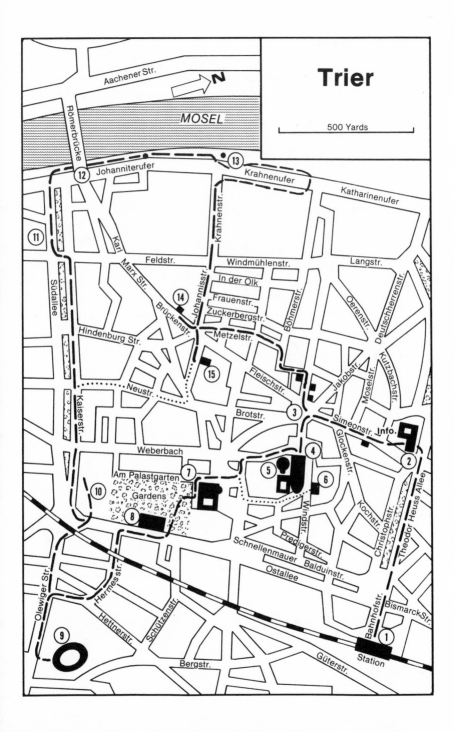

(11) on Südallee. These Roman baths were used for several centuries and were once larger than the Kaiserthermen. What little remains of their past glory is in derelict condition and requires a vivid imagination to visualize, although the effect of really *ruined* ruins can be quite romantic. Take a look from the street before deciding to enter. The opening times are the same as for the Porta Nigra (2), except that it's closed on Mondays and during December.

The **Römerbrücke** (Roman Bridge) (12) is just a few steps away. Its stone piers were built in the 2nd century A.D. and still carry the weight of heavy traffic. The upper parts, originally of wood, were replaced with masonry arches during the 14th century, and again in the 18th. Walk down steps to a path along the Mosel River and follow it past the **Zoll Kran** (Customs Crane), dating from 1774, and the **Alter Kran** (Old Crane) (13), which goes all the way back to 1413. Both are in excellent condition, and the latter's treadmill can be seen by peeking in the window. The busy adjacent street, Krahnenufer, is difficult to cross here, so walk north to the traffic light and return to Krahnenstrasse, which you follow into town.

Of all the people born in Trier, the one who had the greatest impact on society was undoubtedly Karl Marx, who lived from 1818 until 1883. His birthplace at Brückenstrasse 10 is open as the **Karl Marx Haus** (14), where both the life of communism's prophet and the worldwide spread of socialism is traced in minute detail. Perhaps you can find a clue, in the memorabilia or in the house itself, as to why Marx was so tragically mistaken in his understanding of how the world works. It's worth a try, and it can be done on Tuesdays through Sundays, from 10 a.m. to 6 p.m.; and on Mondays from 1–6 p.m., with shorter hours from November through March.

End your tour on a brighter note by paying a visit to the joyful **Spielzeugmuseum** (Toy Museum) (15), installed in three upper floors on Nagelstrasse. Although some of the toys are antiques, the majority are of recent enough vintage to evoke childhood memories. Hidden away in a corner of the third floor is a display of toys from the Third Reich, including a miniature tin Hitler riding in an open Mercedes! The museum is open daily from 10 a.m. to 6 p.m. In November, January, February, and March it's open on Tuesdays through Sundays, from noon until 4 p.m.

Return to the train station via the 11th-century **Frankenturm** at Dietrichstrasse 5—one of the oldest surviving dwellings in Germany—and the Hauptmarkt (3).

*Cologne
(Köln)

The skyline of Cologne is completely dominated by its magnificent cathedral, Germany's largest and one of the greatest on Earth. This ancient city on the Rhine has long been in the center of things. Having begun life as a Roman camp in 38 B.C., it was raised to city status around A.D. 50 and given the name *Colonia Claudia Ara Agrippensium*—a mouthful soon shortened to *Colonia*. After the fall of the Roman Empire this was Germanized to *Köln*, its official designation to this day. With about a million inhabitants, Cologne is now the fourth-largest metropolis in the nation (after Berlin, Hamburg, and Munich) and a world leader in commerce. Excellent transportation facilities make the city a good alternative base for exploring the Rhineland area north of Frankfurt.

GETTING THERE:

Trains, mostly of the EC and IC classes, leave Frankfurt's main station at least hourly for Cologne *(Köln)*, a journey of about 2¼ hours. Return trains run until late evening. Service is slightly reduced on Sundays and holidays.

By car, leave Frankfurt on the A-66 Autobahn, then turn northwest on the A-3 to Cologne *(Köln)*. The distance is 116 miles.

PRACTICALITIES:

Cologne may be explored in any season, but avoid coming on a Monday, when the museums are closed. Apart from the cathedral, these are the city's major attractions. Mass insanity prevails during the **Carnival** season, especially from the Thursday prior to the seventh Sunday before Easter until the start of Lent. The local **Tourist Information Office** *(Verkehrsamt)*, phone (0221) 221-3345, faces the front of the cathedral. Cologne has a **population** of about one million.

FOOD AND DRINK:

Cologne is renowned for its unique dishes such as *Rievkoche* (potato pancakes and applesauce), *Himmel un ärd* (apples and potatoes), *Kölsche Kaviar* (not caviar, but blood sausage with onions), and *Halve Hahn* (not half a chicken, but a fancy cheese sandwich). These are all washed down with *Kölsch,* a light but potent beer served in tiny glasses. Some of the most unusual and enjoyable food is served at inexpensive beerhalls by colorful waiters affectionately called *Köbesse.*

Some good restaurant choices are:

Weinhaus in Walfisch (Salzgasse 13, 2 blocks south of Gross St. Martin Church) Serving traditional local specialties for four centuries. Phone (0221) 257-7879. X: Sat. lunch, Sun., holidays. $$

Alt Köln (Trankgasse 7, between the cathedral and the train station) A favorite old tavern with local dishes. Phone (0221) 13-74-71. $$

Ratskeller (Alter Markt, behind the Old City Hall) Solid German cuisine, indoors or out. Phone (0221) 257-6929. $$

Früh (Am Hof 12, a block south of the cathedral) Cologne specialties in an Old World setting, makes its own beer. Phone (0221) 258-0397. $ and $$

Brauhaus Sion (Unter Taschenmacher 5, a block south of the Roman-Germanic Museum) Traditional local specialties in a Kölsch beer hall. Phone (0221) 257-8540. $ and $$

Museum Cafeteria (in the Wallraf-Richartz-Ludwig Museum) Light, healthy food in a cheerfully modern setting. X: Mon. $

SUGGESTED TOUR:

The **main train station** *(Hauptbahnhof)* (1) is located in the very heart of Cologne, just a few steps from the tourist office. Directly facing this is the ***Cathedral** *(Dom)* (2), one of the world's most stupendous Gothic structures. Begun in 1248 on the site of an earlier cathedral—and a Roman temple—it was far from complete when construction came to a standstill in the early 16th century. After that, not much happened until a wave of romantic nationalism swept the country in the mid-19th century. In the end it was political rather than religious considerations that led to the final completion in 1880. The Protestant rulers of Prussia felt a need to placate the Catholic Rhineland, and the newly united nation would clearly benefit from a symbol embodying the spirit of medieval Germany in its Gothic design.

Enter the cathedral via its magnificent west portal. The sheer verticality of the nave is awe inspiring, as are the medieval stained-glass windows, but the real treasures lie beyond the crossing. In a glass

The Cultural Center and the Rear of the Cathedral

case behind the high altar you will find the most precious object of all. This is the ***Reliquary of the Three Kings** *(Dreikönigenschrein)*, a 12th-century masterpiece of the goldsmiths' art alleged to contain the bones of the Magi, which were brought from Milan in 1164 by Emperor Frederick Barbarossa. It was the veneration of these relics during the Middle Ages that attracted countless pilgrims to Cologne and thus provided the impetus for building the present cathedral.

The medieval **choir** leading up to this has some outstanding stalls and statuary, while in the ambulatory there are two fabulous works of art. The first of these is the ***Gero Cross**, dating from 976, which is regarded as the oldest monumental cross from the Middle Ages and is located in the Cross Chapel to the left of the choir. On the other side, in the Lady Chapel directly across the chancel, is the 15th-century ***Dombild**, a triptych celebrating the Adoration of the Magi and the two patron saints of Cologne—Ursula and Gereon. More riches can be found in the **Treasury**, located just off the north transept and open on Mondays through Saturdays, from 9 a.m. to 5 p.m.; and and on Sundays from 12:30–5 p.m. Before leaving the cathedral, you may want to test your athletic ability by climbing over 500 steps to the top of the **south tower** for a fantastic view. Good luck!

Every time a hole is dug in Cologne there is a very real possibility of striking Roman ruins. An outstanding example of this happened in 1941, when workers were digging a bomb shelter next to the cathedral. What came to light was the wonderfully pagan **Dionysos Mosaic**, a 22-by-34-foot celebration of wine and revelry. In recent years the very modern ***Roman-Germanic Museum** (3) was built around this to display a vast collection of local archaeological finds. Step inside and enjoy the marvelously inspired presentation of life in ancient Colonia, complete with room settings that look as though the Romans had just gone out for a stroll. Don't miss this museum, which is open on Tuesdays through Fridays from 10 a.m. to 4 p.m., and weekends from 11 a.m. to 4 p.m.

The small **Diocesan Museum**, just a few steps away on the same open square, may interest you with its exquisite collection of ancient and medieval religious art. Now walk around to the nearby ***Wallraf-Richartz Museum / Museum Ludwig** (4), two institutions combined to form one of the greatest art galleries in all of Europe. It occupies a large segment of a spectacular cultural center wedged between the cathedral and the Rhine, which also houses the **Philharmonie** concert hall and the **Cinemathek** film theater. Allow plenty of time to peruse the many art treasures of this double museum, ranging all the way from the medieval to an exceptionally rich collection of American Pop. On display are paintings by the Cologne masters of the 14th to 16th centuries, Rembrandt, Dürer, Cranach, Rubens, Van Dyck, and many others. The sections devoted to modern art, called the Museum Ludwig, includes works by Picasso, Kandinsky, Dali, Max Ernst, Oldenburg, Rauschenberg, and Warhol—to name a few. Photographers will enjoy the small **Agfa Foto-Historama** with its collection of old cameras and changing print exhibitions next to the excellent cafeteria on the ground floor. The museum complex is open on Tuesdays through Fridays from 10 a.m. to 6 p.m., and on Saturdays and Sundays from 11 a.m. to 6 p.m.

Return to the front of the cathedral and turn left onto the pedestrians-only Hohe Strasse, the main shopping street. Follow this to Gürzenichstrasse, where you make a left. The **Gürzenich** building, dating from 1441, still fulfills its original purpose as a banqueting hall. Martinstrasse leads to the **Altes Rathaus** (Old City Hall) (5), originally built in the 14th century but considerably altered since. Its Renaissance loggia is particularly attractive. Just in front of this is the open excavation of a 12th-century **Mikwe**, a ritual bath of the Jewish ghetto that was destroyed after the 15th-century expulsion order. You can ask at the City Hall reception desk for a key to see it. Also nearby, at number 1 Kleine Budengasse, is the entrance to the underground **Roman Praetorium** with remains from the 1st through the 4th centuries A.D. It is usually open on Tuesdays through Fridays from 10 a.m. to 4 p.m., and on weekends from 11 a.m. to 4 p.m.

An alleyway next to the City Hall leads to the Alter Markt and then to the imposing **Gross St. Martin Church** (6). Along with the cathedral, this fortress-like structure—begun in 960 and completed in the

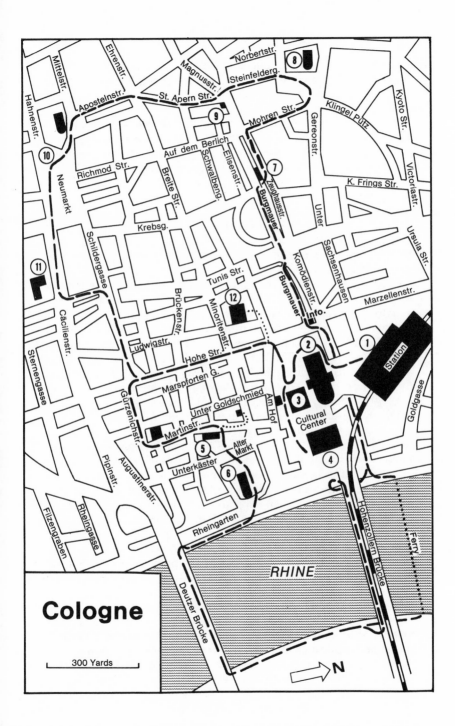

Cologne

300 Yards

N

mid-13th century—is a landmark of Cologne. This is the heart of the historic **Old City**, a maze of narrow, winding streets lined with reconstructed medieval houses and numerous restaurants, taverns, and outdoor cafés.

Stroll through the Fisch Markt and along the river's edge, where a flight of steps will take you up to the Deutzer Bridge. Cross the Rhine on this and turn left on the path along its opposite bank. From here you will have a marvelous view of the renowned Cologne skyline. Return to the city either on the ferry shown on the map, or by walking along the footpath on the south side of the Hohenzollern railway bridge.

You have now seen most of the tourist attractions in Cologne. If time allows, a further exploration can be made by following the map to the **Kölnisches Stadtmuseum** (Cologne Municipal Museum) (7), located in a former arsenal, with its entrance on Zeughausstrasse. The displays here, including arms and armor, are concerned with the history of the city and may be seen on Tuesdays through Fridays from 10 a.m. to 4 p.m., and on weekends from 11 a.m. to 4 p.m.

Continue on to the **Church of St. Gereon** (8), which dates in part from Roman times. Many changes were made since then, making this a particularly interesting structure to visit.

A short stroll down Steinfeldergasse will bring you to the **Römerturm** (Roman Tower) (9), a part of the original town walls built around A.D.. 50. Although small, its mosaic brick patterns are highly intriguing. Now follow St. Apern Strasse, lined with elegant antique shops, and Apostelnstrasse to **Neumarkt** (10). This lively market square is dominated by the massive **Church of the Holy Apostles**, an 11th-century structure in the Rhineland Romanesque style.

Another attraction is the **Schnütgen Museum** (11), housed in the desanctified 12th-century Church of St. Cecilia on Cäcilienstrasse. The superb collection of ancient religious artifacts, many of ivory, gold, or wood, are strikingly displayed in a setting of serene purity. It is open on Tuesdays through Fridays from 10 a.m. to 4 p.m., and on Saturdays and Sundays from 11 a.m. to 4 p.m. From here you can return via Hohe Strasse to the train station, perhaps stopping at the **Museum für Angewandte Kunst** (Museum of Applied Arts) (12). This favorite old institution, long hidden away in an obscure location, has found a magnificent new home for its vast collection of arts and crafts. Alternatively, those with a sweet tooth might want to stroll south along the Rhine, just beyond the Deutzer Bridge, to a delicious new attraction. **Das Imhoff Stollwerck Museum** is devoted entirely to the romance of chocolate, from growing the beans to consuming the product. Samples are included, so indulge yourself.

Düsseldorf

Style is an elusive quality—you either have it or you don't. Düsseldorf does. Perhaps it's the French influence—during their occupation of the city Napoleon called it "my little Paris." Or maybe it's just money, the vast wealth generated in the nearby Ruhr Valley. Whatever the reason, Düsseldorf is Germany's number one trend-setter in matters of fashion and life style. To stroll along the Königsallee, its elegant main street, is to witness another aspect of this kaleidoscopic nation—one that belongs to the world as much as to the *Vaterland*.

Düsseldorf was just a small fishing village until the 13th century, when it acquired city status and eventually became the residence of local nobility. It was their sophisticated affluence that attracted leading artists, musicians, and architects to this then-small town on the Rhine, especially during the early-18th-century reign of Elector Johann Wilhelm II. Within a century, Düsseldorf became a part of Napoleon's France, only to be taken over by Prussia in 1815. After another period of French occupation following World War I and the terrible destruction of World War II, the city reemerged as the state capital of North Rhine-Westphalia as well as a leading center of commerce and culture.

GETTING THERE:
Trains depart Frankfurt's main station at least hourly for the under-three-hour trip to Düsseldorf. Most of these are of the IC or EC class and may require a change at Cologne *(Köln)*. Return service operates until mid-evening.

By car, Düsseldorf is 141 miles northwest of Frankfurt. Take the A-66 Autobahn, then head northwest on the A-3 past Cologne.

PRACTICALITIES:
Avoid coming on a Monday, when most of the museums are closed. A warm, fine day will make the fashionable street life much more enjoyable. The local **Tourist Information Office** *(Verkehrsverein)*, phone (0211) 17-20-20, is across the street from the train station, a bit to the right. Düsseldorf has a **population** of about 570,000.

FOOD AND DRINK:

The *Altstadt,* near the Rhine, is famous for its traditional taverns serving the city's noted dark-brown *Alt Bier* along with local special-ties. Many of the center-city restaurants cater to an international crowd and feature cuisine—and prices—to match. A few good choices are:

> **Zum Schiffchen** (Hafenstr. 5, near the Hetjens Museum) An old traditional favorite in the Altstadt. Reservations advised, phone (0211) 13-24-22. X: Sun., holidays. $$$
>
> **Benrather Hof** (Steinstr. 1, on the corner of Königsallee) Typical German cuisine in the center of things. Phone (0211) 32-52-18. $$
>
> **Im Goldenen Ring** (Burgplatz 21, by the Schlossturm) A beer garden with exceptionally good food. Phone (0211) 13-31-61. $$
>
> **Mövenpick** (Königsallee 60, in the Kö Gallerie mall) This glitter-ing complex includes a full-service restaurant, snack bar, and cafeteria—all with good food at reasonable prices. Phone (0211) 32-06-81. $ and $$
>
> **Im Goldenen Kessel** (Bolkerstr. 44, 3 blocks east of Marktplatz) A popular brewery restaurant in the Altstadt. Phone (0211) 32-60-07. $
>
> **Hausbrauerei zum Schlüssel** (Bolkerstr. 45, 3 blocks east of Marktplatz) Food and beer in the Altstadt. Phone (0211) 32-61-55. $

SUGGESTED TOUR:

Leave the **main train station** (1) and follow Graf-Adolf-Strasse to the foot of the world-renowned ***Königsallee**. This enormously wide tree-lined boulevard, locally known as the *Kö,* is split down the mid-dle by a waterway that was once part of the town moat. The western side is lined with banks and offices, while the sunny east is a continu-ous row of posh shops, luxury restaurants, and sidewalk cafés. Be-sides the wealthy patrons, it is also the province of the *Radschläger,* a species of little boys unique to Düsseldorf. They cartwheel up and down the sidewalks during the summer season, demonstrating a skill learned in school in the hopes of earning a small tip.

At its northern end, the Kö runs into a lovely park called the **Hof-garten** (2), reached via a passageway. Stroll through this and note, to your right, the slab-sided Thyssen building—a modern high-rise that blends in well with its surroundings.

Cross a footbridge and continue along paths through another pas-sageway to the **Goethe Museum** (3) in the 18th-century Schloss Jäger-hof. Fans of Germany's greatest poet and playwright, who lived in

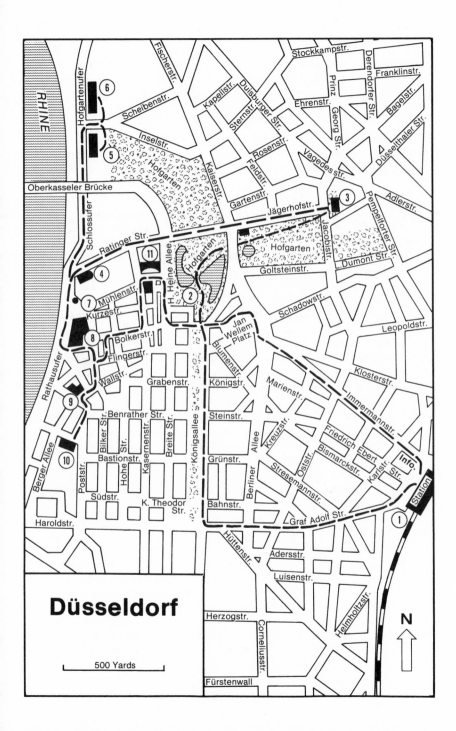

Düsseldorf

500 Yards

N

Düsseldorf for a while, will enjoy seeing the many manuscripts, first editions, and memorabilia associated with his life. It is open daily except on Mondays, from 11 a.m. to 5 p.m.; with Saturday hours being 1–5 p.m.

From here the map leads to the 14th-century **Church of St. Lambertus** (4), whose tower is curiously askew. If you really love museums, you might want to turn north to visit a fine pair. The first of these is the **Landesmuseum Volk und Wirtschaft** (State Museum of People and Economy) (5), a graphic presentation of social and economic conditions around the world. It is open on Mondays through Fridays, from 9 a.m. to 5 p.m.; and on Sundays from 10 a.m. to 6 p.m. On Wednesdays it remains open until 8 p.m. Just beyond this is the **Kunstmuseum** (Fine Arts Museum) (6). Specializing in the 19th-century romantic painting of the Düsseldorf School and 20th-century German Expressionists, the collections also include a balanced selection of other styles ranging from Old Masters to contemporary works. In addition, there is an excellent display of glass from Roman times all the way up to Art Nouveau. The museum is open on Tuesdays through Sundays, from 11 a.m. to 6 p.m.

Return along the river's edge to the **Schlossturm** (Castle Tower) (7), a 13th-century fortification now housing the **Navigation Museum**. You can see the models of inland shipping any day except Mondays, from 10 a.m. to 5 p.m.

A few steps beyond is the **Rathaus** (Town Hall), dating in part from 1573, and the **Marktplatz** (Market Place) (8) with its equestrian statue of the beloved elector Johann Wilhelm II, known in the local dialect as Jan Wellem. It was his leadership that put Düsseldorf on the map, so to speak, by attracting talent from all over the country. You are now in the oldest part of town, the ***Altstadt** . Leading off from here is a maze of lively narrow streets lined with colorful old taverns—the perfect spot for lunch or a break.

Follow Bergerstrasse and Hafenstrasse to the ***Hetjens Museum** (9), otherwise known as the *Deutsches Keramikmuseum*. Located in the former Nesselrode Palace, this incredible collection of ceramic objects from all over the globe spans 8,000 years of history. It is open on Tuesdays through Fridays from noon to 5 p.m., and on weekends from 11 a.m. to 5 p.m. The adjacent **Filmmuseum Düsseldorf** traces the history of the cinema with all sorts of artifacts, equipment, and techniques. You can see it all on Tuesdays through Fridays from 2–8 p.m., or on weekends from 11 a.m. to 6 p.m.

Just beyond this is the **Stadt Museum** (10). Several centuries of local bygones are gathered here, including furniture, art, and household objects; all illustrating Düsseldorf's culture within an historical context. Visits may be made on Tuesdays, Thursdays, Fridays, and

The Marktplatz

Sundays from 11 a.m. to 5 p.m., on Wednesdays from 11 a.m. to 8 p.m., and on Saturdays from 1–5 p.m.

Now stroll back towards the market place (8) and follow the map through some particularly interesting lanes in the Altstadt. The route passes an amusing **musical clock** on Schneider-Wibbel-Gasse, and the birthplace, at number 53 Bolkerstrasse, of the famous poet Heinrich Heine.

An important addition to Düsseldorf's cultural scene is the ***Kunstsammlung Nordrhein-Westfalen** (11), housed in a stunning curved structure of polished black granite on Grabbeplatz. Enter it to enjoy the marvelous North Rhine-Westphalia Collection of 20th-Century Art, one of the finest displays of contemporary art anywhere. Works by Paul Klee, who lived in Düsseldorf in the early 1930s, are exceptionally well represented. The museum is open on Tuesdays through Sundays, from 10 a.m. to 6 p.m. Across the street from it is the **Städtische Kunsthalle**, a municipal art gallery with changing exhibitions.

From here follow the map through Jan-Wellem-Platz and return to the train station.

Limburg

No, this is not the home of the malodorous cheese. *That* Limburg is in Belgium. What is served here is a feast for the eyes rather than the palate. Limburg-an-der-Lahn, to use its proper name, is an extraordinarily well-preserved medieval town where twisting, dreamy lanes wind their way through half-timbered houses to one of the most unusual cathedrals you'll ever see. The view from the river is a scene right out of the Middle Ages—an old engraving come to life.

Yet Limburg is no backwater place. Set astride the Frankfurt-Cologne Autobahn and easily reached by train, it is essentially a thriving modern community that has successfully managed to keep its ancient heritage intact. Excellent rail and road facilities make it possible to combine a daytrip here with one to Koblenz.

GETTING THERE:

Trains on the S-Bahn service (route S-2) depart frequently from Frankfurt's Konstablerwache, Hauptwache, Taunusanlage, and main station (lower level) for Niederhausen, where you change to a local for Limburg. In addition, there are also a few through trains leaving from Frankfurt's main station (street level). The total trip takes a bit over an hour, with good return service until mid-evening.

By car, Limburg is 46 miles northwest of Frankfurt. Take the A-66 Autobahn west, then head north on the A-3, getting off at the Limburg-Süd exit.

PRACTICALITIES:

Good weather is necessary to enjoy this trip, which can be taken any day. Rail service is reduced on weekends and holidays. The local **Tourist Information Office**, phone (06431) 203-222, is behind the town hall at Hospitalstrasse 2. **Bicycles** may be rented at the train station from April through October. Limburg has a **population** of about 31,000.

FOOD AND DRINK:

Dom Hotel (Grabenstr. 57, 2 blocks southwest of the Stadtkirche) Traditional fare in a quiet hotel. Phone (06431) 240-77. X: Sun. eve. $$

St. Georg's Stube (Hospitalstr. 4, a block east of the Rathaus) A nice variety of dishes served in congenial surroundings. Phone (06431) 260-27. $ and $$

In the Altstadt

SUGGESTED TOUR:

Leave the **train station** (1) and follow the map to the **Rathaus** (Town Hall) (2). The open square to the rear of this is enlivened by a contemporary fountain, a new municipal hall, and the beautiful 14th-century **St.-Annakirche** (St. Anne's Church)—noted for its medieval stained-glass windows.

Now cross Grabenstrasse and enter the **Altstadt** (Old Town) proper. As you wander up Plötze through the Fischmarkt you will be engulfed in a world of half-timbered houses *(Fachwerkhäuser)*, many dating from the Middle Ages. Continue up Domstrasse to the ***Cathedral** *(Dom)* (3), a startling sight of almost Oriental appearance. The seven-towered exterior is brightly painted in its original colors—mostly coral and white. Construction began around 1215 on the site of an earlier church, and was ready for consecration as early as 1235.

Step inside for a look at the famous superimposed galleries and the colorful 13th-century frescoes, painstakingly restored in recent years. While the outside of the building is Romanesque, its interior had already made the transition to Gothic during the relatively short period of construction.

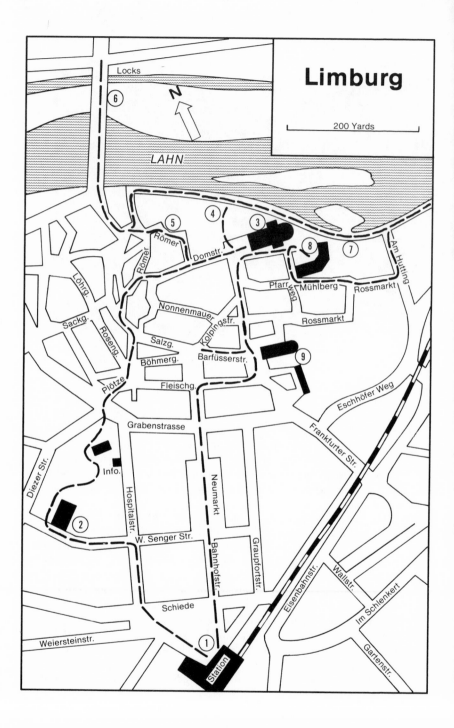

Limburg

200 Yards

Locks

N

LAHN

Am Hutting

Römer

Römer

Domstr.

Pfarr Weg

Mühlberg

Rossmarkt

Löhrg.

Nonnenmauer

Kolpingstr.

Rossmarkt

Sackg.

Roseng.

Salzg.

Böhmerg.

Barfüsserstr.

Plötze

Fleischg.

Eschhöfer Weg

Grabenstrasse

Diezer Str.

Info.

Hospitalstr.

Neumarkt

Frankfurter Str.

W. Senger Str.

Bahnhofstr.

Graupfortstr.

Weiersteinstr.

Schiede

Eisenbahnstr.

Wallstr.

Im Schlenkert

Gartenstr.

Station

Walk out into the **Friedhof** (graveyard) (4) for a splendid panoramic view up and down the Lahn Valley. Now stroll down a back alleyway to the **Römer** (5). The house at number 1 is said to be the oldest inhabited half-timbered house in Germany, and dates from 1296. Continue on past St. John's Chapel and cross the **Alte Lahnbrücke** (Old Lahn Bridge) (6), built of stone in 1315 and still carrying traffic. There is an excellent view of the cathedral from its far end. Tolls collected on this span were a considerable source of revenue to the town until finally being abolished in 1905.

Return across the bridge and follow the river's edge to the left. Beyond the base of the cathedral you will come to a picturesque **old mill** (7), whose waterwheel still turns. A little farther on there is a dock where cruises on the Lahn are offered.

Now turn down Am Huttig and make a right onto Rossmarkt. In one block bear right and climb Mühlberg to the **Schloss** (Castle) (8), a 13th- to 16th-century structure that was once home to the counts of Lahngau. It now houses the **Diözesanmuseum** (Diocesan Museum), where such cathedral treasures as a 10th-century **reliquary** of the True Cross stolen from the Hagia Sophia in Constantinople in 1204 by the crusaders, and the **golden staff** of St. Peter are on display from mid-March through mid-November, on Tuesdays through Saturdays from 9:30 a.m. to 12:30 p.m. and 2–5 p.m.; and on Sundays from 11 a.m. to 5 p.m.

From here follow the map to the **Stadtkirche** (Town Church) (9) on Bischofsplatz. Originally built in the 14th century, it has an interesting Baroque interior that you might want to see. Adjacent to this is the Bishop's Palace.

All of the streets in this area are well worth exploring, especially Barfüsserstrasse, Kornmarkt, and Fleischgasse. Spend some time soaking up the atmosphere, or perhaps stopping at an outdoor café, then return to the station via Neumarkt.

Bad Homburg

Once the haunt of Europe's crowned heads, Bad Homburg is an elegant old spa located just 11 miles from downtown Frankfurt. Today, this genteel turn-of-the-century resort caters more to bankers than to kings, but its casino, hot springs, and lovely Kurpark maintain the ambiance of a world long vanished from most of contemporary Europe. Although this is reason enough for a visit, Bad Homburg also offers an intriguing castle—until 1918 the summer home of Kaiser Wilhelm II—and the utterly fascinating reconstructed Roman fortress dating from the 2nd century A.D. at Saalburg.

GETTING THERE:

Trains on the S-Bahn service depart Frankfurt's Konstablerwache, Hauptwache, Taunusanlage, and main station (lower level) frequently for the 25-minute ride to Bad Homburg. The route number is S-5, going in the direction of Friedrichsdorf. Return trains run until late evening.

By car, Bad Homburg is 11 miles north of Frankfurt via the A-5 Autobahn and the B-456 road.

PRACTICALITIES:

This trip can be made at any time in good weather, but remember that the castle is closed on Mondays and a few major holidays. The local **Tourist Information Office**, phone (06172) 121-310, is in the Kurhaus on Louisenstrasse. Bad Homburg has a **population** of about 52,000.

FOOD AND DRINK:

Bad Homburg offers a broad range of restaurants and cafés, with several places right in the Kurpark. Some good choices are:

Sänger's Restaurant (Kaiser-Friedrich-Promenade 85, near the Russian Chapel) Exceptional cuisine at the town's best restaurant. Reservations advised, phone (06172) 244-25. X: Mon. lunch, Sat. lunch, Sun. $$$

Maritim Hotel (in the Kurhaus on Ludwigstr.) Modern and luxurious. Phone (06172) 280-51. $$$

Saalburg Restaurant (Am Römerkastell, near the B-456 road, at Saalburg) A well-regarded restaurant near the Roman camp. Phone (06175) 10-07. $$

Kartoffelküche (Audenstr. 4, a block west of the Kurhaus) Imaginative meals based on potatoes. Phone (06172) 215-00. X: Sat., Sun. lunch. $

The Siamese Temple

SUGGESTED TOUR:

Before leaving the **train station** (1), check the schedule of buses (line 5) going to Saalburg, which is best visited after seeing the town. Now follow the map on foot to the **Schloss** (Castle) (2). Built on the site of an earlier medieval fortification, of which only the 14th-century **Weisser Turm** (White Tower) remains, the castle as it stands today was begun in 1680 by Landgrave Frederick II of Hesse-Homburg. Famed in literature as *The Prince of Homburg,* he created a Baroque masterpiece that remained the home of his successors until 1866, when the principality was absorbed by Prussia. After that it became the favorite summer residence of Prussian kings and German emperors until the end of World War I.

Be sure to take the guided tour through the castle's interior, which is given in English on request. Unlike many palaces, this one has a rather homey, lived-in quality that is quite endearing. The room settings have been left pretty much as they were when Kaiser Wilhelm II abdicated and fled into a Dutch exile in 1918. Visits may be made on Tuesdays through Sundays, from 10 a.m. to 5 p.m. From November through February the castle closes at 4 p.m. Before leaving the grounds you should stroll out into the courtyard to see the ancient White Tower, which may be climbed.

Continue on past the market place and the modern **Kurhaus**—which houses the tourist office—to the large **Kurpark**. Laid out in the mid-19th century, this gorgeous park contains the **hot springs** that brought fame to Bad Homburg. Among its other attractions is the exotic **Siamese Temple** (3), presented by King Chulalongkorn of Siam after taking the cure.

Shady paths lead to the Kaiser Wilhelm Bad of 1890 and the **Spielbank** (Casino) (4), opened by the famous Blanc brothers of France in 1841. It was so successful that 25 years later they repeated themselves with a similar venture in Monte Carlo. The Russian author Feodor Dostoyevsky came here, lost a fortune, and wrote a novel about the experience called *The Gambler.* You can test *your* luck at the tables every day after 3 p.m., when roulette, blackjack, baccarat, and slots are offered. Adults only, proper dress required.

The spa gained immortality of a sort when Edward VII of England, then Prince of Wales, showed up wearing a new hat style that was quickly dubbed the homburg. A stroll down Brunnen Allee will bring you to the most popular (because of its high salinity) spring of them all, the **Elisabethenbrunnen** (5). Now walk over to the onion-domed **Russian Chapel** (6), built by another patron and member of the royal family, Czar Nicholas II.

Return to the train station via Friedrichstrasse and Bahnhofstrasse. From here a bus on Line 5, leaving from in front of the station, will take you on a 20-minute ride to Saalburg, certainly the most unusual sight in the area. Those with cars will, of course, prefer to drive the four-mile distance north on the B-456 road.

When the Romans invaded Germany in the 1st century A.D., they ran into a slight problem. The local tribes didn't like them. A defensive wall was clearly needed, and slowly one got built. Stretching some 340 miles between a point on the Rhine north of Koblenz to the Danube near Regensburg, this great engineering miracle was called the **Limes**. By A.D. 260, however, the fortifications were abandoned and the frontier moved back to the Rhine, where it remained until the fall of the empire.

*Saalburg (7) was one of the many military camps along the Limes. Built in the early 2nd century A.D., it later fell to ruin and became a convenient quarry during the Middle Ages. Archaeological excavations in the mid-19th century led to a total reconstruction under the leadership of Kaiser Wilhelm II between 1898 and 1907. What resulted is a fantastic, accurate re-creation of Roman life in the provinces. You will want to spend at least an hour exploring the camp and its museum, and take a short stroll to what remains of the great wall itself. An explanatory booklet in English is available, and the site is open daily from 8 a.m. to 5 p.m. Return by bus to Bad Homburg for a train to Frankfurt.

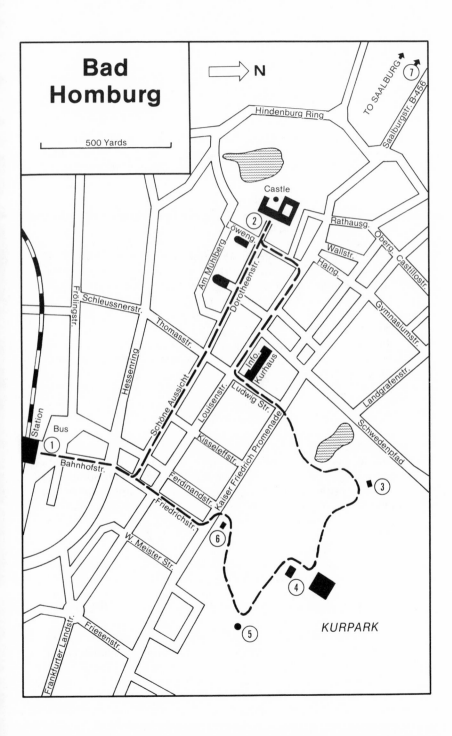

Marburg

Marburg is one of the few examples of a true medieval hill town in Germany. Its narrow, twisting lanes and steep stairways wind their way through a maze of half-timbered houses before finally reaching the ancient castle at its top. The climb can be exhausting, but there are several delightful rewards—and spots to rest—along the way.

A place of holy pilgrimage before the Reformation, Marburg became a center of liberal thinking afterwards. Martin Luther, Ulrich Zwingli, and others held their famous "Colloquy of Marburg" there in 1529, just two years after the world's first Protestant university was founded by the local margrave. That school is still going strong, and still attracts students by the thousands from all over the world. It is their presence that lends a youthful, vital, and international flavor to this otherwise peaceful old market town.

GETTING THERE:

Trains depart Frankfurt's main station almost hourly for Marburg, a run of about one hour. Return service operates until mid-evening.

By car, Marburg is 58 miles north of Frankfurt. Take the A-5 Autobahn to the Giessen-Nord exit, then go to Lollar and take the B-3 to Marburg. Park near the train station or St. Elizabeth's Church as driving in the old part of town is very difficult.

PRACTICALITIES:

Marburg may be visited at any time, but a few of the sights are closed on Mondays, and one on Tuesdays. A colorful **outdoor market** is held on Wednesdays and Saturdays. The local **Tourist Information Office**, phone (06421) 20-12-49, is next to the train station. Marburg has a population of about 75,000.

FOOD AND DRINK:

A wide choice of restaurants will be found along the walking route, many of which feature foreign cuisines. Some choices are:

> **Gasthaus zur Sonne** (Markt 14) An old traditional tavern in a 16th-century half-timbered house. Phone (06421) 253-14. X: Mon. $$

> **Milano** (Biegenstr. 19, 2 blocks north of the University Museum) Italian cuisine in rustic surroundings. Phone (06421) 224-88. X: Tues. $$

> **Zur Krone** (Markt 11) A local favorite for German dishes. Phone (06421) 253-90. $

The Rathaus in the Markt

Brasserie (Reitgasse 8, just north of the old university buildings) Light meals, veggies, beer, and indoor/outdoor tables. $
Zum Alten Brauhaus (Pilrimstein 34, 2 blocks west of the University Museum) A beer restaurant popular with students.
Phone (06421) 221-80. $

SUGGESTED TOUR:

Leave the **train station** (1) and stroll down Bahnhofstrasse, turning
left on Elisabethstrasse to the ***Elisabethkirche** (Church of St. Elizabeth) (2)—said to be the first purely Gothic church in Germany. Built
in the 13th century, it once held the remains of St. Elizabeth, a former
Hungarian princess married to the landgrave of Thuringia. When her
husband died of the plague in 1227 she moved to Marburg and spent
the rest of her short life caring for the sick and needy. After her death
in 1231 and canonization in 1235, the church was erected by the Teutonic Order of Knights as a place of pilgrimage. It continued to serve
that function until the Reformation, when one of her descendants,
Landgrave Philip the Magnanimous—who had converted to Protestantism and founded the local university—abolished the cult of relics
and had her bones removed for reburial elsewhere.

Step into the magnificent interior, which has several outstanding works of art devoted to St. Elizabeth. Don't miss her statue against the left wall near the crossing, her original tomb in the north transept, or especially her exquisite *golden shrine in the sacristy to the left of the high altar. The south transept contains the tombs of the landgraves of Hesse, who were her descendants. One of these is particularly gruesome in its depiction of a worm-ridden corpse. On the way out, stop at the chapel under the north tower for a look at the tomb of President Paul von Hindenburg, the last leader of a democratic Germany prior to Hitler's rise to power.

A short side trip can be made from here to the tiny 13th-century **Chapel of St. Michael** (3) in the lovely pilgrims' cemetery. This involves a rather steep climb but offers a nice view of the castle.

Now follow Steinweg, an unusual street built on three parallel levels, and continue uphill on the pedestrians-only Neustadt and Wettergasse to the **Markt** (Market Place) (4). At the southern end of this stands the early-16th-century **Rathaus** (Town Hall), famous for its clock that for centuries had signaled each passing hour with the simulated crow of a cock. **Farmers' markets** are held in front of this each Wednesday and Saturday. Beyond the **Fountain of St.-George-and-the-Dragon** is the upper market, lined with colorful old houses. Walk through this and climb the steps at the north end.

A left at the top puts you on Landgraf-Philipp-Strasse, which continues ever upwards to the ***Schloss** (Castle) (5). The strategic value of this lofty location was realized as far back as the 11th century, when it held a Franconian watchtower. The present structure, however, is a mixture of buildings dating from the 13th through the 16th centuries, during which time it underwent many changes.

Enter through a door in the courtyard and pick up an explanatory brochure in English. Three of the rooms are particularly interesting. These are the **Gothic Chapel**, now restored to its original 13th-century colors; the **Knights' Hall** *(Rittersaal)*; and the **Landgrave's Study** with its memories of the famous dialogue between Luther and Zwingli in 1529. It was their failure to reach an agreement that helped split the Protestant movement into different sects. The castle is open on Tuesdays through Sundays, from 10 a.m. to 6 p.m.; 11 a.m. to 5 p.m. in winter. Another part of the castle houses the interesting **Museum of Cultural History**.

Return on Landgraf-Philipp-Strasse and descend steps next to the café. A right on Ritterstrasse leads to the Kalbstor gate, where you make a sharp left past the picturesque 15th-century **Kugel Church** (6). From here continue on to the **Church of St. Mary** (7), a Lutheran parish church dating from the late 13th century. The terrace in front of this offers a fabulous view of the town and river valley. Go down the steps and return to the market place (4).

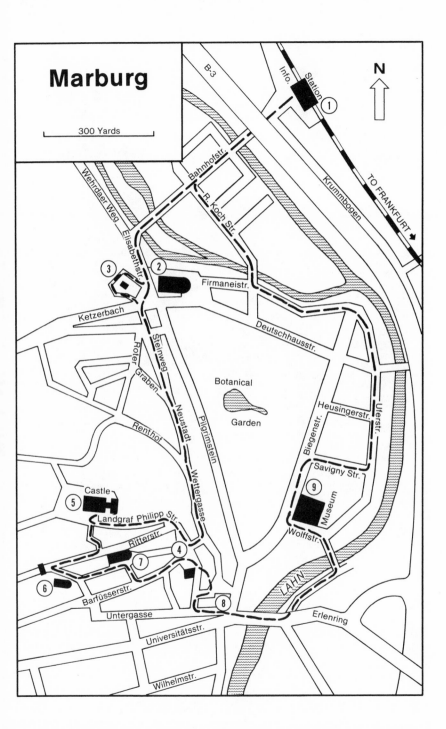

The Kugel Church

Now follow the map past the old buildings of the **Philipp University** (8) and cross the bridge over the Lahn. On the opposite bank there is a path that leads across a footbridge to the **University Museum** (9). Concerned with the history of art and civilization, this unusually fine museum is a must-see for any visitor to Marburg. It is open on Tuesdays through Sundays, from 10 a.m. to 1 p.m. and 2–5 p.m. The route on the map is an especially pleasant way to return to the train station.

Aschaffenburg

Perhaps Aschaffenburg is just too close to Frankfurt. Whatever the reason, it is almost always overlooked by tourists as they speed by on their way to Würzburg or beyond. This exceptionally pleasant small town on the Main has several attractions that make it worth at least a detour, including a huge and quite marvelous Renaissance palace. Much of the town is covered by enchanting parks, and there is a splendid abbey church and museum to see as well.

The curious thing about Aschaffenburg is that it is actually in Bavaria—although well beyond daytrip range of Munich. From the 10th century until the beginning of the 19th, it was under the control of the archbishops of Mainz. Napoleon made it a principality, but after his fall the town was incorporated into the kingdom of Bavaria. Badly devastated in World War II, Aschaffenburg today is a modern, albeit somewhat provincial, place that has managed to hang on to the best of a distinguished past. A trip there could be combined in the same day with one to Miltenberg.

GETTING THERE:

Trains leave Frankfurt's main station at least hourly for Aschaffenburg, with those of the EC class taking only 30 minutes and others a bit longer. Return service operates until late evening.

By car, Aschaffenburg is 25 miles southeast of Frankfurt via the A-3 Autobahn, getting off at the Aschaffenburg-West exit.

PRACTICALITIES:

Avoid coming on a Monday, when the palace is closed. Any other day is fine, although good weather will make this largely outdoor trip much more pleasant. The local **Tourist Information Office**, phone (06021) 39-58-00, is in the new Stadthalle in front of Schloss Johannisburg. Bicycles may be rented at the train station. Aschaffenburg has a population of about 65,500.

FOOD AND DRINK:

Some good restaurant choices along the walking route are:

Hotel Post (Goldbachstr. 19, 3 blocks southeast of the station) A romantic old hotel with a wide selection of excellent cuisine. Phone (06021) 213-33. $$$

Schlossweinstuben (in the palace) A popular wine restaurant with Franconian and other dishes; nice views of the Main Valley. Phone (06021) 124-40. X: Mon. $$

Aschaffenburger Hof (Frohsinnstr. 11, 2 blocks southeast of the station) Local cuisine, with vegetarian dishes available. Phone (06021) 214-41. X: Sat. $$

Wilder Mann (Löherstr. 51, 4 blocks southwest of the Stifts- kirche, near the bridge) Traditional local cuisine. Phone (06021) 215-55. $$

Zum Ochsen (Karlstr. 16, 2 blocks north of the palace) Good- value dining in a small hotel. Phone (06021) 231-32. X: Mon. lunch. $

SUGGESTED TOUR:

Leave the **train station** (1) and follow the map to the palace, ***Schloss Johannisburg** (2). Built between 1605 and 1614 on the site of an earlier castle, it was the summer residence of the electors of Mainz until the Napoleonic period. Many kings and emperors stayed there during the course of their journeys. The palace later became an official residence of King Ludwig I of Bavaria after the town was incorporated into that kingdom. Allow at least an hour to wander through its many rooms, which are filled with superb art, antique fur- niture, and various artifacts. The main floor has a fascinating collec- tion of finely detailed architectural models of classic Roman struc- tures, all rendered in cork during the early 19th century. Go upstairs to see the rest of the treasures. The palace is open on Tuesdays through Sundays, from 9–11:30 a.m. and 1–4:30 p.m., closing at 3:30 in winter.

The palace **gardens**, overlooking the banks of the Main, convey a Mediterranean atmosphere that is at once more Italian than German. Stroll through them to the **Pompeianum** (3), a reproduction of the villa of Castor and Pollux in ancient Pompeii. It was built in the mid- 19th century for King Ludwig I, who fancied the classical era.

Now walk through what little remains of the old part of town, tak- ing the route via Pfaffengasse, Dalbergstrasse, and Stiftsgasse. This will bring you to the **Rathaus** (Town Hall), across the square from the tourist office.

Aschaffenburg's other major sight is the **Stiftskirche** (Church of SS. Peter and Alexander) (4). Dating from the 12th century and much altered over the years, it contains an unexpectedly rich treasure of art including a **Lamentation** by Matthias Grünewald and a **Resurrection** by Lucas Cranach the Elder. The Romanesque cloister, which can be entered from the adjacent museum, is especially lovely. Leave the church proper and visit the small **museum**, housed in the former

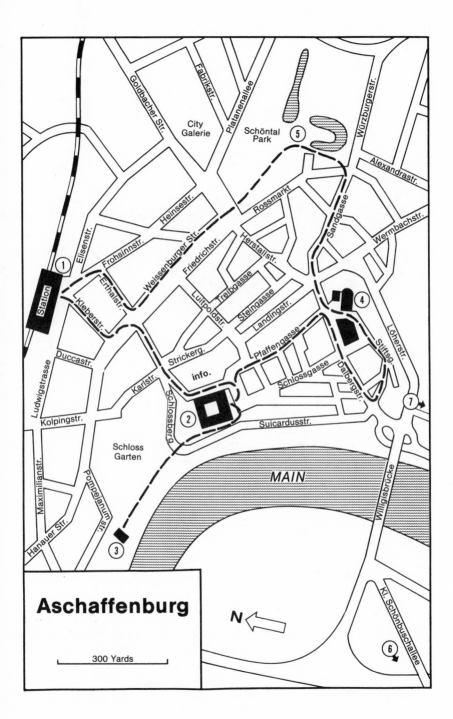

Aschaffenburg

N ←

300 Yards

Schloss Johannisburg
(Photo © Aschaffenburg Tourist Office)

chapter house. More works of outstanding religious art are displayed there, along with a collection of china.

Continue down Sandgasse to **Schöntal Park** (5), a shady and romantic spot laid out in 1780 in the English style. On the other side of the pond you will pass the ruins of an ancient monastery. The park ends at the medieval Herstallturm tower, to the right of which is a modern shopping center. The nicest way back to the station is via the tree-lined Weissenburger Strasse, making a right onto Erthalstrasse.

ADDITIONAL SIGHTS:

An enjoyable short excursion can be made on foot or by car, bike, or bus to **Schönbusch Park** (6), a tranquil place of idyllic beauty. To reach it, cross the Main River on the Willigisbrücke and walk out Kleine Schönbuschallee, a distance of not quite two miles. Cars can get there via Darmstädter Strasse. The main attraction, besides the small temples, gazebos, and follies surrounded by ponds and meandering lanes, is the **Schlösschen** (Little Palace), an 18th-century pleasure retreat of the archbishops.

Sportscar enthusiasts will enjoy a visit to the **Rosso Bianco Automuseum** (7) at Obernauer Strasse 125, reached by city bus number 1. Some 200 magnificent machines cover the history of sports cars from 1907 to the present day, making this perhaps the greatest collection of its kind in the world. Phone (06021) 213-58 for information.

Miltenberg

If a contest were held to choose the most beautiful small town in Germany, Miltenberg would certainly be among the top contenders. Its market place is so astonishingly picturesque that it seems to belong to another world—or a long-forgotten dream.

The Romans had a camp here in the 2nd century A.D. as part of their great defensive wall called the Limes. Around 1200 a castle was begun by the archbishops of Mainz to protect the growing trading post that connected the Rhine-Main area with an overland route to the Danube. The town prospered during the Middle Ages, changed hands several times and ultimately, in 1816, was annexed to Bavaria. Much of old Miltenberg, including its castle, has survived intact to delight us today. A visit here could be combined in the same day with one to Aschaffenburg.

GETTING THERE:

Trains depart Frankfurt's main station several times in the morning for Aschaffenburg, where you connect to a local for Miltenberg. The total trip takes a bit over 1½ hours, with return service until early evening.

By car, Miltenberg is about 50 miles southeast of Frankfurt. Take the A-3 Autobahn to Stockstadt, then head south on the B-469.

PRACTICALITIES:

Visits to Miltenberg should be made from April through October, on any day except Mondays—when the sights are closed. The local **Tourist Information Office**, phone (09371) 400–119, is in the Town Hall on Engelplatz. **Bicycles** may be rented at the train station from April through October, and at other places in town. Miltenberg has a **population** of about 9,500.

FOOD AND DRINK:

The town is very popular with German tourists, and so offers a good choice of restaurants. Among the best are:

> **Altes Bannhaus** (Hauptstr. 211, a block west of the Marktplatz) Excellent dining in an historic building with an arched cellar. Phone (09371) 30-61. X: Thurs. $$$

> **Jagd-Hotel Rose** (Hauptstr. 280, 4 blocks west of St.-Jakobus Church) In a 17th-century house overlooking the river; outdoor tables available. Phone (09371) 400-60. X: Sun. eve. $$$

In the Marktplatz

Gasthaus zum Riesen (Hauptstr. 99) Dine or drink in an historic 16th-century inn. Phone (09371) 672-38. X: Tues. eve., Jan. to mid-March) $$

Mildenburg (Mainstr. 77, 2 blocks west of St.Jakobus Church) Facing the river, with outdoor tables available. Phone (09371) 27-33. X: Mon. $ and $$

Anker (Hauptstr. 31, near the Franciscan Church) Good-value meals at a small inn. Phone (09371) 24-24. X: Fri. $

SUGGESTED TOUR:

Leaving the **train station** (1), follow Brückenstrasse and cross the bridge spanning the Main. Boat trips are offered nearby. Turn right and stroll along the water's edge, then make a left to the ***Marktplatz** (Market Place). One of the most beautiful sights in Germany, this open square is lined with an amazing array of half-timbered houses *(Fachwerkhäuser)*. The Renaissance fountain in its center dates from 1583, while on the left is the **Town Museum** (2), located in the former 16th-century seat of administration. Step inside for a look at the town's history and traditional folk arts. The museum is open from April through October, daily except Mondays, from 10 a.m. to noon and 2–4 p.m.

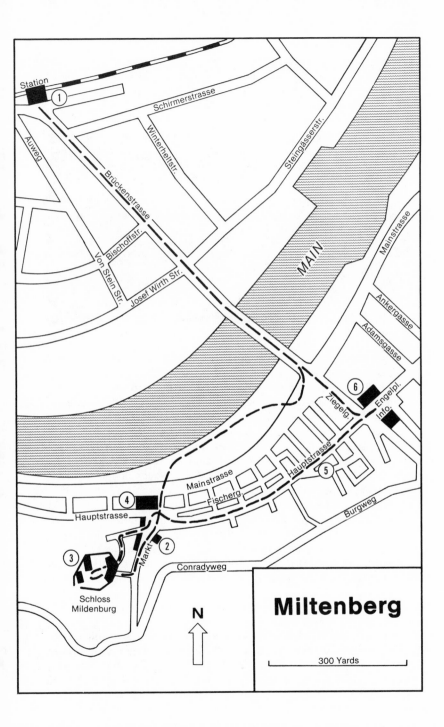

Station

Schirmerstrasse

Winterheltstr.

Steingasserstr.

Auweg

Brückenstrasse

Bischoffstr.

Von Stein Str.

Josef Wirth Str.

MAIN

Mainstrasse

Ankergasse

Adamsgasse

Engelpl. Info.

Ziegelg.

Hauptstrasse

Mainstrasse

Fischerg.

Burgweg

Hauptstrasse

Markt

Schloss Mildenburg

Conradyweg

N

Miltenberg

300 Yards

View from Mildenburg Castle

Now walk uphill through the old town walls to the **Mildenburg Castle** (3), a medieval stronghold built between the 13th and 16th centuries. The view from its tower is spectacular and well worth the climb. In the courtyard you will find the fascinating **Toutonenstein**, a carved stone monument from early Germanic times. The castle may be visited from April through October, but not on Mondays.

Descend the hill via the other path and return to the market place. On its north side stands the 14th-century **Pfarrkirche St.-Jakobus** (St. James' Parish Church) (4), which contains several splendid works of art. The twin towers were added in 1820.

The Hauptstrasse is lined with an impressive variety of old buildings, many of which are half-timbered. Walk past the **Altes Rathaus** (Old Town Hall), a 14th-century stone structure, and continue on to the **Gasthaus zum Riesen** (5). Claiming to be Germany's oldest inn, its guest register reads like a *Who's Who* of European history. The present structure dates from 1590, but some questionable documents seem to show that the inn was doing business since the 12th century and has sheltered Frederick Barbarossa and other greats. In any case, it's a nice place to stay, or just stop for a beer.

Just beyond this is the Engelplatz, where the tourist office is located in the town hall. The Baroque 17th-century **Franciscan Church** (6), on its north side, is a worthwhile stop before spending the rest of your time poking around the narrow alleyways that add so much interest to this ancient town.

Michelstadt

The heart of the Odenwald is Michelstadt, a town of extraordinary beauty set in the enchanted forest of the Nordic god Odin; where once the Nibelungs hunted and Siegfried was killed by Hagen's spear. Or at least in legend. Today's Odenwald is a vacation paradise for the citizens of nearby Frankfurt. The history of its settlement began in Roman times, when the area had to be defended against Teutonic hordes. Michelstadt was first mentioned in A.D. 741 and soon became a place of some importance. The splendid medieval structures still gracing its narrow lanes are a reflection of the great prosperity that blessed the town during the Middle Ages.

By getting off to an early start, it is possible to combine this trip with one to Darmstadt. Those with cars could choose to combine it with Miltenberg instead.

GETTING THERE:

Trains depart Frankfurt's main station about 8 a.m. and noon for the 80-minute ride direct to Michelstadt. There is a direct return service in the early evening. It is also possible to get to and from Michelstadt at other times by changing trains at Darmstadt.

By car, Michelstadt is about 50 miles southeast of Frankfurt by taking the A-5 Autobahn to the Bensheim exit, then the B-47—the famous *Nibelungenstrasse*—into Michelstadt. Shorter routes are possible but not as attractive.

PRACTICALITIES:

Michelstadt may be visited at any time in good weather. Some sights are closed on Mondays. The local **Tourist Information Office** *(Verkehrsamt)*, phone (06061) 741–46, is on the Marktplatz. Michelstadt has a **population** of about 16,000.

FOOD AND DRINK:

Drei Hasen (Braunstr. 5, a block southeast of the Marktplatz) An old inn with superb meals and a beer garden. Phone (06061) 710-17. X: Mon. $$

Grüner Baum (Grosse Gasse 17, just north of the Marktplatz) Traditional cooking in a 17th-century half-timbered house, outdoor tables available. Phone (06061) 24-09. $

Elefantenhaus (Kirchplatz, near the Town Church) Light meals and snacks, vegetarian and otherwise. X: Tues. $

The Marktplatz and Rathaus

SUGGESTED TOUR:

Leave the **train station** (1) and follow the map to the ***Marktplatz** (Market Place). In its center is an ornamental fountain that has been bubbling away since 1575. The ***Rathaus** (Town Hall) (2), directly opposite, is one of the most photographed sights in Germany. Built in 1484, its steeply pointed roof and spired oriel windows resting on massive oak supports combine to form a vision that seems to have been lifted right out of the pages of a fairy tale. The scene is further enhanced by colorful half-timbered houses lining the square, and by the tower of the 15th-century church. During the warm months, outdoor café tables allow you to take it all in while enjoying a drink. The tourist office is adjacent.

Turn right and visit the medieval **Diebsturm** (Thieves' Tower) (3) before crossing the old dry-moat to the public gardens. Stroll through these and into the **Burghof** (4), a courtyard whose origins date from Carolingian times. The present buildings are mostly from the 16th century and now house the interesting **Spielzeugmuseum** (Toy Museum) and the **Odenwald Museum**, whose exhibits range from Celtic finds to the sword of the last town executioner.

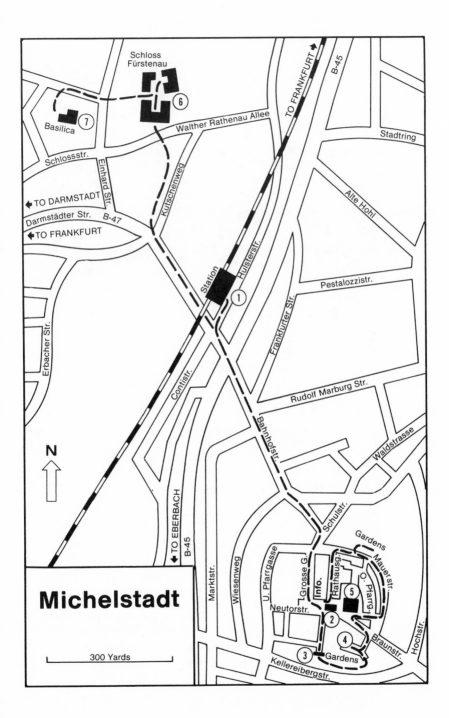

Fürstenau Castle

Now walk over to the **Stadtkirche** (Town Church) (5), a late-Gothic structure begun in 1461. Step inside to see the beautiful old tombs, then follow the map down Mauerstrasse. Along the way you will pass an intriguing 18th-century synagogue before going through the restored **town walls**. Turn left in the gardens, reenter the walls, and return to the market place.

Two fascinating sights lie just outside the town proper. To reach them, return to the train station (1) and continue on until you come to a creek. A trail to the right leads past a lovely old watermill to **Fürstenau Castle** (6). Begun in the 13th century, it grew over the years into a place of immense charm. The magnificent ornamental arch between two of the structures was added in 1588. Although the castle is still a private residence, you can wander around the courtyards and visit the tiny museum.

A path from the central courtyard takes you over the moat to **Einhard's Basilica** (7), an ancient stone church of impressive proportions built in the 9th century by Charlemagne's friend and biographer, Einhard. Once in state of ruin, it has now been partially restored and may be visited on Tuesdays through Sundays from 10 a.m. to noon and 1–5 p.m. From November through February the hours are 11 a.m. to 3 p.m. From here you can retrace your steps back to the train station.

Darmstadt

Creativity has long been the hallmark of Darmstadt, one of those rare places where intellectual curiosity is given a full chance to develop. This medium-size city in the foothills of the Odenwald is among the leading European centers of science, literature, and the arts. There are no tourist attractions in the ordinary sense, but travelers with an interest in architecture will be captivated by its highly unusual—and world-famous—buildings, particularly those in the Art Nouveau style.

An extraordinary amount of the city is devoted to parks, while the pedestrians-only business district has a light and airy quality about it. A Baroque palace and three splendid museums round out this easy daytrip from Frankfurt, which could be combined with a visit to Michelstadt.

GETTING THERE:

Trains leave Frankfurt's main station frequently for the 15-minute ride to Darmstadt. There are also S-Bahn commuter trains that take about one-half hour. Return service operates until late evening.

By car, Darmstadt is 22 miles south of Frankfurt via the A-5 Autobahn.

PRACTICALITIES:

Darmstadt may be visited at any time, but note that some of the museums are closed on Mondays and others on Fridays. The local **Tourist Information Office**, phone (06151) 132-782, is just outside the train station. There is another office, phone (06151) 132-780, at Luisenplatz. Darmstadt has a **population** of about 140,000.

FOOD AND DRINK:

Maritim Hotel (Rheinstr. 105, a block south of the train station) Good dining in a large hotel. Phone (06151) 87-80. $$$

Alt Hamburg (Landgraf-Georg-Str. 17, a block east of the Marktplatz) A well-regarded seafood restaurant. Phone (06151) 213-21. $$

Ratskeller (Am Marktplatz, across from the Schloss) The restaurant in the 16th-century Old City Hall offers solid German fare along with homemade beer. $

SUGGESTED TOUR:

Begin your tour at the **main train station** (1). From here it is a rather uninteresting one-mile walk to downtown, which can be avoided by taking a streetcar or bus to the spacious **Luisenplatz** (2), site of the stunning **Neues Rathaus** (New City Hall) and the towering Ludwig Monument.

Walk straight ahead to the **Marktplatz** (Market Place), where outdoor farmers' markets are held. On its south side you will see the **Altes Rathaus** (Old City Hall), erected in 1598 in the Renaissance style. Dominating the square is the massive **Schloss** (Palace) (3), home to the rulers of the Grand Duchy of Hesse-Darmstadt until 1918. Parts of the palace were once a medieval castle, but many changes and additions made between the 16th and 19th centuries have greatly altered its appearance. Stroll through the main portal to its inner courtyard, where you will find the entrance to the **Schlossmuseum** (Palace Museum). Guided tours lasting an hour are conducted through the beautifully restored rooms, whose treasures include a noted *Madonna* by Hans Holbein the Younger, works by local artists, furniture, costumes, and carriages. The museum is open on Mondays through Thursdays, 10 a.m. to 1 p.m. and 2–5 p.m.; and on Saturdays and Sundays from 10 a.m. to 1 p.m.

Now follow the map along a garden path to the ***Mathildenhöhe** (4). Developed around the turn of the century as an artists' colony by the visionary Grand Duke Ernst-Ludwig, this low hill overlooking the city is famous for its unusual structures. Rising above all is the very symbol of Darmstadt, the **Hochzeitsturm** (Wedding Tower), an acknowledged masterpiece of *Jugendstil* (German Art Nouveau) architecture built in 1906 but appearing to be much younger than that. You can ride an elevator 150 feet up to its top for a good view, on Tuesdays through Sundays from 10 a.m. to 6 p.m. Next to the tower, the gold-domed **Russian Chapel** of 1899 seems wildly out of place—a strong addition to an already surrealist landscape. Built by Czar Nicholas II for his Hessian bride, it is still used as an Orthodox church and may be visited.

Don't miss the stunning new ***Museum Künstlerkolonie** *(Artists' Colony Museum)* in the Ernst-Ludwig-Haus of 1901, whose curved entrance is flanked by huge statues of Adam and Eve. Built to house studios, it now exhibits creative works of the *Jugendstil* era, especially in the applied arts field. It's open on Tuesdays through Sundays, from 10 a.m. to 5 p.m. Industrial design of a more contemporary nature can be seen at the nearby **Braun Design Collection** in the Institute of New Technical Form at Eugen-Bracht-Weg 6.

From here you can take a pleasant walk by heading east past the railway line to the tranquil **Rosenhöhe Park** (5). Go through the lion-topped gateway of 1914 and wander past the secluded artists' homes, then return to the center of town via the Mathildenhöhe.

Back at the palace (3), turn north and visit the ***Hessisches**

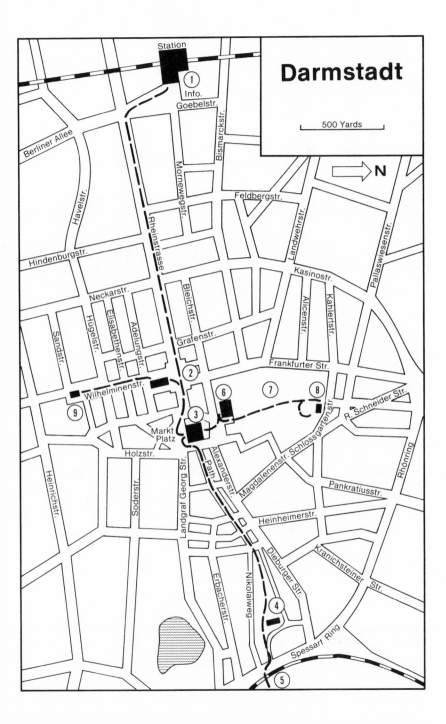

The Hochzeitsturm and Russian Chapel

Landesmuseum (Hessian State Museum) (6). The exhibitions in this huge institution—one of Europe's oldest—encompass a wide scope of subjects ranging from art to natural history. Of particular interest are the outstanding collections of medieval, Renaissance, and modern paintings. Allow at least an hour to sample the highlights, and be sure to see the marvelous display of **Jugendstil* and **Art Nouveau** objects in the basement. The museum is open on Tuesdays and Thursdays through Saturdays from 10 a.m. to 7 p.m.; on Wednesdays from 10 a.m. to 1 p.m. and 2–9 p.m.; and on Sundays from 11 a.m. to 5 p.m.

Continue on through the **Herrngarten** (7), a lovely city park in the English style. At its far end is **Prince George's Palace** (8), an early-18th-century summer residence of the dukes. It now houses an exquisite collection of porcelain, which is temporarily closed pending renovation. The side of the palace facing the park has an immensely charming garden that should not be missed.

Return to Luisenplatz (2) and visit the bold Luisen Center on its south side. This large structure is home to both the new city hall and an indoor shopping mall. Amble through it and continue south on Wilhelminenstrasse to **St. Ludwig's Church** (9), an imposing 19th-century building with an enormous dome modeled on the Pantheon in Rome. Take a look at its unusual interior, then return to Luisenplatz where you can board a streetcar or bus back to the train station.

*Heidelberg

More a romantic state of mind than an actual place, old Heidelberg has captured the hearts of countless tourists. First-time visitors are often filled with a sense of *deja-vu*, that feeling that somehow they've been here before. In their thoughts they probably have, for who hasn't heard of the *Student Prince?*

Half a million years ago these hills were home to the Heidelberg Man, a pre-human whose jawbone was found nearby. Celtic tribes settled the area around 400 B.C., were succeeded by Teutons, and eventually by the Romans. A series of rival kingdoms followed, monasteries were built, and in 1196 the first documented reference to *Heidelberch*—then the political center of the Palatinate—was made.

Heidelberg University, the oldest in Germany, dates from 1386. During the Reformation it became a stronghold of Protestantism. In 1622, at the height of the Thirty Years War, General Tilly's Catholic army captured the town after a destructive two-month seige.

In an effort to bring peace to the Rhineland, the new ruler, Karl-Ludwig, married his daughter to the Duke of Orléans—the brother of France's Louis XIV. When Karl-Ludwig's son died heirless in 1685, the "Sun King" claimed the Rhineland-Palatinate as his own, precipitating a war that left Heidelberg almost totally leveled. Later rebuilt in stone, the town lost status when the court moved to Mannheim in 1720. The final blow to its castle came in 1764 in the form of a lightning bolt that reduced it to the ruin it is today.

Heidelberg's glory faded in those last smoldering ashes; but its university lived on, eventually escaping into a never-never land of romanticism—a world of writers, artists, poets, and musicians. This was the *milieu* of the Student Prince; the ambiance of beer drinking, songs, and duels that still fires the imagination of today.

With its many hotels and good transportation, Heidelberg makes an excellent alternative base for exploring the Rhineland south of Frankfurt.

GETTING THERE:

Trains depart Frankfurt's main station frequently for the one-hour ride to Heidelberg. Return service operates until late evening.

By car, Heidelberg is 56 miles south of Frankfurt via the A-5 Autobahn.

PRACTICALITIES:

Heidelberg may be visited at any time. The Kurpfälzisches Museum is closed on Mondays and the Student Jail on both Sundays and Mondays. The local **Tourist Information Office**, phone (06221) 213-41, is in front of the train station. **Bicycles** may be rented at the station from April through October. Heidelberg has a **population** of about 135,000.

FOOD AND DRINK:

This much-visited town offers a huge variety of restaurants in all price ranges, including:

Kurpfälzisches Museum Restaurant (in the Kurpfälzisches Museum at Hauptstr. 97) Superb meals and courtyard dining in an atmospheric wine restaurant. Phone (06221) 240-50. $$ and $$$

Hotel zum Ritter (Hauptstr. 178, west of the Marktplatz) Traditional German specialties and atmosphere in a 16th-century mansion. Phone (06221) 242-72. $$

Hackteufel (Steingasse 7, by the Old Bridge) A romantic old inn with good German cooking. Phone (06221) 271-62. $$

Perkeo (Hauptstr. 75, 3 blocks west of the Kurpfälzisches Museum) An old and thoroughly German restaurant with plenty of atmosphere. Phone (06221) 16-06-13. $$

Zum Sepp'l (Hauptstr. 213, east of Karlsplatz) An historic student tavern since 1634. Simple food and noisy fun. Phone (06221) 230-85. $

Schnookeloch (Haspelgasse 8, a block north of the Heiliggeist Church) An historic tavern and beer garden, near the Old Bridge. Phone (06221) 227-33. $

SUGGESTED TOUR:

Start your tour at the **main train station** (1). From here it is a rather boring one-mile walk to **Bismarck Platz** (2), where the Old Town begins. You may prefer to take a streetcar (route 1), a bus (routes 11 or 33), or a taxi instead.

Continue down the pedestrians-only Hauptstrasse to the **Old University** (3) on Universitäts Platz. This is the oldest surviving building of the school, having been erected in the early 18th century. Walk around its rear façade and visit the **Studentenkarzer** (Student Jail) at number 2 Augustinergasse. The lockup was used until 1914 for the incarceration of campus rowdies, who got to spend anywhere from one to five weeks on bread and water for their misdeeds. Actually, serving time here was considered a mark of honor and, given the cleverness of students, the water usually turned out to be beer. Many of the "convicts" immortalized their enforced leisure by covering the cell walls with amusing graffiti, which can be seen today. The jail is open on Tuesdays through Saturdays from 10 a.m. to noon and 2–5 p.m., but closed on Saturday afternoons in winter.

Escaping the pokey, stroll across to the New University, built in 1931 with American funds. In its courtyard you will find the 14th-century **Hexenturm** (Witches' Tower) (4), all that remains of the medieval town walls. Now climb a few steps and turn right on Seminarstrasse to the **Universitäts-Bibliothek** (University Library) (5). Here you can visit the exhibition gallery, containing a priceless collection of medieval manuscripts and illuminations along with other treasures. The library is open on Mondays through Saturdays, from 10 a.m. to 7 p.m. From Easter through October it's also open on Sundays and holidays, from 11 a.m. to 4 p.m.

St. Peter's Church (6), dating from the 15th century, serves the academic community. Wander through its tranquil yard and follow the map past the Jesuit Church of 1712 to **Kornmarkt** (7), from which you get a lovely view of the castle. The 18th-century Prinz-Karl Inn on the west side of the square is now a town hall annex, but in its heyday housed such luminaries as Mark Twain, Kaiser Wilhelm I, and Bismarck.

At the corner of Burgweg stands the house of Count Graimberg, a French artist who was responsible for the preservation of the castle ruins during the 19th century. Just a few steps beyond is the lower station of the **funicular** (Bergbahn). Board this and ride up to the **Schloss** (Castle). Alternatively, you could walk up the rather steep Kurzer Buckel.

You are now at Heidelberg's stellar attraction, its ***Castle**. Follow the path to the **Rondell** (8), once a gun battery and now an excellent spot for closeup views of the town below. Beyond it lies the remains of the **Dicker Turm** (Fat Tower), which was blown up by the French in 1689. Return along the other path through the **Elizabeth Gate**, built in 1615—allegedly in one night—by Friedrich V as a present for his wife, Elizabeth Stuart, the daughter of England's James I.

Stroll over to the castle's main entrance and cross the moat into the **courtyard** (9). From here you can take a one-hour guided tour through the complex, partly in a state of ruin and partly restored. Tours are offered daily from 9 a.m. to 4 p.m. If you don't feel up to this, at least see the **Grosses Fass** (Great Vat), which may be visited separately. This is the world's largest wine cask, once guarded by the court jester Perkeo, a dwarf with a monumental capacity for the juice. A statue of him—glass in hand—may be seen opposite the vat. Another attraction that may be visited without taking the tour is the ***Deutsches Apothekenmuseum** (German Pharmaceutical Museum), a fascinating collection of ancient apothecary equipment complete

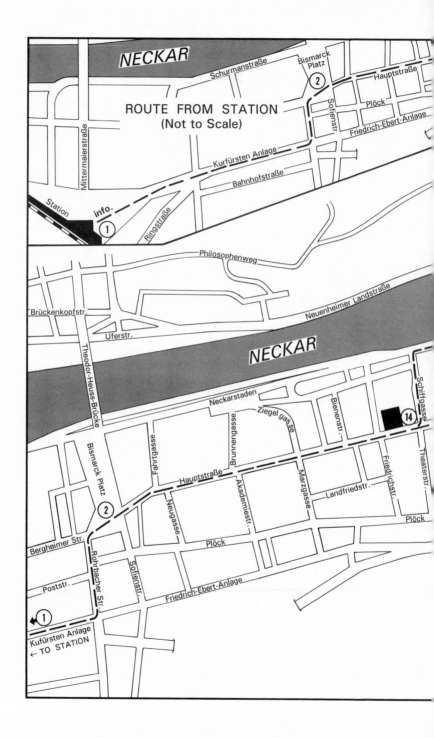

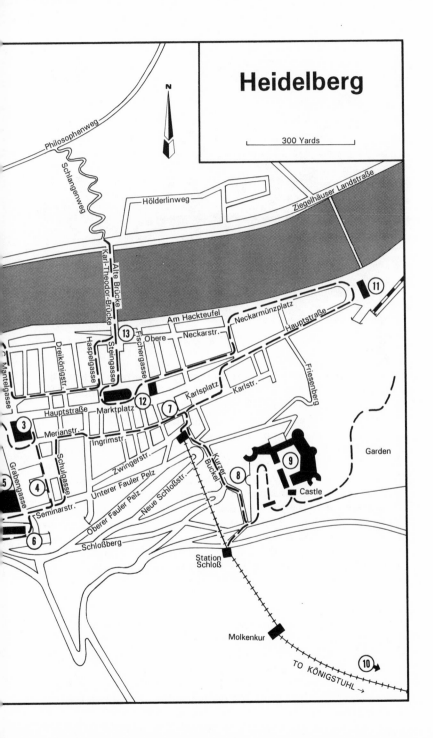

Heidelberg

300 Yards

Philosophenweg

Schlangenweg

Hölderlinweg

Ziegelhäuser Landstraße

Karl-Theodor-Brücke

Alte Brücke

11

Am Hackteufel

Neckarmünzplatz

Hauptstraße

Obere Neckarstr.

13

Fischergasse

Dreikönigstr.

Haspelgasse

Steingasse

Mantelgasse

Friesenberg

Karlsplatz

Karlstr.

12

Hauptstraße

Marktplatz

7

3

Merianstr.

Ingrimstr.

Kurzer Buckel

Garden

9

8

Castle

Schulgasse

Zwingerstr.

Grabengasse

4

Unterer Fauler Pelz

Neue Schloßstr.

5

Seminarstr.

Oberer Fauler Pelz

6

Schloßberg

Station
Schloß

Molkenkur

10

TO KÖNIGSTUHL →

The Courtyard of Heidelberg Castle

with an alchemist's laboratory. From mid-March through October it's open daily from 10 a.m. to 5 p.m., and from November through mid-March on Saturdays, Sundays, and holidays from 11 a.m. to 5 p.m. Outside again, a walk through the beautiful **gardens**, originally laid out around 1620, will complete your visit to the castle.

An interesting side trip can be made by returning to the funicular and riding it all the way up to the **Königstuhl** (10), changing cars at Molkenkur along the way. The panoramic view from here is spectacular, and is even better from the top of the TV tower *(Fernsehturm)*.

Return to town via the funicular or the Kurzer Buckel, a narrow stepped lane leading back to Kornmarkt (7). Now turn right and follow Karlstrasse to **Karlsplatz** . Opposite this, on Hauptstrasse, are two famous old student inns—the Roter Ochsen and Zum Sepp'l. Continue on to **Karlstor** (11), a neoclassic archway from 1775. Turn left and walk along the river, noting the locks that enable Rhine traffic to reach as far as Stuttgart, then make a left on Leyergasse and a right onto Heiliggeiststrasse.

Marktplatz (12), the main square, is the scene of a farmers' market held on Wednesday and Saturday mornings. It bustles with activity on other days as well, with several outdoor cafés in good weather. On its east end is the Baroque **Rathaus** (Town Hall), which features a daily *glockenspiel* recital at 7 p.m. Walking along the south side of the church, you will come to the **Haus zum Ritter**. Now a hotel, it was built in 1592 by a wealthy merchant and was the only mansion to survive the French invasion of 1693. It fantastically elaborate façade is well worth studying.

The **Heiliggeist Kirche** (Church of the Holy Ghost), dominating the square, also made it through the devastation. Erected during the early 15th century, it was both Protestant and Catholic from 1705 until 1936; the two faiths being separated by a wall between the nave and choir. The unusual merchants' stalls along the outside walls have been there since medieval days.

Stroll through Fischmarkt and follow Steingasse to the **Alte Brücke** (Old Bridge) (13), a.k.a. Karl-Theodor-Brücke. Four earlier bridges had occupied this same site since the Middle Ages, all succumbing to flood, ice, or fire. The present span was completed in 1788, blown up in 1945, and rebuilt in 1947. Walk across it for the classic **view of Heidelberg**. Those with both time and abundant energy may want to continue up the steep Schlangenweg path to the famed ***Philosophenweg**, from which many a great thinker has contemplated the ravishing sights around sunset. You might prefer to return here later.

Now follow the map through colorful old streets to the ***Kurpfälzisches Museum** (Palatinate Museum) (14), housed in an early-18th-century mansion, the Palais Morass. Among the best of the smaller German museums, its collections range from the jawbone cast of the original Heidelberg Man of a half-million years ago—the earliest evidence of man in Europe—through Roman finds and goes all the way up to Romantic and contemporary art. The real treasure, however, is the *Altarpiece of the Twelve Apostles*, carved by the renowned Tilman Riemenschneider in 1509. The museum is open on Tuesdays through Sundays, from 10 a.m. to 5 p.m., remaining open until 9 p.m. on Wednesdays. From here it is an easy walk back to Bismarck Platz (2), where you can board a streetcar, take a taxi, or hike back to the train station.

Worms

For over a thousand years, Worms played a pivotal role in German history—and has the monuments to prove it. Although the town had been settled since the Stone Age and was a major Roman garrison, its time of glory really began in the 5th century A.D. when, according to legend, the Burgundians made it their capital. Out of a cloudy past came the greatest of German epics, the *Nibelungenlied,* replete with such heroes and villains as Siegfried, Brunhild, Gunther, Hagen, and even Attila the Hun. Twisted almost beyond recognition in Richard Wagner's *Ring Cycle,* the original story takes place mostly in and around Worms, and is partly based on historic events.

The town flourished when Charlegmagne made it a major center of the Holy Roman Empire. Slowly losing prestige as succeeding emperors became weaker, it had its final moment on the world stage in 1521 when Martin Luther's incipient Reformation was solidified at the Diet of Worms. Events after that, especially the Thirty Years War and the French Revolution, reduced Worms to the status of a small market town. World War II brought vast destruction, but in the decades since then the town has prospered and grown. Happily, most of its ancient treasures survived intact and today make Worms a fascinating place to explore. This trip can be combined in the same day with one to Mainz.

GETTING THERE:

Trains depart Frankfurt at frequent intervals for Mainz, where you change for Worms. Refer to page 161 for more details. The total journey takes up to 90 minutes. Return service operates until mid-evening. Be sure to check the schedule as there are other possible routes.

By car, Worms is about 50 miles southwest of Frankfurt. Take the A-5 Autobahn, then switch to the A-67 and head south to the Lorsch exit. From there the B-47 road leads into Worms.

PRACTICALITIES:

A visit to Worms may be made at any time, but note that some of the museums are closed on Mondays and holidays. The local **Tourist Information Office**, Phone (06241) 853-560, is at Neumarkt 14, behind the cathedral. Worms has a **population** of about 82,000.

St. Peter's Cathedral

FOOD AND DRINK:

   Bacchus Restaurant (in the Dom Hotel at Obermarkt 10, just east of the Luther monument) Regional dishes and wines. Phone (06241) 69-13. X: Sat. lunch, Sun. $$$

   Kriemhilde (Hofgasse 2, just east of the cathedral) Dining at a small inn. Phone (06241) 62-78. X: Sat. $$

   Tivoli (Adenauer Ring 4, just west of St. Martin's Church) Italian cuisine. Phone (06241) 284-85. X: Tues., July. $$

SUGGESTED TOUR:

Leave the **main train station** (1) and follow Wilhelm-Leuschner Strasse to Lutherplatz. The massive **Luther Monument** (2), erected in 1868, is inscribed with the famous words *"Here I stand, I cannot do otherwise. God help me. Amen."* It commemorates Martin Luther's appearance before the Diet of Worms in 1521, which is regarded as the turning point of the Reformation. At his feet are other leaders who set out to reform the Church—Hus, Savonarola, Waldus, and Wycliffe.

Continue on to ***St. Peter's Cathedral** *(Dom)* (3), one of the glories of the High Romanesque style. Begun in the 11th century, it has an outstanding interior with fine sculptures and an 18th-century Baroque **high altar** by Balthazar Neumann.

While in the area, you may want to want to visit the small **Heylshof Museum** (4), located in a mansion on the site of the former Bishop's Palace. The collections include 15th- to 19th-century paintings and sculptures, porcelains, ceramics, and medieval stained glass. It is open daily from May through September, from 10 a.m. to 5 p.m.; and the rest of the year on Tuesdays through Saturdays from 2–4 p.m. and on Sundays from 10 a.m. to noon and 2–4 p.m.

Now stroll down the shady Lutherring to the **Judenfriedhof** (Jewish Cemetery) (5), in use since the 11th century and the oldest in Europe. A walk through this highly evocative spot with ancient tombstones recalls the time when Worms was a major center of Jewish culture.

The Willy-Brandt-Ring leads around a corner to the former 12th- to 13th-century St. Andrew's Monastery, which now houses the **Museum der Stadt Worms** (Municipal Museum) (6). Step inside to see magnificent displays encompassing the entire long history of Worms, from prehistoric days to the present. The room devoted to Luther is especially interesting. Visits may be made on Tuesdays through Sundays, from 10 a.m. to noon and 2–5 p.m.

Walk straight ahead past the **Church of St. Magnus**, begun in the 9th century and now the oldest Lutheran church in southwest Germany. The route reveals a splendid view of the cathedral, then continues on to the tourist office, the Siegfried Fountain, and the colorful **Marktplatz** (Market Place) (7). Next to this is the **Dreifaltigkeitskirche** (Church of the Holy Trinity), an 18th-century Baroque structure with an exceptionally nice interior.

Follow the map along a complicated route through Old Worms to the 11th-century **Raschi Tor** (8), a medieval gate in the old town walls. Close to this is the oldest **synagogue** (9) in Germany, originally built in 1034, with a 13th-century women's synagogue added next to it. The Jewish community once accounted for 30 percent of Worms' population. There is an interesting **Jewish Museum** just behind this; open daily except on Mondays, from 10 a.m. to noon and 2–5 p.m.

From here you could make a short side trip to the **Liebfrauenkirche** (Church of Our Lady) (10), a 15th-century church surrounded by vineyards. This is where the original *Liebfrauenmilch* wine comes from, not the pale imitation sold as Liebfraumilch—which can be any Rheinhessen wine at all.

Continue on to **St. Martin's Church** (11), dating from the 12th century and noted for its beautiful west portal. A walk through the pedestrians-only shopping district will finish the tour and return you to the train station.

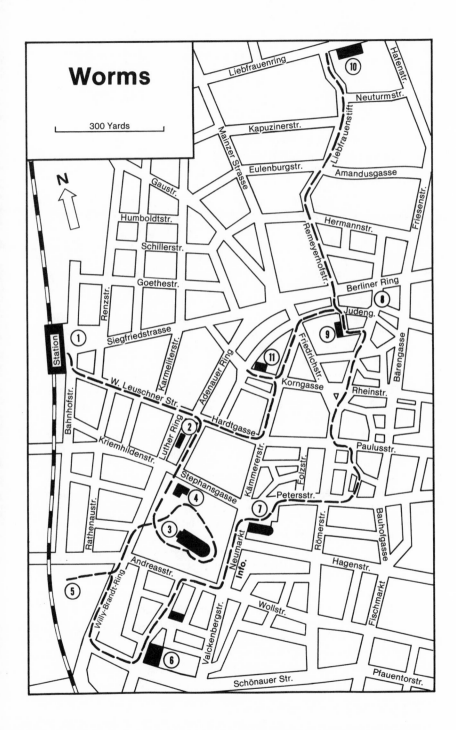

Baden-Baden

There are very few places in the world like Baden-Baden. By far the most elegant spa in Germany, it was known as the "summer capital of Europe" during the 19th century. Today it caters less to aristocrats than to wealthy businessmen and celebrities, but its gold-plated ambiance remains as glittering as ever. To go there is to experience an aspect of Germany that is quite at odds with the usual image of bustling cities, quaint old villages, and natural splendor.

The Romans, who loved to take baths, were here first and called the place *Aquae Aureliae*. Their emperor Caracalla came for the cure, and was followed by countless other crowned heads down through the centuries. What really put Baden-Baden on the map, though, was not the healing waters but the casino, opened in 1838. This attracted the international set, particularly those from nearby France. Since World War II Baden-Baden has regained its prestige, and is now on an equal footing with Monte Carlo.

GETTING THERE:

Trains depart Frankfurt's main station at least hourly for the under-two-hour ride to Baden-Baden. Most of these are of the EC, IC, or IR class. Return service operates until mid-evening.

By car, Baden-Baden is 112 miles south of Frankfurt via the A-5 Autobahn.

PRACTICALITIES:

You can visit Baden-Baden at any time, although it is much more pleasant in warm weather when the gardens are in bloom. A few minor sights may be closed on Mondays. The local **Tourist Information Office**, phone (07221) 275-200, is on Augusta Platz. **Bicycles** may be rented at the train station from April through October. Baden-Baden has a permanent **population** of about 53,000.

FOOD AND DRINK:

Although the town has many elegant and expensive restaurants, you can dine well for much less around Leopoldsplatz and into the Old Town. Some choices are:

> **Stahlbad** (Augusta Platz 2, in the northwest corner) Contemporary French and German cuisine served in an elegant mansion. Dress nicely and reserve. Phone (07221) 245-69. X: Sun., Mon. $$$

Along the Oos Stream

Schwarzwald Stube (in Brenner's Park Hotel, Schillerstr. 6, 3 blocks southwest of Augusta Platz) One of the great hotel restaurants of Europe. Phone (07221) 90-00. $$$

Münchner Löwenbräu (Gernsbacherstr. 9, just southeast of the Rathaus) Regional specialties at a Bavarian restaurant, outdoor beer garden. Phone (07221) 223-11. $$

Bratwurstglöckle (Steinstr. 7, a block southeast of the Stiftskirche) Hearty German fare in traditional surroundings. $

SUGGESTED TOUR:

The **train station** (1) is quite a distance from the town. Take a bus (routes 1 or 3) or taxi from the front of the station to **Augusta Platz** (2), where the tourist office is located. You could also rent a bicycle and pedal there.

Follow the map across the Oos stream to the **Kurhaus** (3), a white colonnaded building of 1821. Its splendid interior houses the **Casino**, ballrooms, a luxury restaurant, a bistro, and a buffet. Guided tours through the luxurious casino are held daily between 10 a.m. and noon. Gambling, which includes roulette, baccarat, and blackjack, begins at 2 p.m. and lasts until early morning. Proper dress—meaning jacket and tie for men—is required at that time. There is a small entrance fee but no obligation to gamble.

In front of the Kurhaus you will notice a bandstand where spa concerts are given in good weather—otherwise they are held indoors. You may want to check the posted schedules and perhaps come back for one of these. Now continue on to the **Trinkhalle** (Pump Room) (4), a marvelously elegant 19th-century building whose colonnade features frescoes of Black Forest legends. Step inside and sample the healing waters.

From here you can take a pleasant side trip up the Michaelsberg to the **Stourdza-Kapelle** (Romanian Chapel) (5), a lovely spot with nice views.

Now follow the map into the colorful old part of town. Stroll down the pedestrians-only Lange Strasse and turn left on Gernsbacher Strasse to the **Rathaus** (Town Hall) (6), then around to the market place. The **Stiftskirche** (Collegiate Church) (7), partly dating from the early 13th century, contains some exceptional works of art including a remarkable sandstone **crucifix** of 1467 and the highly ornate **tomb** of Margrave Ludwig Wilhelm, both of which are in the chancel.

Leave the church and climb the steps opposite to the 15th-century **Neues Schloss** (New Palace) (8), home of the excellent Zähringer Museum. Paintings, porcelains, china, and exquisite objects of art are well displayed in several magnificent room settings. Walk around to the **palace gardens** for a good panoramic view of Baden-Baden.

Return to town via Schloss Strasse and Marktplatz to the sumptuous **Friedrichsbad**, where many of the spa's best hydrotherapy facilities are located, and where you can sample them in as little as two hours for a reasonable price. Next to this, covered by a modern structure, are the **Römische Badruinen** (9), the ruins of the 2nd-century Roman baths. Go in for a fascinating stroll through the excavations, open daily from 10 a.m. to noon and 1:30–4 p.m.; then walk around Römerplatz past the strikingly contemporary **Caracalla-Therme**, another of the spa's water-cure establishments.

From here, the tree-lined Sophienstrasse brings you back to the Kurhaus area. Cross the Oos stream and turn left onto the world-famous ***Lichtentaler Allee**, a fashionable promenade lined with exotic trees. You will soon pass the small **Kunsthalle** (Art Museum) (10), which features changing exhibitions of 20th-century art. It is usually open on Tuesdays through Sundays, from 10 a.m. to 6 p.m.

The path continues on for quite a distance, but you will probably want to turn around and return along the stream before reaching its end at the Lichtental Abbey. In any case, be sure to go by the renowned **Brenner's Park Hotel** (11), almost universally regarded as one of Europe's poshest hostelries. An anachronism in this changing world, it still retains the quiet elegance of an age long vanished, and in its way is the very symbol of Baden-Baden. Now stroll back to the Augusta Platz and board a bus to the train station.

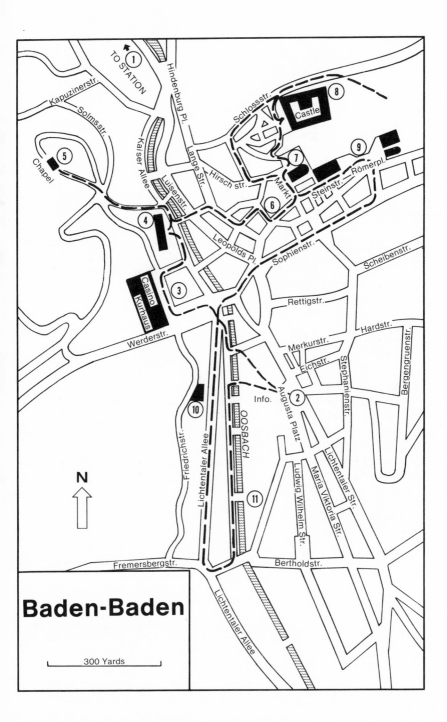

Baden-Baden

300 Yards

N

Triberg

The legendary Black Forest lies tucked away in a remote corner of Germany, often overlooked by foreign tourists. Simple geography keeps them away. One glance at the map shows you how difficult it is to include this enchanted region—known in German as the *Schwarzwald*—into any practical itinerary. But that doesn't rule out sampling at least a bit of its magic on a lengthy but delightful daytrip from Frankfurt.

Triberg is probably the best spot for a first-time visit to the Black Forest. It has just about everything—waterfalls, mountain trails, a *gemütlich* atmosphere, good restaurants, and a fabulous museum filled with cuckoo clocks. It is easy to reach by rail, and not too difficult to get to by car. You could make the journey more worthwhile by staying overnight in the region and also visiting Freiburg, described in the next few pages.

GETTING THERE:

Trains of the comfortable new IR class leave Frankfurt's main station at 2-hour intervals for the direct 3-hour ride to Triberg, offering spectacular scenery during the last half-hour. Return service operates until early evening. Other routings are possible by making a change at Offenburg. Railpass holders will get their money's worth on this trip!

By car, Triberg is 165 miles south of Frankfurt. Take the A-5 Autobahn to the Offenburg exit, then continue on the B-33 road.

PRACTICALITIES:

Triberg should be visited in the warm season, when all the trails around the waterfall are sure to be open. Good weather is important. The local **Tourist Information Office,** phone (07722) 95-32-30, is in the Kurhaus near the waterfalls entrance. Triberg has a **population** of about 6,000.

FOOD AND DRINK:

There are many places to eat and drink in this popular mountain resort. Some good choices are:

> **Parkhotel Wehrle** (on the Markt Platz) Elegant, with trout prepared 20 different ways, along with wild game and other dishes. Phone (07722) 860-20. $$$

In the Heimat Museum

Hotel Pfaff (Hauptstr. 85, near the waterfalls entrance) Known for its trout dishes. Outdoor tables available. Phone (07722) 44-79. X: Wed. in off-season, Nov. $$

Krone (Schulstr. 37, behind the Rathaus) A small inn with simple meals. Phone (07722) 45-24. $

Zur Lilie (at the waterfalls entrance) A rather rustic but enjoyable place with simple food. Phone (07722) 44-19. X: Fri. in winter. $

SUGGESTED TOUR:

The **Triberg Train Station** (1) is isolated in a forested valley. From there you can either take a DB bus (railpasses accepted), a taxi, or just walk slightly uphill for three-quarters of a mile to the **Markt Platz** (Market Place) (2). The Gutach stream, a few yards to the right of the main street, pokes its rushing waters between a clutter of inns, restaurants, and shops—none very elegant but all quite appealing. The **Rathaus** (Town Hall) (3) is worth a short visit to see the exceptionally rich wood carvings in its council chamber, a true reflection of the local folk art of which the town is so proud.

Continue uphill past a multitude of cuckoo-clock shops and enter the woods. In a few yards you will see an attractive café with a small watermill. Just beyond this is a **tollhouse** (4) where you pay a small fee to visit the **waterfalls.** From this point upwards, the Gutach stream tumbles down over seven cascades into a romantic glen for a drop of over 500 feet, making it the highest *Wasserfälle* in Germany.

Climb the path alongside the rushing torrent until you reach the top. Once there, descend a short distance to a bridge with a sign pointing the way to the Wallfahrtskirche. Cross it and pass another tollhouse. You are now on the **Panorama Weg,** a woodland trail with stunning views of the surrounding mountains and forests. Going past an onion-domed church, you will soon come to a **boating pond** (5), where an outdoor café invites you to stop for lunch or a drink.

Now follow the map to the **Wallfahrtskirche** (Church of Our Lady of the Pines) (6), which you saw from the path. Built in 1705, this small pilgrimage church has a marvelously Baroque interior. Its beautifully carved high altar is particularly outstanding.

Continue down the street to the ***Heimat Museum** (Local History Museum) (7), one of Germany's best. Here you can get a good impression of Black Forest life in the hard times before the region became a tourist center. Woodcarving, clock-making, and mining were the predominant industries, and all are well represented in the museum. Individual rooms re-create the workshops and homes of long ago, while a hundred-foot-long tunnel offers a small taste of what the mines must have been like. Another section traces the development of a more modern local industry, radio communications, over the years. The best exhibits, however, are the ***mechanical music machines**, ranging from huge orchestrions to tiny bird-call boxes. Many of these can be operated by inserting a coin, and are an absolute delight to watch and hear. The most famous products of the Black Forest—**cuckoo clocks**—are also displayed in great variety. Triberg is a good place to purchase one of these noisy contraptions, should you feel so inclined. The museum is open daily from May through September, 9 a.m. to 6 p.m.; and daily during the rest of the year, from 10 a.m. to noon and 2–5 p.m., but closed from mid-November to mid-December.

Crossing the Hauptstrasse, walk down Luisenstrasse to the **Kurhaus** (8), a modern structure housing a concert hall, a restaurant, and the tourist office. Here you can rest in a pleasant garden before returning to the train station.

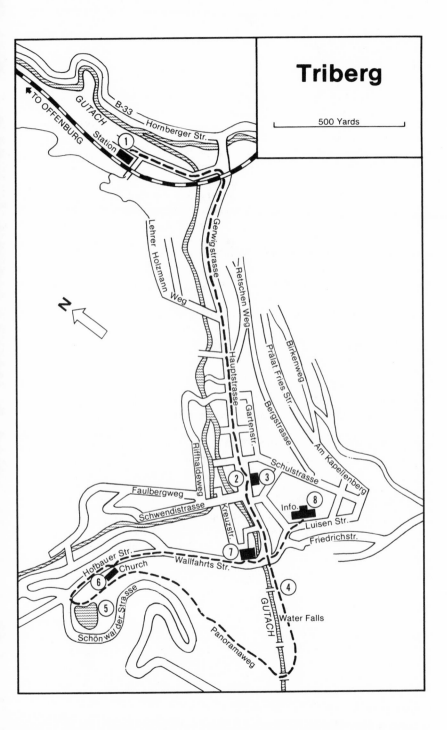

Triberg

500 Yards

TO OFFENBURG

GUTACH Station

B-33 Hornberger Str.

Lehrer Holzmann Weg

Gerwigstrasse

Retschen Weg

Prälat Fries Str.

Birkenweg

Hauptstrasse

Gartenstr.

Bergstrasse

Am Kapellenberg

Riffhaldeweg

Schulstrasse

Faulbergweg

Kreuzstr.

Info.

Schwendistrasse

Luisen Str.

Friedrichstr.

Hofbauer Str.

Wallfahrts Str.

Church

Schönwalder Strasse

Panoramaweg

GUTACH

Water Falls

N

1 2 3 4 5 6 7 8

Freiburg

One of Germany's most appealing cities remains unspoiled by mass tourism. Located in the extreme southwest corner of the country, Freiburg-im-Breisgau (its official name) lies far enough off the beaten path to discourage most travelers from even considering going there. Those who do go are in for a real discovery. This delightful place on the edge of the Black Forest is not only exceptionally attractive, but also has plenty of character—and eccentricities. Where else do forest streams run down the gutters of the streets? How many other towns have a mountain right in their very center? Freiburg's main attraction, however, lies in the sunny disposition of its people, who manage to be easygoing and cosmopolitan at the same time; a heritage, no doubt, from over four centuries of Austrian rule as well as strong ties to nearby France and Switzerland. The presence, since 1457, of a major university also adds a certain youthful vitality.

Although this is a one-day trip, you might prefer to stay overnight and combine it with nearby Triberg, described in the last chapter. There is both rail and road transportation between them.

GETTING THERE:

Trains of the ICE, IC, and EC classes depart Frankfurt's main station hourly for the 2¼-hour run to Freiburg. A change at Mannheim is sometimes necessary. Good return service operates until early evening, with other trains running all night long.

By car, Freiburg is 168 miles south of Frankfurt via the A-5 Autobahn. Use the Freiburg-Nord exit.

PRACTICALITIES:

Most of Freiburg's museums are closed on Mondays. The town claims to get more sunshine than any other city in Germany, so you'll probably enjoy good weather. The local **Tourist Information Office**, phone (0761) 368-9090, is at Rotteckring 14, opposite Colombi Park. Bicycles may be rented at the train station from April through October. Freiburg has a population of about 200,000.

FOOD AND DRINK:

Freiburg abounds in good restaurants, a few of which are:

> **Zum Roten Bären** (Oberlinden 12, near the Augustiner Museum) Traditional Black Forest specialties in one of Germany's oldest and most atmospheric inns. Phone (0761) 369-13. $$$

Münsterplatz and the Cathedral

Schlossberg Dattler (at the top of the cable car) A large, rustic place with a great view and outdoor terraces. Phone (0761) 317-29. X: Tues. $$

Bier und Speck (Münsterplatz 18, by the cathedral) Black Forest dishes, substantial and tasty. Phone (0761) 343-67. $$

Grosser Meyerhof (Grünwälderstr. 7, 2 blocks northeast of the Martinstor) A beer hall with good food. Phone (0761) 225-52. X: Mon., Tues. $

Salatstuben (Löwenstr. 1, near the Martinstor) A popular vegetarian cafeteria. Phone (0761) 351-55. X: Sun. $

A very cheap lunch can be had from one of the many vendors at the farmers' market in Münsterplatz, held daily except on Sundays.

SUGGESTED TOUR:

Leave the **main train station** *(Hauptbahnhof)* (1) and follow Eisenbahnstrasse to the tourist office at the corner of Rotteckring. Continue down the pedestrianized Rathausgasse to **Rathausplatz** (2), a very charming old square bordered on the west by both the new and old town halls. The statue in its center is of a Franciscan friar, Berthold Schwarz, who is supposed to have invented gunpowder here in 1353. Enter the picturesque courtyard of the **Neues Rathaus** (New Town Hall), which was created by linking together two 16th-century houses. A carillon plays folk tunes here each day at 12:03 p.m.

Turn right on Franziskanerstrasse and pass the 13th-century St. Martin's Church, noted for its beautiful Gothic cloisters. Opposite this is the famous **Haus zum Walfisch.** Originally built in 1516 as a home for Emperor Maximilian I, it later served as a refuge for the humanist, Erasmus of Rotterdam, and is now a bank. Note the magnificent oriel window above its doorway.

Continue on to the ***Cathedral** *(Münster)* (3), widely regarded as one of the great masterpieces of Gothic architecture. Its superb 380-foot-high **tower** is among the very few in Germany to have been completed during the Middle Ages. It may be climbed on Tuesdays through Saturdays from 10 a.m. to 5 p.m., and on Sundays from 1–5 p.m. Construction on the cathedral began around 1200 and took over 300 years to complete, resulting in a rather engaging mixture of styles. The interior has several excellent works of art, including an early 16th-century triptych of the *Coronation of the Virgin* by Hans Baldung on the ***high altar.** This and other treasures can be seen better by taking one of the guided tours from the south transept entrance. Another outstanding altarpiece, this by Hans Holbein the Younger, is in the University Chapel to the right. The **stained-glass windows** in the side aisles date mostly from the 13th century.

A lively ***farmers' market** is held in the adjacent area every day except Sundays and some holidays, from 7 a.m. to 1 p.m. **Outdoor cafés** line the square in good weather, making this a wonderful place to sit down and enjoy all the activity. Some of the buildings have survived the ages and are still in good condition, especially the blood-red, turreted 16th-century **Kaufhaus** (Merchants' Guild House) on the south side.

Now follow the map to the lower station of the **Schlossberg Seilbahn** (cable car) (4), which carries you to the top of Freiburg's downtown mountain. Purchase an "up" ticket *(Bergfahrt)* only, since you will be walking down. Stroll along the trail overlooking the city and descend to the medieval **Schwabentor** (Swabian Gate) (5), a part of the old fortifications. Take a look at the street leading into town—Oberlinden—which has the characteristic *Bächle*, or little streams running in the gutters that formed the medieval sewage system. Unwary pedestrians and drivers keep falling into these traps.

From the gate, the route goes through a colorful old district alongside a canal to the ***Augustiner Museum** (6). Housed in a former 13th-century monastery, its magnificent collections span over ten centuries of art. At least an hour will be needed to even sample the treasures on display, including some of the most illustrious names in painting. The museum is open on Tuesdays through Fridays, from 9:30 a.m. to 5 p.m.; and on Saturdays and Sundays from 10:30 a.m. to 5 p.m.

You may be interested in the nearby **Natur und Völkerkundemus**

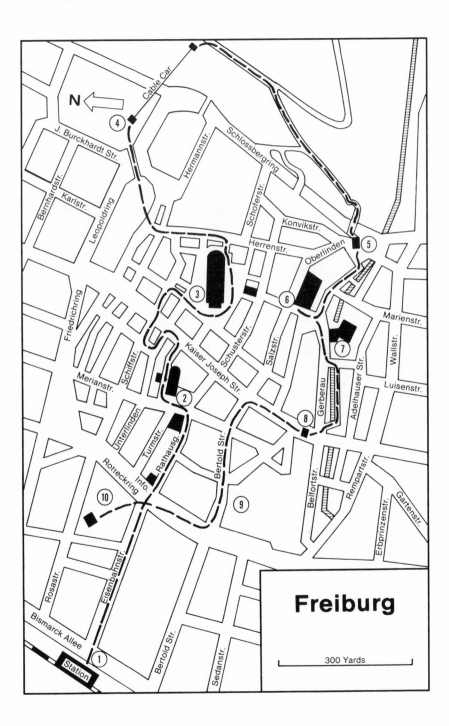

Freiburg

300 Yards

The Martinstor Town Gate

Museum (Natural History and Ethnology Museum) (7), also occupying an old monastery. Continue along the canal to the magnificently medieval **Martinstor** (8), the other surviving town gate.

Turn left on Bertoldstrasse and go by the main buildings of the **University** (9), which was founded as far back as 1457 and is now among the leading centers of higher education in Germany. Wander around them and follow Rotteckring to **Colombi Park** (10), a nice place to rest before returning to the train station.

Section IV

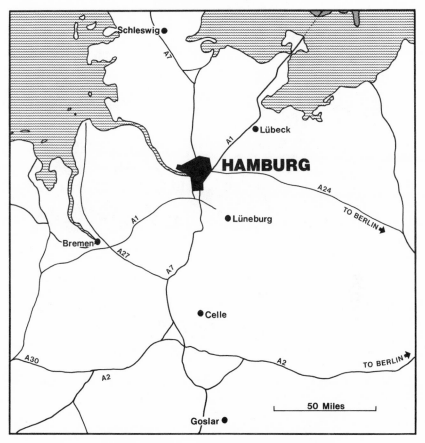

THE NORTH

Northern Germany is a world apart—and all too often overlooked. You won't find many castles here, or towering mountains. The landscape is mostly flat and sometimes even bleak. More akin to Scandinavia—or Holland—than to Bavaria, its true beauty lies in its people, and the intriguing civilization they have created over the centuries.

This is the land of the great merchant cities, a prosperous place that developed around trade rather than kings or the Church. Its inhabitants have always been fiercely independent; attuned more to the outside world than to the *Vaterland*.

Hamburg's Harbor

Hamburg is the natural center of the north. Superb accommodations, a cosmopolitan atmosphere, and excellent transportation make it the ideal base for probing this fascinating region. Before setting out on any adventures, however, you should really take a look at the great metropolis itself—the subject of the next chapter.

Most of the daytrips in this section can also be made from Hannover, which is centrally located and enjoys equally good transportation. Ambitious travelers may want to combine the trips to Lüneburg and Celle in the same day.

Hamburg

Proudly proclaiming itself as the Free and Hanseatic City of Hamburg, Germany's greatest port and second-largest metropolis—after Berlin—is a state in its own right. It possesses its own parliament and has never had much use for kings, emperors, or even archbishops. Merchants run the show here, as they have since the founding of the Hanseatic League in the 13th century. The goal of its citizens is to make money, a trait they were always quite adept at.

Hamburg is perhaps best known for its notorious St. Pauli district and the famous Reeperbahn, an area filled with fleshpots and raunchy bars. Yet this in only a very small part of a very large picture. It is also one of the Continent's most elegant cities, as well as a leader in culture and the arts. A visit to its bustling port facilities is always exciting. Virtually nothing of the city's ancient history has survived the great fire of 1842 and the wholesale devastation of the last war, but in its place a handsome new metropolis has risen—one whose many facets are at least partially explored on the suggested tour that follows:

GETTING THERE:

Trains from all over Germany and northern Europe arrive at Hamburg's three major stations: **Hauptbahnhof** (main station), **Dammtor**, and **Altona**. Most expresses stop at all three, but check the schedules to make sure. Built in 1906, the Hauptbahnhof has recently been modernized and is centrally located in an area of moderately-priced and inexpensive hotels. Dammtor Station, an Art Nouveau masterpiece of 1903, is close to some leading hotels and the convention center. Altona Station, in the western part of the city, opened in 1979 and is thoroughly modern. Frequent S-Bahn commuter trains connect all three.

By car, Hamburg lies at the hub of major Autobahns coming from all directions. To find the city center, just follow the "Stadtmitte" signs. Driving in town is not as difficult as in other German cities.

By air, flights from all over Europe and the world arrive at Hamburg's **Fuhlsbüttel Airport**, 6 miles north of the city center. A special airport bus runs between the terminals and the downtown main train station *(Hauptbahnhof)* at 20-minute intervals.

GETTING AROUND:

The route shown involves about five miles of walking, which can be reduced by using the excellent public transportation system *(HVV)* part of the way. This consists of **U-Bahn** subways, **S-Bahn** subways which continue on as commuter trains, **buses**, and **ferries**. A map and instructions are available at the tourist information office next to the main train station. The system operates very much the same as Frankfurt's (see page 153), and the same rules generally apply. One-day passes can be purchased at the tourist offices or from vending machines in the stations. Tourist offices also sell the economical **Hamburg Card**, which covers all public transportation, gives free admission to 11 museums, and discounts on various top attractions. It is available for either individuals or groups, for either one or three days.

PRACTICALITIES:

Hamburg is at its best from April through September, although even the winter season is much milder than you might expect. The museums are closed on Mondays. The local **Tourist Information Office**, phone (040) 30-05-12-45, is just outside the northeast corner of the main train station; with branches in the station, at the airport, and at the St. Pauli docks. **Bicycles** may be rented at the main tourist office from May through September. Hamburg has a **population** of about 1,700,000.

FOOD AND DRINK:

Great restaurants abound in this internationally minded city, some of them very expensive. Among the best choices in all prices ranges near the walking route are:

Schümann's Austernkeller (Jungfernstieg 34, near the inner lake) A traditional Old World restaurant famed for its seafood for over a century. Proper dress expected, for reservations phone (040) 34-53-28. X: Sun., holidays. $$$

Zum Alten Rathaus (Börsenbrücke 10, 2 blocks south of the Rathaus) A famous seafaring place in a vaulted cellar. Reservations advised, phone (040) 36-75-70. X: Sat. lunch, Sun., holidays. $$$

Deichgraf (Deichstr. 23, 3 blocks southwest of the Nikolaikirche) An elegant place for North German specialties, overlooking the ancient harbor. Reservations advised, phone (040) 36-42-08. X: Sat. lunch, Sun. $$$

Mövenpick (Grosse Bleichen 36, 2 blocks southwest of the Jungfernstieg) Always ultra reliable, this local outlet of the Swiss chain has several dining rooms with varying menus. Phone (040) 341-0032. X: Sun. $$ and $$$

Ratsweinkeller (in the Rathaus) A wide choice of dishes served amid antique ship models in the vaulted cellars of the City Hall. Phone (040) 36-41-53. X: Sun., holidays. $$

Nikolaikeller (Cremon 36, by the Hohe Brücke) *The* place for herring, served in an old-fashioned tavern. Phone (040) 36-61-13. X: Sun. lunch. $$

Old Commercial Room (Englische Plank 10, by St. Michael's Church) Traditional Hamburg cooking, specializing in *Labskaus*. Phone (040) 36-63-19. $$

Sagres (Vorsetzen 46, 4 blocks east of St. Pauli docks) A favorite with local dockworkers; Portuguese and Spanish specialties. Phone 37-12-01. $

Fischerhaus (Fischmarkt 14, 5 blocks west of St. Pauli docks) A simple place long popular for its local seafood dishes. Phone (040) 31-40-53. $

SUGGESTED TOUR:

Begin your walk at the **Jungfernstieg** (1), easily reached on foot or by U- or S-Bahn subway. This elegant boulevard is bordered on the north by the **Binnenalster**, a large boat basin created centuries ago by damning up the Alster River. Delightful cruises through a complex network of waterways are available here, but this treat is better saved for the end of the day.

Stroll through the lovely Alsterarkaden to the **Rathaus** (City Hall) (2). Built in the Renaissance style during the 1890s atop some 4,000 oak piles, its 367-foot-high tower dominates the adjacent market place. Guided tours through the richly, if heavily, decorated interior are conducted frequently on Mondays through Thursdays, from 10 a.m. to 3 p.m.; and on Fridays through Sundays from 10 a.m. to 1 p.m. While these don't visit all 647 rooms, they do take a full hour.

Now follow the map past the **Börse** (Stock Exchange) and along several ancient canals, including Hamburg's first harbor, the 700-year-old Nikolai Fleet. The ruined **Nikolaikirche** (Church of St. Nicholas) (3), originally dating from 1195 and rebuilt several times, was destroyed during World War II and is now preserved as a monument. Its steeple, at 482 feet, is the third-highest in Germany.

Cross the pedestrian bridge spanning busy Ost-West Strasse and wander down **Deichstrasse**, an intriguing street lined with old merchants' homes—many of which are now occupied by restaurants specializing in traditional Hamburg dishes. A stroll over Hohe Brücke and around **Cremon** (4) will take you past old warehouses and a former crane on the edge of the harbor. The massive 19th-century **Speicherstadt** warehouses across the canal to the south are in a customs-controlled duty-free zone, but the guards won't mind if you wander

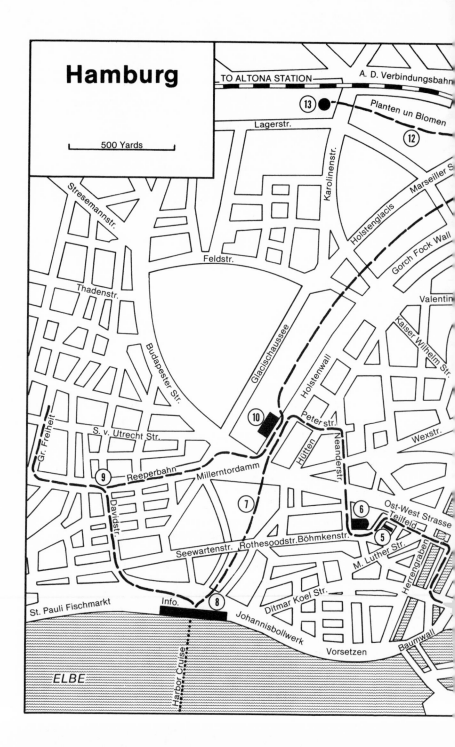

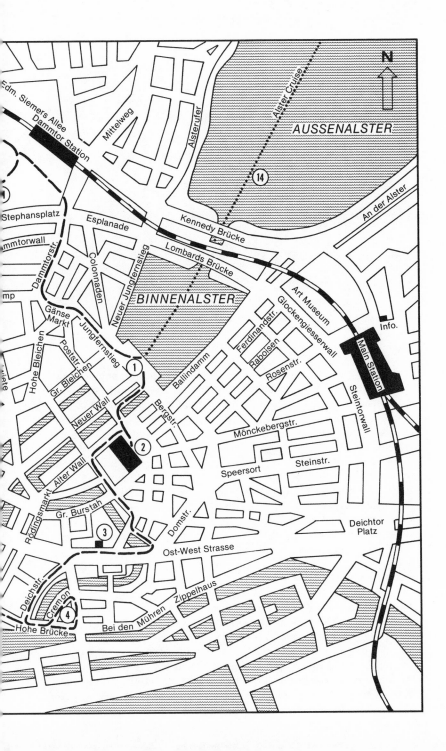

In the Krameramtswohnungen

around on foot there as long as you don't try to smuggle anything out.

Continue along the route to number 10 Krayenkamp and enter its courtyard. The 17th-century ***Krameramtswohnungen** (Mercers' Guild Houses) (5) were built to house the widows of guild members, and have been converted into restaurants, art galleries, boutiques, and the like. This is a delightful place to stop for refreshments. House "C" was restored to its original condition by the History Museum and may be visited on Tuesdays through Sundays, from 10 a.m. to 5 p.m.

From here it is only a few steps to the landmark ***Michaeliskirche** (St. Michael's Church) (6), a marvelously Baroque structure from the 18th century. Its spacious white-and-gold interior has a highly unusual layout with an amazing **pulpit**. Popularly known as "Michel," its **spire** is 434 feet high and is decorated with the largest tower clock in Germany. You can ride an elevator (or climb steps) to the **viewing platform**, which offers the best panoramic view of Hamburg and its vast harbor. From here a trumpet is played every day at 10 a.m. and 9 p.m., with a whole wind ensemble on festival days.

Now follow Neanderstrasse and Peterstrasse past some beautifully restored old houses. A left on Holstenwall brings you into a park on the site of the former town walls. Stroll by the **Bismarck Monument** (7) and continue down steps to the **St.-Pauli Landungsbrücken** (8), the main passenger terminal for the docks. From here you can take a ***harbor cruise** *(Hafenrundfahrt)* offered by the HADAG company and

In the Michaeliskirche

other firms, easily one of the highlights of any visit to Hamburg. These take about one hour and give you an excellent closeup view of the port's extensive facilities. Don't miss this treat! While at the harbor you might want to visit the 19th-century East Indies windjammer *Rickmer Rickmers*, now restored as a museum ship and docked at Pier 1.

If your ancestors emigrated from northern Europe between 1850 and 1914, you may also be interested in stopping at the **Historic Emigration Office** located at the passenger terminal, between piers 4 and 5. Records are kept here on all persons who passed through Hamburg en route to America. These can be traced for a fee if you already know your ancestor's name and year of emigration. The office is open on Mondays through Saturdays, from 9 a.m. to 6 p.m., with shorter hours in winter.

From here the route enters the notorious **St. Pauli district**, where prostitution is open and legal. Although it looks rough, you are perfectly safe as long as you stick to the main streets. Stroll up Davidstrasse, perhaps getting in the mood by visiting the new **Erotic Art Museum** at the intersecting Bernhard-Nocht-Strasse, number 69. Over 500 works by famous artists from the 16th century to the present are beautifully displayed, and there's an appropriate gift shop. The museum is open daily, from 10 a.m. to midnight.

Continuing on Davidstrasse, you'll soon come to a barrier on the left that seals off the end of Herbertstrasse. A police notice forbids entry to this side street to women and children. If you're male and over 18 you can go in for a peek, but don't try to take pictures.

Turn left onto the world-famous **Reeperbahn** (9), a wide street lined with sleazy bars and porno shops. The tamer night spots, which are still pretty raw, are on the Grosse Freiheit—the street of "great freedom." Return on the Reeperbahn to Millerntor Platz. Along the way you will pass the **Panoptikum**, an interesting wax-works museum.

Continue on to the ***Museum für Hamburgische Geschichte** (Museum of Hamburg History) (10). The fine exhibits here are concerned with shipping through the ages, development of the port, and reproductions of Old Hamburg. There is even an exciting **model railway layout** where scale models of historic trains run on a re-creation of the original Hamburg-to-Harburg line. Visits may be made on Tuesdays through Sundays, from 10 a.m. to 6 p.m.

The route now leads through a lovely park to the **Old Botanical Gardens** (11), where you can wander through tropical plants in a large climate-controlled structure. A little farther on is the delightful **Planten un Blomen Park** (12), whose strange-sounding name is in the old Hamburg dialect. The **Fernsehturm** (Television Tower) (13) offers splendid views from its observation deck, reached by elevator. There is also a revolving restaurant and a self-service cafeteria.

Now return to Jungfernstieg (1), either on foot or by subway from Stephansplatz. Several ***boat cruises** are available from the landing alongside the Alster Pavilion. Of these, the least expensive and longest, but perhaps the most interesting, ride is to take one of the regular commuter ferries that make stops along the Binnenalster and **Aussenalster** (14) and then continue up the creeks to the north. Just ride all the way to the end, and come back on the same boat. Try to get an outdoor seat for the best views. This is the perfect end to a busy day of exploring.

NEARBY SIGHTS:

Hamburg has several other attractions, which are best saved for another day. Among them are the **Kunsthalle** (Art Gallery) and the **Museum für Kunst und Gewerbe** (Arts and Crafts Museum) at either end of the main train station. **Hagenbecks Tierpark** (Zoo), reached via the U-2 subway, is world-renowned. If you happen to be in town on a Sunday morning, you may want to visit the ***Altona Fish Market** around 8 a.m. (or earlier) for some excitement. Even if you don't especially want to buy a fish, there are all kinds of other things for sale. The show is over by 10 a.m., and it can be reached by U- or S-Bahn to Landungsbrücken.

*Bremen

Standing defiantly in Bremen's market place is a tall statue of the valiant knight Roland. With sword drawn, he stares at the medieval cathedral opposite, as he has done since 1404. His bearing summarizes the attitude of most *Bremers*. These are a people who do not like to be told what to do—not by the Church, not by the government, not by anyone. Still calling itself the Free Hanseatic City of Bremen, this ancient seaport has its own parliament and is, in fact, Germany's smallest self-governing state.

Bremen's history goes back at least 1,200 years. In 787, during the reign of Charlemagne, it was made the seat of a bishop. Already a major shipping center, the growing town joined the Hanseatic League in 1358. Along with Hamburg and Lübeck, it virtually controlled northern trade and grew very rich as a result. Further independence came in 1646 when Bremen became a Free Imperial City, and later a sovereign city-state—a status it held well into this century.

Despite its size, Bremen is an eminently walkable city. Just about everything of interest lies in the compact area between the train station and the river, while the fascinating docks can be seen at closeup range on a boat tour.

GETTING THERE:

Trains, mostly of the IC class, depart Hamburg's main station at least hourly for the one-hour run to Bremen. Most of these may also be boarded a few minutes earlier at Hamburg's Altona or Dammtor stations. Return service operates until late evening.

By car, Bremen is 74 miles southwest of Hamburg via the A-7 and A-1 Autobahns. There are several parking lots behind the train station.

PRACTICALITIES:

The best time to visit Bremen is from late March through October, when the harbor tour operates. Most of the museums are closed on Mondays. The local **Tourist Information Office**, phone (0421) 30-80-00, is in front of the train station. Bremen has a **population** of about 550,000.

FOOD AND DRINK:

In a city famous for its good food, some choice restaurants are:

Das Flett (Böttcherstr. 3, across from the Roselius House) Classic German dishes in an inviting setting. Phone (0421) 32-09-95. X: Sun. $$$

Ratskeller (in the Rathaus) Over 600 German wines (but no beers!) are available in this centuries-old bastion of traditional North German cuisine. Phone (0421) 32-16-76. $$ and $$$

Friesenhof (Hinter dem Schütting 12, a block southeast of the Roselius House) A brewery restaurant with hearty meat dishes. Phone (0421) 32-16-61. $$

Alte Gilde (Ansgaritorstr. 24, by the Gewerbehaus) Good-value lunches in the vaulted cellar of an historic house. Phone (0421) 17-17-12. X: Sun. $ and $$

Kleiner Ratskeller (Hinter dem Schütting 11, a block southeast of the Roselius House) Traditional German food in a cozy setting. Phone (0421) 32-61-68. $

SUGGESTED TOUR:

Leave the **main train station** (1) and walk across the square to the tourist office, where you can confirm schedules for the town hall and harbor tours. Continue straight ahead and cross the old city moat. Until the early 19th century, Bremen was surrounded on three sides by defensive bastions—since replaced by lovely gardens and waterways.

Stroll down Sögestrasse, a pedestrians-only shopping street, past a charming group of bronze pigs that children love to play on. At the end bear left to the 13th-century **Liebfrauenkirche** (Church of Our Lady) (2). A delightful flower market is held each morning along its outer walls.

Just a few more steps and you are in one of Europe's most beautiful squares, the ***Marktplatz**. To the left stands the elegant ***Rathaus** (Town Hall) (3), dramatically proclaiming the wealth of Old Bremen. Originally built in 1409, it was given a magnificent new façade in the Weser Renaissance style during the early 17th century. On its west side, near the church, you will find a statue of the **Bremen Town Musicians**—a donkey, dog, cat, and cock who figured in the famous fairytale by the Brothers Grimm.

Enter the Town Hall and take the 45-minute **guided tour** of its Upper Hall, the richest interior in this affluent city. The splendid spiral staircase of 1620, Renaissance decorations, and wonderful models of early sailing ships are its main attractions. Tours are held on Mondays through Fridays at 10 a.m., 11 a.m., and noon; and on weekends at 11

The Rathaus and St. Petri Dom

a.m. and noon; except during civic functions. From November through April there are tours on weekends only, at 11 a.m. and noon.

A huge **statue** of the knight Roland, symbol of Bremen's independence, stands proudly in the market square. Since 1404 he has guarded its citizens against encroachment by the Church or anyone else who would attempt to rule them. Roland was obviously successful at this task, for his face wears a smile of self-satisfaction.

St.-Petri Dom (St. Peter's Cathedral) (4) towers over the square. Begun in 1042, it occupies the site of an earlier church built in 787 at the request of Charlemagne. Be sure to see its oldest parts, the **crypts**, and especially the **Bleikeller** (Lead Cellar), which contains nine curiously preserved corpses dating from the 16th to the 18th centuries. This is open from May through October. There is also a small **museum** of artifacts and a **tower** that may be climbed. The cathedral is closed on Saturday afternoons and Sunday mornings.

The ugly modern structure next to the cathedral is Bremen's own parliament. To the right of it is the **Schütting**, a 16th-century merchants' guildhall in the Flemish style.

Now stroll over to the famous ***Böttcherstrasse**, a crowded narrow passage teeming with visual excitement. Once a tradesmen's alleyway, it was transformed during the 1920s into an idealistic art cen-

On the Harbor Cruise

ter by the wealthy coffee merchant Ludwig Roselius, who had invented decaffeinated coffee in 1907. A porcelain **carillon** in the tiny square to your left plays tunes at noon, 3, and 6 p.m. Adjoining this, at number 6, is the **Roselius House** (5), a 16th-century mansion filled with masterpieces of North German art and period furniture. It connects internally with the adjacent **Paula Becker-Modersohn House**, a museum dedicated to the early Expressionist painter who worked in the Bremen area. Both are open on Tuesdays through Sundays, from 11 a.m. to 5 p.m.

Continuing along Böttcherstrasse, you will pass other buildings of the development, some of which house shops, restaurants, cafés, and even a gambling **casino**. The overall style is a strange blend of Gothic and *Jugendstil* (German Art Nouveau), an overpowering combination rarely encountered.

Stroll down to the **Martini Dock** (6), where you can take a fascinating 75-minute ***cruise** *(Hafenrundfahrt)* of Germany's second-largest harbor. Boats operate from late March through October, departing daily at 11:30 a.m., 1:30 p.m., and 3:15 p.m. From April through September there are also departures at 10 a.m. and 4:45 p.m.

When you return, take a look at the unusual 13th-century **Martinikirche** (St. Martin's Church), just a few steps to the northwest. It is noted for its organ of 1619, its modern stained-glass windows, and its tower carillon. Then follow the map to the ***Schnoor District** (7), which was home to Bremen's fishermen since the late Middle Ages. Little changed over the past three centuries, it has been restored and is now inhabited by craftsmen and artists. Wander down its main al-

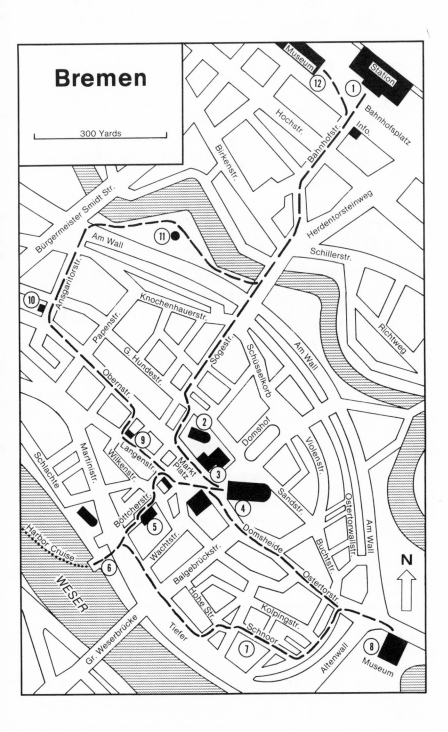

In the Schnoor

leyway, **Im Schnoor**, and explore the labyrinth of narrow passageways and tiny squares that cut off to the sides. The area is filled, as you might expect, with cafés, restaurants, galleries, and boutiques.

While in the area, you might want to visit the **Kunsthalle** (Art Museum) (8). Its collections are particularly rich in Old Masters, French Impressionists, and works by modern German painters. Visits may be made on Tuesdays from 10 a.m. to 9 p.m.; and on Wednesdays through Sundays from 10 a.m. to 5 p.m.

Now return to the Marktplatz and head down Langenstrasse. Note the magnificent **Stadtwaage** (9), a weights-and-measures office erected in 1587. A right on Grosse Waagestrasse leads to Obernstrasse, a pedestrians-only shopping street. Turn left and then make a right on Ansgaritorstrasse, passing the 17th-century **Gewerbehaus** (10), once a retail merchants' guildhall. Beyond the busy thoroughfare, Am Wall, lie the peaceful gardens that replaced the former fortifications. Stroll along the pathway to the last **windmill** (11) in the Old Town.

From here it is only a short walk to the **Überseemuseum** (Overseas Museum) (12), featuring interesting displays of exotic cultures and world trade. It is open on Tuesdays through Sundays, from 10 a.m. to 6 p.m. The train station is right next to this.

Schleswig

Schleswig is haunted by memories of the Vikings, who founded their great trading post here over a thousand years ago. Even today, the town seems more Danish than German. Relatively few foreign tourists find their way to this ancient settlement, but those who do are in for a delightful experience.

Located at the end of a long arm of the Baltic, Schleswig was the link that enabled trade to cross the Jutland peninsula from the North Sea, thus avoiding dangerous waters to the north. Then known as *Sliesthorp* or *Haithabu,* the town was first mentioned in 804. Two centuries later it moved to the opposite bank of the Schlei and prospered throughout the Middle Ages. A cathedral and a castle got built, both of which dominate Schleswig today. The town's greatest attraction, though, lies in its charming provincial character—and in the opportunity to sample a small taste of Scandinavia while remaining in Germany.

GETTING THERE:

Trains depart Hamburg's **Altona Station** several times in the morning for the 90-minute trip to Schleswig. There is an S-Bahn connection to Hamburg's main station. Check the schedule carefully as a change at Neumünster may be needed. Return service operates until early evening.

By car, Schleswig is 77 miles north of Hamburg on the A-7 Autobahn. Get off at the Schleswig-Jagel exit and continue into town, parking near the cathedral. You will probably prefer to drive to Gottorf Castle and the Viking Museum.

PRACTICALITIES:

The summer season is the best time to visit Schleswig. Avoid coming on a Monday or major holiday, when the castle is partially or fully closed. You'll have a better time if the sun shines. The local **Tourist Information Office**, phone (04621) 248-78, is at Plessenstrasse 7, just west of the cathedral. Ask them about getting to the Viking Museum at Haithabu. **Bicycles** may be rented at the train station from April through October. Schleswig has a **population** of about 28,000.

FOOD AND DRINK:

Some choice restaurants are:

Senator-Krog (Rathausmarkt 9, near the Rathaus) Local specialties in an atmospheric setting, outdoor service in summer.
Phone (04621) 222-90. $$

Schleimöwe (Süderholmstr. 8, in Holm, near the cemetery) Re-
gional seafood specialties in a quaint setting. Phone (04621)
243-09. $$

Waldhotel (Stampfmühle 1, a half-mile northwest of the castle)
A secluded place for pleasant meals. Phone (04621) 232-88. X:
Thurs. in winter. $$

Patio (Lollfuss 3, between old town and castle) An attractive
place for light lunches. Phone (04621) 299-99. $

SUGGESTED TOUR:

Schleswig's **train station** (1) is located a little over a mile and a half
from the old part of town *(Altstadt)*. You can get there by bus, taxi, or
rented bicycle, although the walking route on the map is very pleas-
ant. In any case, begin at the tourist office, just a block from the ca-
thedral.

*St. Peter's Cathedral *(Dom)* (2) is an unusually attractive brick
Gothic structure. Begun around 1100, it was not completed until the
15th century and only acquired its present tower in the late 19th. Enter
by the south portal, which is capped by a marvelous stone tympanum
from 1170. In the chancel you will see the renowned ***Bordesholm
Altar**, carved from oak during the early 16th century by Hans Brügge-
man. A masterpiece of the woodcarvers' art, it contains some 392 fig-
ures. Other treasures include the noted *Blue Madonna* painting on a
pillar on the north side of the nave and fine medieval cloisters decor-
ated with 13th-century frescoes.

Now follow the map along the harbor to the picturesque fish-
ermen's district of **Holm** (3). Its lanes, very reminiscent of Scandinavia,
are lined with tiny cottages and converge at a small cemetery. Stroll
down a passageway called Fuss-am-Holm to the water's edge, then
take a look at the **Johanniskloster** (St. John's Convent) (4), which was
founded in the 12th century. You can arrange a visit there by first
phoning them at (04621) 242-36.

Return to town via Norderholmstrasse and Fischbrückstrasse. The
Rathausmarkt (5) is a lovely open square bordered by the 18th-cen-
tury **Rathaus** (Town Hall), itself incorporating a well-restored 13th-
century monastery. You're welcome to stop in and explore the
ground floor, which is interesting for the way in which the ancient
monastic cells are put to modern use. Continue up Lange Strasse and

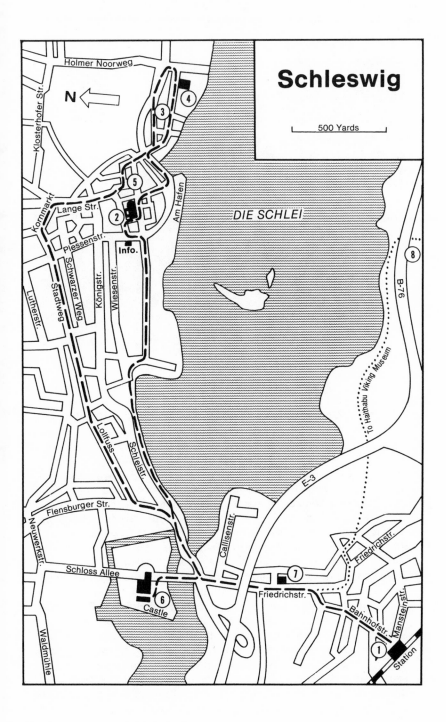

The Bordesholm Altar

turn left into Kornmarkt. From here the pedestrians-only Stadtweg and Lollfuss lead to the castle.

*Schloss Gottorf (Castle) (6) was first built around 1150, although virtually all of the present structure dates from the 16th and 17th centuries. For over 400 years it was home to the dukes of Schleswig-Holstein-Gottorf, a dynasty that gave Russia its czars in the 18th century. Today it houses the two major museums of Schleswig-Holstein, which are worth the trip in themselves. One admission covers both.

The **Archaeological Museum** contains one of the most fantastic archaeological finds in Germany, the 4th-century ***Nydam Boat**, on display in a separate building next to the castle. Discovered in 1863, this remarkably well-preserved craft required 36 rowers to man its oars, and is of the type used by the Angles and Saxons on their conquest of Britain. Other exhibits, some here and others in the castle, include prehistoric corpses, runic stones, and Viking artifacts.

Also in the castle is the splendid ***Schleswig-Holstein State Museum**, which has rich collections of local art and culture from the Middle Ages to the present. Among the most outstanding rooms are the Gothic **Royal Hall** and the Renaissance **chapel**. Allow at least an hour to sample some of its treasures. If you have more time, there are usually some interesting changing exhibitions in the outer buildings. Both museums are open daily from March through October, from 9

In the Fishermen's District of Holm

a.m. to 5 p.m., though only partially open on Mondays. From November through February they are open on Tuesdays through Sundays, from 9:30 a.m. to 4 p.m.

You can return to the train station by bus from the corner of Gottorfstrasse. Those walking the half-mile distance may want to stop at the **Stadtmuseum** (Municipal Museum) (7), located in a 17th-century mansion on Friedrichstrasse. Its displays are concerned with local history and may be seen on Tuesdays through Sundays, from 10 a.m. to 5 p.m.

From here it is only a short walk to the station, or you could continue on to the **Haithabu Viking Museum** (8) at the nearby "Haddeby Noor" archaeological digs, where exciting discoveries have been made in recent years. A Viking ship is presently being reconstructed as visitors watch. The museum is open from April through October, daily from 9 a.m. to 6 p.m.; and the rest of the year on Tuesdays through Fridays from 9 a.m. to 5 p.m. and weekends from 10 a.m. to 6 p.m. During the summer it can also be reached by boat from the town pier just south of the cathedral, or you could rent a bike and pedal there.

Lübeck

Free and Imperial Lübeck, Queen of the Hansa; in the Middle Ages the capital of the Hanseatic League and one of the most powerful mercantile cities on Earth. What a place it must have been at the height of its glory! Fortunately for the traveler, its gradual decline and location well off the mainstream of German life have combined to preserve much of the city's medieval flavor. Here you can still walk back in time to another age when its merchants brought untold prosperity to the mighty little republic that rose from the ruins of the Holy Roman Empire.

Lübeck was founded in 1143 as a trading post on an easily defended island in the Trave and grew in importance, becoming a Free Imperial City in 1226. Gradually, however, expanding trade with the New World favored ports on the North Sea. This, along with the collapse of the Hanseatic League in the 17th century, weakened Lübeck's position. It slowly became a backwater port, no longer rich enough to rebuild, and had to be content with remaining in the fabric of its medieval past. The final blow came in 1937, when the proud old city lost its last claim to independence. Since the end of World War II it has shared in Germany's rebirth, and once again stands to prosper under reunification with the nearby East.

GETTING THERE:

Trains depart Hamburg's **main station** at least hourly for the 40-minute run to Lübeck. Return service operates until late evening.

By car, Lübeck is 41 miles northeast of Hamburg via the A-1 Autobahn.

PRACTICALITIES:

Lübeck is a city for all seasons, but note that some of its museums are closed on Mondays. The local **Tourist Information Office**, phone (0451) 122-81-06, is on the market place by the Rathaus, with a branch in the train station. Lübeck has a **population** of about 217,000.

FOOD AND DRINK:

The city is well endowed with restaurants evoking an Old World atmosphere. Among the best known are:

> **Zimmermann's Lübecker Hanse** (Am Kolk 3, just northwest of the Petrikirche) Regional and French cuisine in an old-time favorite restaurant. Reservations advised, phone (0451) 780-54. X: Sat., Sun. $$$

The Holstentor

Das Schabbelhaus (Mengstr. 48, 2 blocks west of the Marien-kirche) Traditional Hanseatic meals in an elegant old mansion. World famous, so reserve by phoning (0451) 720-11. X: Sun. $$$

Schiffergesellschaft (Breitestr. 2, in the Mariners' Guild House) An historic and highly atmospheric restaurant in the heavy Hanseatic tradition. Phone (0451) 767-76. X: Mon. $$ and $$$

Stadtrestaurant (in the train station) Continental cuisine in a traditional old *Bahnhof* restaurant. Phone (0451) 840-44. $$

Ratskeller (in the Rathaus) Many choices in different price categories, including inexpensive vegetarian dishes. Phone (0451) 720-44. $ and $$

Schweinske (Untertrave 90, 4 blocks west of the Marienkirche) Good-value pork dishes. Phone (0451) 15-16-77. $

SUGGESTED TOUR:

Leave the **main train station** (1) and follow the map to the ***Holsten-tor** (2), a gigantic fortified gate built in 1477. This symbol of Lübeck's former power now houses an intriguing **museum** of the city's history. Be sure to see the large model of the town as it appeared in 1650, as well as the grim **torture chamber** in the basement. It is open on Tuesdays through Sundays, from 10 a.m. to 5 p.m.; closing at 4 p.m. in winter. To the right of the gate, along the water, stands a colorful

The Rathaus

row of salt warehouses from the 16th and 17th centuries. Salt from Lüneburg was once stored there before being exported to Scandinavia.

Cross the bridge and continue on to the **Petrikirche** (St. Peter's Church) (3). Built between the 13th and 15th centuries, it was badly damaged during World War II and is being rebuilt. Its **tower**, however, has been restored and may be ascended by elevator for a marvelous view.

A left off Kohlmarkt leads to the **Marktplatz** (Market Place) (4), bordered by the splendid old **Rathaus** (Town Hall). This highly ornate structure with its needle-like spires and arcaded promenade was begun in 1250 and modified in the centuries since. The strange round holes in its 15th-century façade are there to reduce wind resistance. Guided tours of the interior are offered on Mondays through Fridays at 11 a.m., noon, and 3 p.m. The tourist office is on the north side of the square.

The ***Marienkirche** (St. Mary's Church) (5), just a few steps away, is the finest in Lübeck and a triumph of the Brick Gothic style. Serving as a prototype for many other churches in the Baltic region, it was erected during the 13th and 14th centuries. Its **Briefkapelle** chapel, with star vaultings supported by only two slender columns, is particularly lovely. The composer Buxtehude was organist here; both Bach and Handel came to hear him play. During the war, the church was

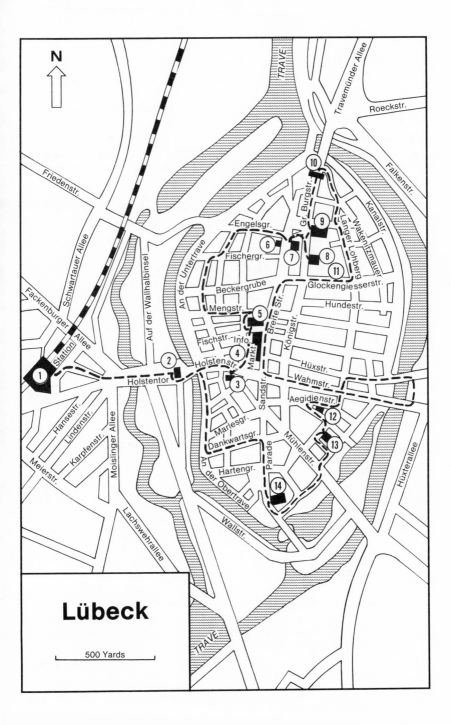

N

Roeckstr.

Friedenstr.

Schwartauer Allee

Fackenburger Allee

Station

1

Hansestr.

Lindenstr.

Karpfenstr.

Moislinger Allee

Meierstr.

Lachswehallee

Auf der Wallhalbinsel

An der Untertrave

TRAVE

Travemünder Allee

Falkenstr.

Kanalstr.

Wakenitzmauer

Langer Lohberg

Gr. Burgstr.

10

9

Engelsgr.

6

Fischergr.

7

8

11

Beckergrube

Glockengiesserstr.

Mengstr.

Hundestr.

Fischstr.

Info.

5

4

Markt

Breite Str.

Königstr.

2

Holstenstr.

Holstentor

3

Sandstr.

Hüxstr.

Wahmstr.

Aegidienstr.

12

Marlesgr.

Dankwartsgr.

An der Obertrave

Hartengr.

Parade

Mühlenstr.

13

Hüxterallee

14

Wallstr.

TRAVE

Lübeck

500 Yards

bombed and two great bells fell, smashed to bits, and became embedded in the floor under the south tower. The pieces were left there as a silent memorial to the war dead.

Opposite the church, at Mengstrasse 4, is the Baroque **Buddenbrooks House** where Thomas Mann was born in 1875. It played a role in his novel of the same name, and is now a museum devoted to his life. Tours and videos in English are offered. Visits may be made on Tuesdays through Sundays, from 10 a.m. to 5 p.m. Continue down the street past the **Schabbelhause**, a pair of elegant merchants' homes at numbers 48 and 50, which house a famous restaurant. Now follow the map through some interesting old streets to the **Haus der Schiffergesellschaft** (Mariners' Guild House) (6). Built in 1535, it houses an historic restaurant noted for its splendid interior, whose ambiance recalls the glorious days of the Hanseatic League.

The **Jakobikirche** (St. James' Church) (7) is directly across the street. A visit to this dark, atmospheric 14th-century hall church—noted for its Gothic organs—will be in complete contrast to others in Lübeck. Under the north tower there is a chapel dedicated to sailors lost at sea. It contains a lifeboat, the sole survivor of a 1957 shipwreck when a local barque went down with all hands.

Walk through the little alleyway between the church and its vicarage and then turn right on Königstrasse. The **Behnhaus Museum** (8), located in a magnificent 18th-century mansion, specializes in 19th- and 20th-century art, particularly the works of Friedrich Overbeck and Edvard Munch. It is open on Tuesdays through Sundays, from 10 a.m. to 5 p.m., closing at 4 p.m. in winter.

Now retrace your steps to the ***Heiligen-Geist-Hospital** (9), one of the most outstanding structures in town. It was built in 1286 as a charity hospital and later used as an old-age home. The entrance opens directly into a spacious chapel. Next to this is a huge hall containing four rows of tiny rooms that were once the patients' quarters. You can examine some of these medieval stalls, whose proximity to the chapel underlines the religious character of charity in those days. It is open on Tuesdays through Sundays, from 10 a.m. to 5 p.m., closing at 4 p.m. in winter.

Grosse Burgstrasse leads to the 15th-century **Burgtor** (10), a fortified gate that defended the only land approach to Lübeck. Walk under it and follow the map through a quiet old part of town. Along Glockengiesserstrasse you will pass several examples of the residential alleys and courtyards (*Wohngänge* and *Höfe*) for which the city is noted. Beginning in the late Middle Ages, these were built to alleviate an increasing demand for space on the small island. The **Füchtingshof** (11) at number 25 is a particularly nice one.

Turn left on Breite Strasse, a pedestrians-only shopping street, and

The Salt Warehouses

note the elegant 16th-century Dutch Renaissance staircase on the side of the town hall. Opposite this is the shop and café of **I. G. Niederegger**, famous throughout the world for its delicious *Lübecker Marzipan* confections since 1806. This is the perfect spot for a break, or to purchase an edible souvenir.

A left on Wahmstrasse leads to Balauerfohr, from which a pleasant **side trip** can be made by following the route on the map through a park on the far side of the river.

The small 13th-century **Aegidien Church** (12) is famous for its magnificent Renaissance rood screen. Now stroll down St.-Annen-Strasse to the **St.-Annen-Museum** (13). Housed in a former convent, it has a fabulous collection of ecclesiastical art and period room settings that should not be missed. The museum is open on Tuesdays through Sundays, from 10 a.m. to 5 p.m., closing at 4 p.m. in winter.

Continue on to the restored **Cathedral** *(Dom)* (14). Built between the 12th and 15th centuries, its delightful interior is well worth a visit before heading back to the station via the route on the map.

Lüneburg

It was salt that made Lüneburg rich. This well-preserved medieval town dates from the discovery of its saline springs at least a thousand years ago. In those days salt was needed for food preservation, especially in Scandinavia—which has no deposits of its own and borders on a distinctly un-briny sea, the Baltic. From Lüneburg, the Old Salt Road led to Lübeck, where the white gold was put on ships headed for ports as distant as Russia.

Lüneburg joined the Hanseatic League in the 14th century and became immensely wealthy. Fine homes, churches, and public buildings were constructed, mostly of brick. Then, in the 16th century, trade began to decline. After that the town remained a poor, backwater place until fairly recent times, when new industry and the development of its spa brought a measure of prosperity. Today, the town remains much as it was in the 15th and 16th centuries, a living museum of life in the late Middle Ages. This trip can be combined in the same day with one to Celle.

GETTING THERE:

Trains depart Hamburg's main station frequently for the half-hour trip to Lüneburg. These same trains can also be boarded a few minutes earlier at Hamburg's Altona and Dammtor stations. Return service operates until late evening.

By car, Lüneburg is 34 miles southeast of Hamburg via the A-7 Autobahn and the B-4 road.

PRACTICALITIES:

Lüneburg may be visited at any time, but avoid coming on a Monday if you want to see the museum or the inside of the town hall. The local **Tourist Information Office** *(Verkehrsverein)*, phone (04131) 30-95-93, is in the Rathaus on the Market Square. Lüneburg has a population of about 65,000.

FOOD AND DRINK:

Some choice restaurants are:

Zum Heidkrug (Am Berge 5, 2 blocks south of the Roter Hahn) Romantic dining in a 15th-century inn. Phone (04131) 312-49. $$$

Mills by the Old Port

Ratskeller (in the Rathaus on the Market Square) Local specialties highlight a well-rounded menu, served in an Old-World
atmosphere. Phone (04131) 317-57. X: Wed. $$

Bremer Hof (Lüner Str. 13, a block east of St. Nikolaikirche)
Comfortable dining in an old hotel. Phone (04131) 360-77. $$

Kronen Brauhaus (Heiligengeiststr. 39, 3 blocks west of St. Jo-
hanniskirche) A popular brewery restaurant with a beer garden. Phone (04131) 71-32-00. $ and $$

Kartoffeln Keller (Auf dem Kauf, a block east of the Roter Hahn)
Imaginative potato-based dishes. Phone (04131) 39-14-64. $

SUGGESTED TOUR:

Leave the **train station** (1) and follow the map to the colorful ***Old
Port** (2) in the *Wasserviertel* quarter on the Ilmenau River. On your
left, looking like a fantastic bird, is the **Alter Kran** (Old Crane), a
strange wooden contraption built in 1797. Similar cranes have stood
here since at least the 14th century. There are some ancient warehouses in the same area and, across the harbor, a group of 16th-cen-
tury merchants' houses. Stroll along Am Fischmarkt and cross the tiny
footbridge over the millstream. One of the old watermills here continues to grind flour as it has done for centuries.

Walk straight ahead and turn right on Rotehahnstrasse. Midway down the block, at number 14, is the **Roter Hahn** (3), a medieval old-folks' home. Step into its very lovely courtyard, then continue on to the **St.-Nikolaikirche** (St. Nicholas' Church) (4), consecrated in 1409 and noted for its star-vaulted ceiling.

A left on Bardowicker Strasse leads to the **Marktplatz** (Market Place) (5), with its Luna Fountain of 1530. Outdoor farmers' markets are held here on Wednesdays and Saturdays. The splendid ***Rathaus** (Town Hall), facing the square, has an ornately decorated façade. Actually a complex of buildings dating from the 13th through the 18th centuries, it is considered to be among the finest in Germany. Guided tours through its magnificent interior are held several times daily, except on Mondays. For specific times, ask at the tourist office located on the side facing the square.

Now follow the map to the **Michaeliskirche** (St. Michael's Church) (6) on Johann Sebastian Bach Platz, where the great composer is supposed to have gotten his start as a boy soprano at the age of 15. From here you can make a pleasant side trip to the **Kalkberg** (7), a small mound that offers a good view of the town.

Continue down Auf der Altstadt and Schlägertwiete. This ancient part of town has slowly subsided as the salt deposits below were worked until recent decades. Some of the houses lean at odd angles, and cracks develop in their walls. An interesting little side trip can be made to the former salt works, now home to the **Deutsches Salzmuseum** (8). Here you can learn everything you ever wanted to know about this precious mineral, and see how it was refined throughout the ages.

Heiligengeiststrasse leads to the **Brauereimuseum** (9), where beer has been brewed from 1485 until recently. It's free, so pop in for a look. Another nearby attraction, on Ritterstrasse, is the **Ostpreussisches Landesmuseum** (10), which explores the history of East Prussia.

You are now at Am Sande, a large open area lined with some beautiful old buildings. The most outstanding of these is the **St.-Johannis-Kirche** (St. John's Church) (11), a 14th-century brick structure with a slightly skewed tower. Go inside for a look at the fine altarpiece and choir stalls, and especially at the partly 16th-century "Bach" organ.

At this point you might want to amble around the picturesque streets between here and the market place, or follow the map to the **Museum für das Fürstentum Lüneburg** (Museum of the Principality of Lüneburg) (12), whose superb displays are concerned with local history and culture. It's open on Tuesdays through Fridays, from 10 a.m. to 4 p.m.; and on weekends from 11 a.m. to 5 p.m. The train station is only a few blocks away.

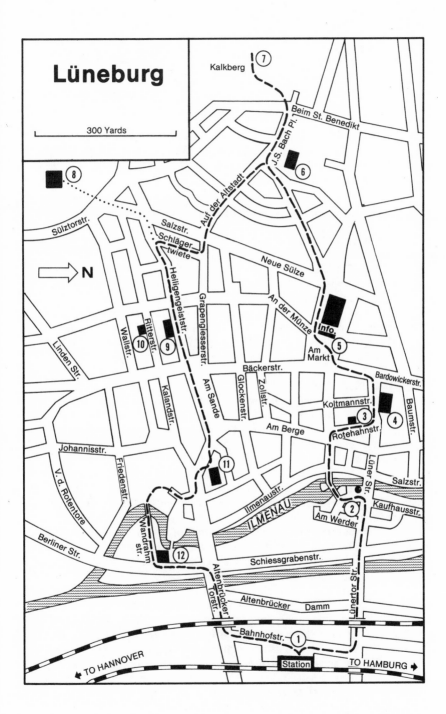

Celle

If Celle were in Bavaria, it would be mobbed with tourists. Fortunately, its location on the fringe of the Lüneburg Heath has spared it that fate. Pronounced *Tz-ella,* this delightful old town has a refreshing atmosphere, a lightheartedness often missing in other holdovers from the Middle Ages. This is a place to savor, not for any famous sights—there are precious few—but for its remarkably enjoyable ambiance. A trip here could easily be combined in the same day with one to Lüneburg.

GETTING THERE:

Trains, mostly of the IR or E class, depart Hamburg's main station several times in the morning for Celle, a ride of about 75 minutes. These may also be boarded a few minutes earlier at Hamburg's Altona or Dammtor stations. Return service operates until late evening.

By car, Celle is 74 miles south of Hamburg. Take the A-7 Autobahn to the Soltau-Süd exit, then the B-3 road.

PRACTICALITIES:

Celle may be visited at any time, but a fine day in the warm season will make it much more enjoyable. The museum is closed on Mondays. The local **Tourist Information Office,** phone (05141) 12-12, is at Markt 6, across from the Rathaus. Celle has a population of about 73,000.

FOOD AND DRINK:

The town offers a selection of restaurants in all price ranges. Among the best are:

Endtenfang (in the Hotel Fürstenhof, Hannoversche Str. 55, 4 blocks southwest of the castle) Renowned cuisine in a famous hotel that was once a castle. Phone (05141) 20-10. $$$

Historischer Ratskeller (under the Rathaus at Markt 14) An exceptionally fine *Ratskeller* with regional and other cuisine in historic surroundings. Phone (05141) 290-99. X: Tues. $$

Städtische Union Celle (Thaerplatz 1, 3 blocks southwest of the castle) Seasonal specialties in a stylish restaurant overlooking the castle and its park. Phone (05141) 60-96. X: Sun. $$

Schwarzwaldstube (Bergstr. 14, 2 blocks southeast of the Hoppener House) A good value in fine German food. Phone (05141) 21-73-41. X: Mon. $$

The Herzogliches Schloss

SUGGESTED TOUR:

The **train station** (1) is about one mile from the old part of town. Although you can get there by bus or taxi, the walk—going through a park most of the way—is actually very pleasant.

Turn left on Schlossplatz to the impressive ***Herzogliches Schloss** (Duke's Castle) (2), formerly the residence of the dukes of Brunswick and Lüneburg. Begun in 1292 as a fortification, it was later rebuilt in the Renaissance and Baroque styles. The castle has a strange relationship with British royalty. Sophie-Dorothea, the daughter of the last duke to live in Celle, was married to her cousin, the elector of Hannover, who in 1714 became the German-speaking King George I of England. He later divorced her for infidelity and had her imprisoned for life, but before that unhappy event they had two children. One of these became England's George II and the other, Sophie, the mother of Frederick the Great. George III fits into the story, too. His sister, Caroline Mathilda, married the mentally unstable king of Denmark, and later had an affair with one of his ministers. For this she was banished for life to Celle Castle, where she died in 1775.

Enter the castle and take one of the **guided tours** through its splendid interior, which begin at 10 and 11 a.m., noon, and 2, 3, and 4 p.m. daily except on Mondays. From November through March the tours are offered at 11 a.m. and 3 p.m. only. The most interesting rooms are the kitchen, the highly eccentric Renaissance ***chapel**, and the magnificent Baroque **court theater**—still in use today.

The *Bomann Museum (3), just across the street, has an utterly fascinating display of life in Lower Saxony. Reconstructed farm houses, utensils, costumes, and toys compete for your attention with a sizeable collection of art and antiques. Be sure to see all of the floors, including the basement, and don't miss the charming *Biedermeier house in the courtyard, reached from an upper floor of the museum. Visits may be made from 10 a.m. to 5 p.m., daily except Mondays; closing earlier on winter Sundays.

Now follow the Stechbahn, once a medieval tournament ground, to the Stadt Kirche (Town Church) (4). This was consecrated in 1308 and renovated in the Baroque style during the 17th century. The dukes are buried here, along with the unfortunate Caroline Mathilda. A trumpet is played from its tower every day at 8:15 a.m. and 5:15 p.m. From April through October, on Tuesdays through Saturdays, you may climb the tower for a nice view, but only between 3 and 4 p.m.

From here the narrow Kalandgasse leads past the Old Latin School of 1602 to Kanzleistrasse. Make a right and stroll down to the Markt, where a carillon with revolving figures plays tunes at 10 and 11 a.m., noon, and 3, 4, and 5 p.m. Continue along Schuhstrasse, a gorgeous pedestrians-only street lined with restored half-timbered houses. A colorful farmers' market is held on Wednesday and Saturday mornings at Brandplatz.

Return via Neue Strasse, again lined with a profusion of ancient houses, to the Rathaus (Town Hall) (5). This ornately elegant structure was begun in the 14th century and enlarged in the 16th. Note the fabulous north façade with its Weser Renaissance gable.

Continue up Zöllnerstrasse, a pedestrian shopping street with medieval houses, interesting shops, and outdoor cafés. At its end turn right and wander down Mauernstrasse to the Hoppener House (6) at the southwest corner of Poststrasse. Built in 1532, this is the most ornate dwelling in a town jam-packed with elaborately decorated houses. Its richness sums up what Celle is all about—the Middle Ages could never have been this colorful, but the fantasy created is very inviting.

Now follow the map to the Französischer Garten (French Park) (7), a thoroughly delightful spot to relax. At its far end you will come to the Bieneninstitut (Bee Institute) (8), a state facility devoted to research on apiculture. Visitors are welcome on Mondays through Fridays, except on holidays, from 9 a.m. to noon and 2–4 p.m. Don't get stung before returning to the station!

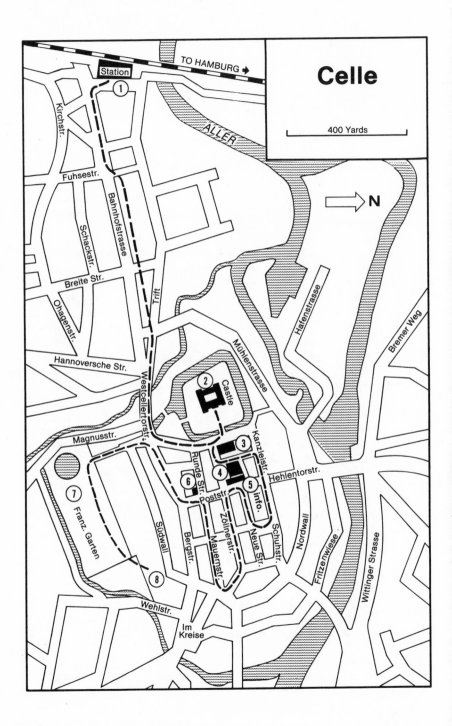

TO HAMBURG →

Station

ALLER

Celle

400 Yards

N

Kirchstr.

Fuhsestr.

Schackstr.

Breite Str.

Ohagenstr.

Bahnhofstrasse

Trift

Hannoversche Str.

Westcellertorstr.

Magnusstr.

Mühlenstrasse

Hafenstrasse

Bremer Weg

② Castle

Kanzleistr.

③

Runde Str.

④

⑥

Poststr.

⑤ Info.

Hehlentorstr.

⑦

Franz. Garten

Südwall

Bergstr.

Zöllnerstr.

Mauernstr.

Neue Str.

Schuhstr.

Nordwall

Fritzenwiese

Wittinger Strasse

⑧

Wehlstr.

Im
Kreise

*Goslar

Easily one of the most fantastic medieval towns in Germany, Goslar lies tucked away at the foot of the Harz Mountains, miles from the nearest Autobahn. Relatively few foreign tourists venture this far off the beaten path, but those who do are in for a visual treat that rivals even Rothenburg.

Goslar is over a thousand years old—and looks it. Virtually untouched by time, it was the favorite residence of the Holy Roman emperors during the 11th and 12th centuries. Rich deposits of silver, lead, copper, and even some gold brought great wealth; and in the 13th century the prospering town joined the Hanseatic League. By 1340 it had become a Free Imperial City, remaining powerful well into the 16th century. After that, however, religious wars and the loss of its mining rights to the Duke of Braunschweig brought on the inevitable decline. Goslar went into a long sleep, from which it did not awaken until the 19th century. Today, the real gold comes from vacationing Germans, who flock to the nearby mountains by the thousands.

GETTING THERE:

Trains depart Hamburg's main station in the morning for either Hildesheim or Hannover, where you can change to a local for Goslar. The trip takes about 3 hours. Be sure to check the current schedules carefully, preferably the day before as an early start is necessary. Return service runs until mid-evening.

By car, Goslar is about 150 miles southeast of Hamburg. Take the A-7 Autobahn past Hannover and Hildesheim to the Rhüden exit, then the B-82 into Goslar. This makes a good stopover on a trip between northern and central Germany, or into the former East area.

PRACTICALITIES:

Goslar may be visited at any time. The major sights are open daily, except that the Goslarer Museum closes on Sunday afternoons. The local **Tourist Information Office**, phone (05321) 28-46, is at Marktplatz 7. Goslar has a population of about 46,000.

FOOD AND DRINK:

Being the center of a popular resort area, Goslar offers a fine selection of restaurants, including:

The Marktplatz, Kaiserworth, and Rathaus

Kaiserworth (Marktplatz 3, opposite the Rathaus) Hearty German cooking in the dining room or medieval cellar of this 15th-century guildhall, now a hotel. Phone (05321) 211-11. $$

Das Brusttuch (Hoher Weg 1, opposite the Marktkirche) A heavily decorated 16th-century inn noted for its regional specialties. Phone (05321) 210-81. $$

Der Achtermann (Rosentorstr. 20, 2 blocks southeast of the train station) The Old World dining room and bierstube of this noted hotel are set in a restored historic structure. Phone (05321) 210-01. $$

Schwarzer Adler (Rosentorstr. 25, a block southeast of the train station) Indoor and outdoor dining in a small hotel. Phone (05321) 240-01. X: Mon., Tues. $$

Ratskeller (Marktplatz 1) An atmospheric, vaulted cellar for good-value lunches and fancier dinners. Phone (05321) 455-66. $ and $$

SUGGESTED TOUR:

Leave the **train station** (1) and follow the map to the ***Marktplatz** (Market Place) (2), where the tourist office is located. Ask them about visits to the ***Bergbau Museum**, an ancient mine that ceased operations in 1988 after over a thousand years of continuous digging. Now a museum, it features subterranean tours and is open daily. It's a bit out of town, but can be reached by bus or car.

An outdoor farmers' market is held here on Tuesdays and Fridays until 1 p.m. In the center of the square stands a 13th-century **fountain** adorned with the town's emblem, an imperial eagle that unfortunately looks more like a fat chicken trying to fly. On the east side, a carillon with mechanical figures puts on a free show depicting the history of mining in the region at 9 a.m., noon, 3 and 6 p.m. **Outdoor café** tables are set up in the square during the summer. The 15th-century **Kaiserworth**, now a hotel, is a remarkably picturesque structure. Take a look at its famous **Ducat Man**, a somewhat obscene figure of a man excreting golden coins, below the statue of Abundance on the side near the corner.

The ***Rathaus** (Town Hall) (3), on the west side of the square, also dates from the 15th century. Enter it by way of the outdoor staircase and take a short guided tour that includes the **Huldigungssaal** (Chamber of Homage), a small room covered with lavish medieval decorations. The Rathaus is open daily from 10 a.m. to 5 p.m., closing at 4 from November through March.

Now stroll over to the **Marktkirche** (Market Church) (4). Begun in the 12th century, it was expanded over the years and contains some wonderful Romanesque stained-glass windows, a 16th-century brass baptismal font, and other treasures. Next to this, at the corner of Hoher Weg, stands the 16th-century **Brusttuch** (5). One of Goslar's most outstanding dwellings, this curiously named structure is now an inn.

From here the route leads to the **Siemens House** (6), the ancestral home of the famous industrialist family. Built in the 17th century, this mansion may be visited by appointment only, phone (05321) 238-37.

Continue via Bergstrasse, Forststrasse, and Frankenberger Strasse through a delightful square to the **Frankenberg Church** (7). Originally built in the 12th century, it was remodeled during the 1700s and is renowned for its 13th-century murals and elaborately decorated nuns' gallery.

The walk now goes through a very colorful old part of town along the Gose stream, across which is the **Kaiserpfalz** (Imperial Palace) (8). Once a residence of the Holy Roman emperors, it was the scene of many imperial diets until the 13th century. The immense structure was first built around 1050, altered many times, and almost completely reconstructed during the late 19th century as a memorial to the First Reich. Enter the enormous **Reichssaal** (Imperial Hall) with its overly-romantic 19th-century murals depicting great events in German history. While there, be sure to see the 12th-century ***Chapel of St.**

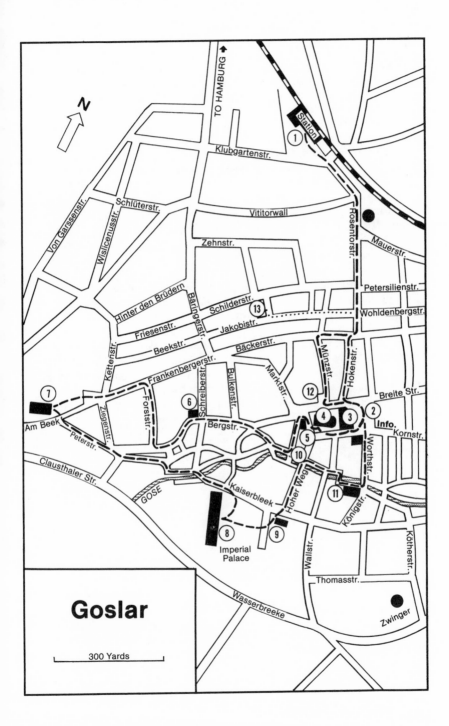

TO HAMBURG

Station

①

Klubgartenstr.

Vititorwall

Rosentorstr.

Mauerstr.

Von Garssenstr.

Wislicenusstr.

Schlüterstr.

Zehnstr.

Petersilienstr.

Hinter den Brüdern

Bäringstr.

Schilderstr.

⑬

Wohldenbergstr.

Friesenstr.

Jakobistr.

Kettenstr.

Beekstr.

Bäckerstr.

Münzstr.

Hokenstr.

Frankenbergerstr.

Schreiberstr.

Bulkenstr.

Marktstr.

⑫

Breite Str.

⑦

Forststr.

⑥

④ ③

②

Info.

Am Beek

Ziegenstr.

Bergstr.

⑤

Kornstr.

Peterstr.

⑩

Worthstr.

Clausthaler Str.

GOSE

Kaiserbleek

Hoher Weg

⑪

Königstr.

Köthenstr.

⑧

⑨

Imperial
Palace

Wallstr.

Thomasstr.

Wasserbreeke

Zwinger

Goslar

├─── 300 Yards ───┤

Ulrich, the final resting place for the heart of Heinrich III, an 11th-century emperor. The rest of Henry is buried in Speyer. Visits to the palace may be made any day from 10 a.m. to 5 p.m., closing at 4 in winter.

Goslar once had a cathedral, but this was demolished in 1820. All that remains today is its 12th-century **Domvorhalle** (north porch) (9), which can be visited. Walk down Hoher Weg, perhaps stopping at the delightful **Musikinstrumente und Puppenmuseum** (10), where you can examine a fabulous collection of really unusual musical instruments along with a lot of dolls.

Turn right along the stream, passing a charming old mill. The **Goslarer Museum** (11), a few steps beyond, has fascinating displays of life in old Goslar as well as treasures from the former cathedral. It's open on Tuesdays through Sundays from 10 a.m. to 5 p.m., closing at 4 in winter.

Return to the Marktplatz (2), where several outdoor cafés invite you to stop for a rest. On the way back to the station be sure to go through the **Schuhhof** (12), a marvelous square lined with half-timbered houses. Continue on via Münzstrasse, possibly stopping at the interesting **Zinnfiguren Museum** at number 11, which features over a thousand pewter figures in a hundred settings. It's open daily from 10 a.m. to 5 p.m. Lovers of modern art might want to make a left turn at Jakobistrasse and follow it to the **Mönchehaus** (13), a superb gallery of contemporary creations that's open on Tuesdays through Saturdays, from 10 a.m. to 1 p.m. and 3–5 p.m.; as well as Sundays from 10 to 1.

Section V

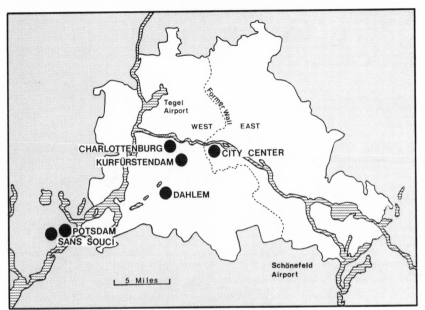

Tegel
Airport

WEST | EAST

CHARLOTTENBURG
KURFÜRSTENDAM

CITY CENTER

DAHLEM

POTSDAM
SANS SOUCI

Schönefeld
Airport

5 Miles

BERLIN
AND THE EAST

In all the world, there's hardly a city as intriguing as today's Berlin.
Germany's official capital teems with excitement as enormous trans-
formations sweep through the former communist state that until recently surrounded it. Many of these changes can be witnessed first-
hand on daytrips to the various neighborhoods—East and West—of
the immensely varied city itself, to its beautiful suburbs, and to the
nearby Potsdam region. One-day excursions to more distant places
such as Dresden or Leipzig are now possible, but remain problematic
for the time being.

Berlin
*City Center

Being divided in the aftermath of World War II was nothing new for Berlin, which began life in the late 12th century as two rival towns on opposite sides of a narrow crossing point on the Spree River. Known as Berlin and Cölln, these were located in the very heart of what until 1990 was communist East Berlin.

By the 15th century Berlin-Cölln was the seat of the electors of Brandenburg-Prussia, and was made the capital of the newly-formed Kingdom of Prussia in 1701. In 1710 the two towns and their suburbs were finally completely merged into one city. This became the capital of the new German Empire (the Second Reich) pieced together by Bismarck in 1871, which lasted until 1918; then of the Weimar Republic from 1919 until 1933; and finally of Hitler's Third Reich until 1945.

When Berlin was again divided after World War II, nearly all of its historic core and many of its most interesting areas fell within the sector allocated to Soviet domination. While the newly-prosperous West replaced its bombed-out rubble with modern buildings, the poorer communist East had to make do by patching up many of the ruined structures, eventually restoring some. Thus the former East Berlin, isolated behind its infamous Wall, has actually preserved quite a bit of the Prussian past for visitors to experience today. Here you will still find traces of what Berlin must have been like in its heyday. Between these old survivors stand block after block of sterile Socialist Modern building from the 1960s and 70s, which were intended to be a showcase for the virtues of communism but wound up speaking volumes about the cold barrenness of its bureaucracy.

Beginning at the historic Reichstag building in the west, this walking tour goes by way of the Brandenburg Gate and scanty remnants of the Wall to the renowned Unter den Linden boulevard, which leads to a fine set of world-class museums on an island in the Spree. Two powerful emblems that promised a bright socialist Utopia, the frighteningly ordered Alexanderplatz and the landmark Television Tower, are followed by a visit to the oldest part of Berlin, the beautifully-restored Nikolaiviertel with its 13th-century church. The walk ends at the elegant Gendarmenmarkt, near which are both U- and S-Bahn stations.

GETTING THERE:

Trains from major cities in Germany and other places throughout Europe arrive at Berlin's two major stations, **Zoologischer Garten** ("Zoo Station") in the west and **Hauptbahnhof** in the east, possibly making other stops in the city. Day trains from Munich take about 8 hours, from Frankfurt about 5 hours, and from Hamburg a bit over 3 hours.

By car, Berlin is 363 miles north (and slightly east) of **Munich** via the A-9 Autobahn to Hof and then the E-51 highway. It is 352 miles northeast of **Frankfurt-am-Main** by way of the A-5 and A-4 Autobahns, followed by the E-51. From **Hamburg**, take the A-24 and E-26 Autobahns into Berlin, a distance of 180 miles to the southeast.

Flying is the fastest way into Berlin. **Lufthansa** offers flights from all major German cities including Frankfurt, Munich, Hamburg, Cologne, Düsseldorf, Nürnberg, Stuttgart, Bremen, and Kiel. They also provide direct service with other European cities, and connecting flights worldwide. Other airlines offer similar services. Berlin has three airports: **Tegel** (TXL) in the northwest, **Templehof** (THF) south of the city center, and **Schönefeld** (SXF) well to the southeast. All are connected to downtown points by frequent and inexpensive buses. In addition, Templehof is served by U-Bahn subway and Schönefeld by S-Bahn commuter trains.

GETTING AROUND:

The public transportation system of Berlin, formerly divided into east and west with few interconnections, was reorganized as a single system operated by the Berlin Transport Authority (**BVG**). It is now quite easy to get to any destination in town or in the suburbs, which is great because distances in this spread-out city tend to be enormous. Unless you have a car, you'll find public transportation to be an essential part of your visit. The unified system consists of the:

S-Bahn—Commuter trains, usually running above ground, which connect central city locations with the farthest reaches of Berlin and its suburbs. Until 1984, the S-Bahn in West Berlin was operated by the East German railroad, which allowed it to become dilapidated. Much of the entire S-Bahn network has now been renovated and is once again an excellent way to get around.

U-Bahn—Subways providing a local service with many stops throughout the inner city and nearby suburbs. Several of its stations are beautifully-maintained architectural gems, while the trains are bright, clean, and punctual.

Buses—Surely the best views of Berlin are those from the upstairs front seats of its many double-decker buses. Bus stops are well marked and have amazingly accurate posted schedules.

FARES, TICKETS, and PASSES—The easiest and probably the most economical plan is to purchase a **Berlin Ticket**, which entitles you to unlimited use of the entire transit system throughout Berlin, and to Potsdam and some other suburbs for a period of 24 hours after beginning your first ride. Costing less than four single fares, it is sold at major stations and BVG information offices, and is available for both adults *(Erwachsene)* and children between the ages of 6 and 14 *(Kinder)*. The ticket must be validated when starting the first ride by inserting into a red time-stamping machine *(Entwerter)* in stations or on board buses.

Single Tickets *(Einzelfahrschein Normaltarif)*, valid for two hours of continuous travel anywhere in the system, are sold by machines and by bus drivers. The **Multiple Ticket** *(Sammelkarte)* is in effect four single tickets sold at a reduced price. All tickets must be validated in the time-stamping *Entwerter* machines before beginning a journey, and shown to bus drivers when making transfers.

A simple **route map** of the S- and U-Bahn lines is available free at tourist offices, or you can purchase a complete one that includes all bus lines, called a *Liniennetzplan*, at ticket offices in the stations. For **additional information** about all services phone (030) 752-7020.

PRACTICALITIES:

Avoid making this trip on a Monday, when most of the sights are closed. The main Berlin **Tourist Information Office**, phone (030) 262-6031, is on the ground floor of Europa Center, facing Budapester Strasse, at the eastern end of the Kurfürstendamm. There are branch offices at both Zoo and Hauptbahnhof train stations, and at Tegel Airport. Berlin has a population of about 3,900,000, making it by far the largest city in Germany.

FOOD AND DRINK:

Some good places for lunch along this walking route are:

Borchardt (Französische Str. 47, near the Gendarmenmarkt) An elegant re-creation of Berlin in its heyday. Reservations advised, phone (030) 229-3144. $$$

Französischer Hof (Jägerstr. 56, by the Französischer Dom) Continental cuisine, with outdoor dining in season. Phone (030) 229-3969. $$

Telecafé (in the Fernsehturm) Enjoy the view along with a light lunch in this revolving restaurant high atop the TV tower. Phone (030) 242-3333. $$

Arkade (Französische Str. 25, near the Gendarmenmarkt) Indoor/outdoor dining; both a café and a grill restaurant. Phone (030) 200-4241. $ and $$

The Reichstag Building
(Photo courtesy of Berlin Tourist Office)

Zur Letzten Instanz (Waisenstr. 14, 4 blocks east of the Niko-laikirche) Traditional Berlin cooking in the city's oldest res-taurant, founded in the 17th century. Very popular, reserva-tions suggested, phone (030) 242-5528. $

Zur Rippe (Poststr. 17, a block south of the Nikolaikirche) A café with simple meals in the heart of the historic district. Phone (030) 24-31-32-34. $

Alt-Cöllner Schankstuben (Friedrichsgracht 50, on the banks of the Spree Canal, 6 blocks southwest of the Nikolaikirche) Traditional food in a genuine *Alt-Berlin* setting. Phone (030) 242-5972.

SUGGESTED TOUR:

This tour begins at the Reichstag Building, which is most easily reached by taking bus number 100 from the Zoo train station, or by walking a few blocks southeast from the Lehrter Stadtbahnhof station of the S-Bahn.

Opened in 1894 as a home for the Imperial Parliament of Kaiser Wilhelm II's German Empire, the imposing **Reichstag Building** *(Reichstaggebäude)* (1) has a past as troubled as that of the nation it represents. Ironically, the words above its entrance, *Dem Deutschen Volke* (To the German People), were added only during World War I, a conflict that the parliament proved powerless to prevent. Following the defeat of the Reich in 1918, the ill-fated Weimar Republic was pro-claimed from a Reichstag balcony while at the same time a rival Socialist Republic was announced just down the street to the east. It was this battle between right and left ideologies, along with deteriorating social conditions, that paved the way for the rise of Nazism during the late 1920s.

On February 27th, 1933, the Reichstag Building was badly damaged in a mysterious fire that was blamed by the Nazis on the communists, although there is some evidence that Hitler's own people started the blaze. This single event led to the draconian measures that solidified Hitler's grip on the nation.

Further damaged by bombing and ground warfare, the Reichstag was rebuilt between 1957 and 1971. It is now used for parliamentary meetings, and will eventually house the Bundestag when that body moves here from Bonn. In the meantime there's an excellent public exhibition called **Questions on German History** *(Fragen an die deutsche Geschichte).* Covering the years 1800 to the present, this takes an honest look at the rise of empire, the stark reality of the Third Reich, and the postwar consequences. The exhibition is open on Tuesdays through Sundays, from 10 a.m. to 5 p.m., and admission is free.

The ignominious **Wall** *(die Mauer),* which imprisoned half of the city from 1961 until 1989, ran directly behind the Reichstag. Tiny portions of it still stand, at least until the tourists are done hacking it to pieces for souvenirs. Continue on to the nearby ***Brandenburg Gate** *(Brandenburger Tor)* (2), which stood just inside East Berlin but was for decades inaccessible to either side. Long a symbol of Berlin, it was built in 1791 for King Frederick William II of Prussia as a triumphal gateway marking the western end of the city's grandest boulevard, the Unter den Linden. Atop the structure stands a postwar reproduction of the famous **Quadriga**, a four-horse chariot driven by the goddess of Peace, who was at first stark naked but soon clothed by Prussian morality with decent copper garments. The original statue was stolen in 1806 by a victorious Napoleon but later returned, and was destroyed during World War II.

Just south of the gate, in what had been the death strip, or no-man's land, a slight mound of earth marks the location of the Führer Bunker, the underground air-raid shelter in which Hitler committed suicide on April 30th, 1945, during the final *Götterdämmerung* of the Third Reich.

From here, the **Unter den Linden** leads into the heart of Old Berlin. This broad, shady avenue, whose name means "Under the Lime Trees," is nearly a mile long and was laid out in 1647. Enlarged by Frederick the Great in 1734, it connected the former Imperial Palace with the Tiergarten hunting grounds in the west. During the 19th century the Unter den Linden became the most fashionable promenade

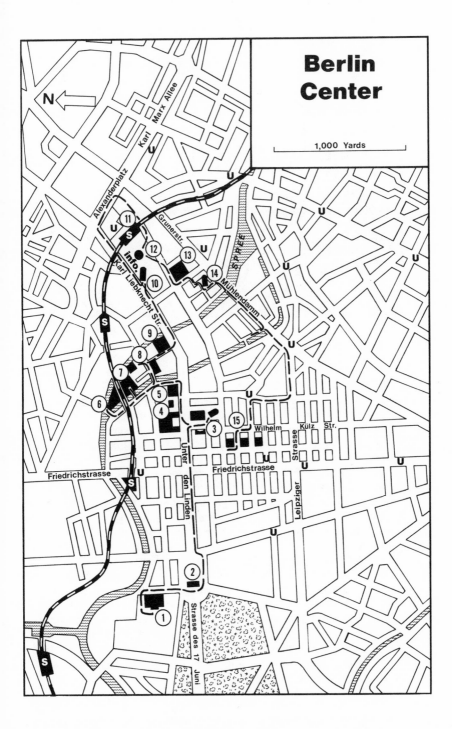

Berlin
Center

1,000 Yards

N

Karl Marx Allee

Alexanderplatz

Grunerstr.

SPREE

Karl Liebknecht Str.

Mühlendamm

info.

Friedrichstrasse

Unter den Linden

Friedrichstrasse

Wilhelm Külz Str.

Strasse

Leipziger

Strasse des 17 Juni

The Bode Museum

in Berlin, soon acquiring street lighting, cafés, shops, and later banks and luxury hotels. Throughout the Weimar and Nazi eras it remained a street of pleasure—right up until the very moment the bombs fell and reduced its ornate buildings to rubble. After the war, the earlier structures at the eastern end were beautifully restored by the East German government. Modern embassies, office buildings, and shops now line the western stretch. Although the street is still quite elegant, over 40 years of communist rule have drained it of the joyous atmosphere it once thrived on; slowly this is now returning.

You will soon come to the equestrian **statue of Frederick the Great**, the enlightened ruler of 18th-century Prussia. To the left of this is **Humboldt University**, once the University of Berlin, which counts among its former students both Marx and Engels. It was founded in 1810 by Wilhelm von Humboldt, the younger brother of the explorer Alexander von Humboldt. Statues of both flank the entrance.

Directly across the street is **Bebelplatz** (3), also known as Opernplatz. On May 11th, 1933, this was the scene of a ceremonial book burning in which thousands of volumes that conflicted with Nazi doctrine went up in smoke. On the west side of the square is an old library popularly called the "Kommode" (after irs curved façade), where Lenin studied in the reading room during 1895. The **State Opera** *(Deutsche Staatsoper)*, on the east side, was first built in 1743 and reconstructed several times after fires and bombings. Behind this

Alexanderplatz

stands **St. Hedwig's Cathedral**, a Baroque masterpiece begun in 1747 and modeled on the Pantheon in Rome. It has been the seat of the Roman Catholic bishop of Berlin since 1930.

Back on the Unter den Linden, you are only steps from the **Neue Wache** (4), a Prussian guardhouse built in 1818 in the style of a Greek temple. Since 1960 it has served as a memorial to the victims of fascism and militarism, with an eternal flame, ashes of resistance fighters, earth from the concentration camps, and the *Mother with Dead Son* statue by Käthe Kollwitz.

Just beyond this is the **Zeughaus** (Arsenal) (5), a stunning late-17th-century Baroque building once used to store war booty and later as a museum glorifying the Prussian army. Since 1952 it has housed the **Museum of German History** *(Deutsches Historisches Museum)*, a fascinating collection of artifacts from 1789 until the recent past. Be sure to visit the inner courtyard with its *****sculptures** of dying warriors in agony, an early indictment of the horrors of war. The museum is open daily except Fridays, from 10 a.m. to 6 p.m.

Now follow the map to the Spree Canal, passing an inviting outdoor café, and continue along to the *****Bode Museum** (6). Located at the northern tip of **Museum Island** *(Museuminsel)*, the old and wonderfully preserved museum complex between the canal and the river, the Bode is world famous for its *****Egyptian antiquities** and also possesses splendid collections of early Christian and Byzantine art, European sculptures and paintings, and prehistoric artifacts. The museum is open on Tuesdays through Sundays, from 9 a.m. to 5 p.m. A bargain one-day admission card *(Tageskarte)* covering nearly all of the attractions on Museum Island is available here and at the other museums.

Return along the canal and cross a small footbridge to the fabulous ***Pergamon Museum** (7), one of the greatest institutions of its type on Earth. Built in the early 20th century to display a multitude of treasures from the ancient world that were unearthed by German archaeologists, its greatest single attraction is the monumental ***Pergamon Altar**, dating from at least 160 B.C. and discovered in Turkey in 1876. Among the other riches are the Processional Way and Ishtar Gate from ancient Babylon, the Roman Market Gate of Miletus, a mosaic wall from 3000 B.C., and a vast collection of Islamic and Far Eastern art. Don't miss this special treat, which is open on Tuesdays through Sundays, from 9 a.m. to 5 p.m.

Continue back along the canal and cross it onto Bodestrasse. The **National Gallery** *(Alte Nationalgalerie)* (8) has a comprehensive collection of 19th-century, mostly German art. It's open on Tuesdays through Sundays, from 9 a.m. to 5 p.m. Just across the street stands the **Old Museum** *(Altes Museum),* mostly devoted to special exhibitions with variable opening times and admission prices. The nearby **New Museum** *(Neues Museum),* which is actually older than the Altes but only very recently brought back to life, also accommodates special exhibitions.

Next to the museum complex stands the **Berlin Cathedral** *(Berliner Dom)* (9), a neo-Renaissance structure completed in 1905 for Kaiser Wilhelm II. The main Protestant church of Berlin, it contains in its Hohenzollern Vault the remains of many of the rulers of Prussia. A balcony inside allows a wonderful view of the recently restored interior, and there's a small museum.

The hideous modern monstrosity across the street is the **Palast der Republik**, once the seat of the former East German parliament. Occupying the site of the Kaiser's Imperial Palace, the bronze-colored building is presently closed and will likely be torn down.

Cross the Spree River and follow Karl-Liebknecht-Strasse to the **Marienkirche** (St. Mary's Church) (10), a 13th-century Gothic structure that looks wildly out of place in its almost surrealist setting. Inside, however, it has been beautifully restored and features a 74-foot-long *Totentanz* (Dance of Death) fresco, probably dating from a 15th-century outbreak of the plague.

Continue along Karl-Liebknecht-Strasse and turn right on Karl-Marx-Allee (formerly Stalin Allee, and due for another name-change) to what was the center of activity in East Berlin, the **Alexanderplatz** (11). This enormous, windswept pedestrian plaza, lined as far as the eye can see with featureless modern boxes, is at least enlivened with a few sculptures including the unusual World Time Clock, surely the brainchild of a mad sputnik scientist. Before World War II, the "Alex" was a very different place, a crowded area of small shops that throbbed with street life. Its colorful ambiance was beautifully captured in Alfred Döblin's 1929 novel of human vices and passions, *Berlin-Alexanderplatz*, later made into a dark, lengthy film by Fassbinder.

Go through the passage next to the elevated train station to Berlin's most visible landmark, the **Fernsehturm** (Television Tower) (12). Built in 1969 as a proud symbol of socialist prosperity, it is 1,197 feet high and sports the inevitable revolving restaurant. You can ride an elevator to the observation level for a terrific view, and to the Telecafé for a light lunch or refreshments. One curious aspect of the tower is that when the sun shines on its metallic globe it forms a reflection in the shape of a cross that can be seen across the city; in what was officially a secular communist state this phenomenon became known as the "Pope's Revenge."

Just south of the tower, directly across from the **Neptune Fountain** of 1891, stands the **Berliner Rathaus** (13) of 1869, once the Town Hall for East Berlin and now the seat of local government for all Berlin. It is often called the *Rotes Rathaus,* as much for the color of its bricks as for its left-wing politics even in the time of the empire. Berlin's history is depicted on an exterior frieze of 36 plaques running clear around the building.

The very heart of Old Berlin, the ***Nikolaiviertel**, lies just around the corner. Most of this historic district was totally demolished by World War II bombs, but the Gothic ***Nikolaikirche** (St. Nicholas' Church) (14), partially dating from 1230 and the oldest building in Berlin, made it through the devastation and was restored in the mid-1980s. It now houses a **museum of medieval Berlin**, open on Tuesdays through Sundays from 9 a.m. to 5 p.m. Several other venerable structures in the immediate neighborhood, most notably the rococo **Ephrain-Palais** and the 18th-century **Knoblauchhaus**, have been restored and are used for exhibitions. Surrounding these are replicas of *Alt-Berlin* taverns and shops, and other recent buildings that somehow convey a feeling of the past.

Now follow the map across the Spree River and into what was Old Berlin's rival town of Cölln during medieval times. Little of its past remains; however you might want to take a look at the Friedrichsgracht along the east bank of the Spree Canal, and at some of the surrounding streets.

Continue on to **Gendarmenmarkt** (15), an elegant square of restored classical buildings. In its center is the **Schauspielhaus**, a notable theater built in 1821 that reopened as a major concert hall in 1984.

The domed Protestant church to its right is the **Französische Dom**, which has served Berlin's large Huguenot community since 1705. The story of these refugees who fled Louis XIV's France in 1685 and contributed much to Berlin's development is detailed in the small **Huguenot Museum** in the basement. From here it is a short stroll back to the Unter den Linden, or you can get a subway from the nearby station.

Berlin
Kurfürstendamm
and Charlottenburg

When Berlin was divided after World War II, the Soviets took over the urban heart of the city while the three western powers administered large areas that were essentially residential or suburban. This walking tour explores the liveliest and most famous of these, the Kurfürstendamm shopping and entertainment district, and then continues on to a great palace complex from the 17th century that is easily the most significant historical attraction in what had been West Berlin.

GETTING THERE:

The start of this tour, Zoo Station, can be reached by taking the **S-Bahn** train (route S-3) or the **U-Bahn** subway (routes U-1 or U-9) to the Zoologischer Garten stop. **Bus** routes 9, 19, 29, 54, 60, 69, 73, 90, and 94 also go there, or you can take a **taxi**. For further transit details see "Getting Around" on page 299.

PRACTICALITIES:

Avoid making this trip on a Monday if seeing the interior of the Charlottenburg Palace or the Bröhan Museum is important. The Prehistoric, Egyptian, and Antiquities museums are closed on Fridays. Most of the shops in the Kurfürstendamm area close around 2 p.m. on the second, third, and fourth Saturdays of each month except December, and remain closed all day on Sundays. The main Berlin **Tourist Information Office**, phone (030) 262-6031, is on the ground floor of Europa Center, facing Budapester Strasse. There is also a branch office in Zoo Station.

FOOD AND DRINK:

One of the great pleasures of Berlin is to sit at an outdoor café on the Ku'damm (as the Kurfürstendamm is usually called) and just watch the world go by while nursing a cup of coffee or a refreshing *Berliner Weisse*. The latter is a light wheat beer with a shot of raspberry syrup or green woodruff. For a more substantial lunch, try one of the following:

Alt Nürnberg (in Europa Center) Bavarian and Old Berlin specialties in a colorful setting. Phone (030) 261-4397. $$

Hecker's Deele (Grolmanstr. 35, a block southeast of Savignyplatz) Westphalian specialties with atmosphere. Phone (030) 889-00. $$

Kaufhaus des Westens (in the KaDeWe department store at Wittenberg Platz) A variety of restaurants, delis, and bars on the top floor of Berlin's leading store. All are good values. Phone (030) 212-10. $ and $$

Novo Skopje (Kurfürstendamm 23, 2 blocks southeast of Savignyplatz) An old-time favorite for Macedonian food, with plenty of atmosphere. Phone (030) 883-8549. $ and $$

Cour Carré (Savignyplatz 12) A romantic little French bistro. Phone (030) 443-6552. $ and $$

Hardtke (Meinekestr. 27, 3 blocks southwest of the Kaiser Wilhelm Church) This old-fashioned restaurants serves ample portions of traditional Berlin food. Phone (030) 881-9827. $

Dicke Wirtin (Carmerstr. 9, just northeast of Savignyplatz) A boisterous, lively pub with cheap stews and soups. Phone (030) 312-4952. $

SUGGESTED TOUR:

Begin your tour at **Bahnhof Zoologischer Garten** ("Zoo Station") (1), the mainline train station for western Berlin and a hub for commuter trains, subways, and city buses. The area around it is not quite as seedy as it was in years past, but is still populated by some rather colorful characters. Directly across from the station is the main entrance of the *Zoologischer Garten** (2), the oldest zoo in Germany. Destroyed during the war, it was rebuilt using the most advanced ideas of presenting animals in natural surroundings. This program has been so successful that even rare species are now routinely bred. There is also a large **Aquarium**, which can be entered from inside the zoo or from Budapester Strasse. Both attractions are open daily from 9 a.m. to 6 p.m., although the zoo closes at dusk when that is earlier. Exit through the famous old **Elephant Gate** onto Budapester Strasse. Since an enjoyable visit here will take several hours, you may prefer to return on another day instead.

Follow the map to the attractive **Wittenbergplatz** (3), a large open square in the center of which stands Berlin's oldest existing U-Bahn (subway) station. Built in 1913, this has been meticulously restored to its original appearance, even down to the early advertising posters on the walls. Step inside for a look. The imposing structure on the southwest corner of the square is the largest department store on the Continent, the world-famous **Kaufhaus des Westens**. First opened

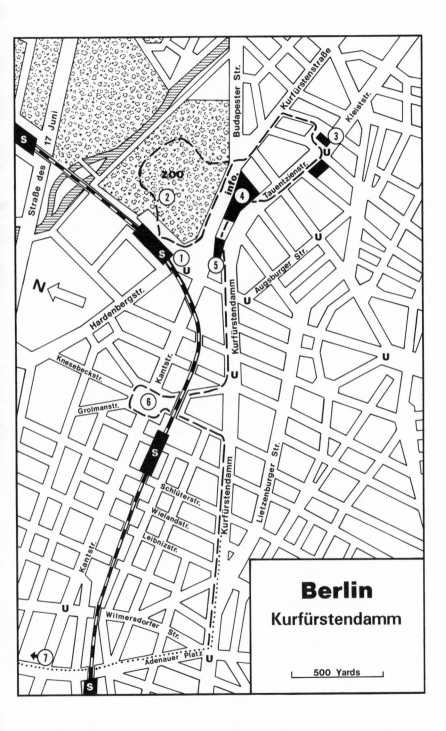

Berlin
Kurfürstendamm

500 Yards

in 1907 and rebuilt in 1950, it has been known to generations of luxury-loving Berliners simple as the **KaDeWe**. Even if you're not shopping, you might want to visit its top floor to sample the exotic food delicacies or have a drink.

A short stroll west on Tauentzienstrasse brings you to **Europa Center** (4), a huge and rather flashy indoor shopping mall topped with a 22-story office tower with a revolving Mercedes star. Besides housing over 70 shops, the center has a gambling casino, a cabaret, restaurants, cafés, pubs, theaters, various entertainments, and the main **Tourist Information Office**.

Cross the pedestrian island to the broken remains of the **Kaiser Wilhelm Gedächtniskirche** (Memorial Church) (5), a sad testament to the destructiveness of war. Built in 1895, it perished in a 1943 air raid and its ruins have since been joined by a modern octagonal chapel with blue glass windows and a separate matching bell tower.

You are now at the eastern end of the famed **Kurfürstendamm**, a broad tree-lined boulevard known to all Berliners simply as the **Ku'damm**. Stretching two miles to the west, this is Berlin's main showcase of capitalist prosperity, a promenade of quality shops, outdoor cafés, theaters, hotels, and top restaurants. It is definitely where the action is, day and night.

Stroll down the avenue, perhaps taking a refreshment break at the famous **Café Kranzler**, an *Alt Berlin* establishment that moved here from the Unter den Linden shortly after the Russians arrived.

As a little side trip, a right turn on Grolmanstrasse leads to the **Savignyplatz** (6), one of the most colorful and enjoyable squares in Berlin. Lined with bookshops, inexpensive restaurants, and friendly pubs *(Kneipen)*, this is where the locals go to escape the tourists. Return to the Ku'damm via Knesebeckstrasse and turn right, following the main street for another few blocks.

At some point before reaching Adenauer Platz you can board bus number 9 in the direction of Flughafen Tegel and ride it as far as the **Luisenplatz/Schloss-Charlottenburg** stop, or take the subway (line U-7) from Adenauer Platz to Richard Wagner Platz and walk there via Otto Suhr Allee. It is also possible to hike the entire mile-and-a-half distance along Kaiser Friedrich Strasse.

However you get there, ***Schloss Charlottenburg** (7) is one of the major attractions of Berlin and should not be missed. It was begun in 1695 as a country estate for Sophie-Charlotte, wife of the future King Frederick I of Prussia. Nearly a half-century later the mansion was transformed into a royal palace for another king, Frederick the Great. Badly damaged during World War II, it has been restored and is now the centerpiece of a wonderful museum-and-garden complex.

The magnificent **equestrian statue** in the central courtyard is of the

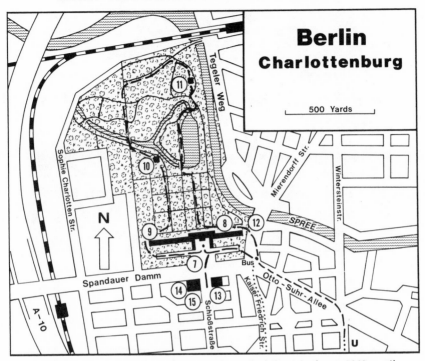

Great Elector, Frederick William, who ruled Prussia from 1640 until 1688. One of the finest sculptures of the entire Baroque period, it originally stood by the Royal Town Palace at the east end of the Unter den Linden.

Walk straight ahead to the main entrance. Most of the sumptuous interiors can only be seen on **guided tours**, which are conducted in German. These are still highly worthwhile even if you don't understand the language, and an English guide booklet is available. The palace is open on Tuesdays through Fridays from 9 a.m. to 5 p.m., and on Saturdays and Sundays from 10 a.m. to 5 p.m.

In addition to the royal apartments, the palace building contains two museums that might interest you. The first of these, in the east wing, is the **Galerie der Romantik** (8), a fine collection of 19th-century paintings from the German Romantic school, including works by Caspar David Friedrich. It is open at the same times as the palace, above. The west wing houses the **Museum für Vor- und Frühgeschichte** (Museum for Pre- and Protohistory) (9), a fascinating survey of artifacts from the Stone Age to the High Middle Ages that can be seen on Mondays through Thursdays from 9 a.m. to 5 p.m., and Saturdays and Sundays from 10 a.m. to 5 p.m.

Schloss Charlottenburg from the Park

The **Park** (*Schlosspark*) extending to the north is laid out in the English manner and remains one of Berlin's most popular free public parks. A stroll through its woods and lovely gardens will take you past the **Royal Mausoleum** (10); the 18th-century **Belvedere** (11) with its noted collection of Berlin porcelains; and finally the **Schinkel Pavilion** (12), a simple summer residence of King Freidrich Wilhelm III. Admission to these buildings is covered by the complete palace tour ticket.

The two former barracks buildings of the royal guards just south of the palace also house some first-rate attractions. Start with the splendid ***Ägyptisches Museum** (Egyptian Museum) (13), world famous for its spectacular *Bust of Nefertiti* of about 1350 B.C. Among the many other treasures from along the Nile are the *Kalabsha Gate* and a priest's head sculpted in green stone. Across the street is the **Antikenmuseum** (Museum of Antiquities) (14), which specializes in art and artifacts from ancient Greek and Roman times. Both museums are open on Mondays through Thursdays from 9 a.m. to 5 p.m., and on Saturdays and Sundays from 10 a.m. to 5 p.m.

One last treat that might interest you is just a few steps down the street. The **Bröhan Museum** (15) is quite small and often overlooked, but it houses a terrific collection of Jugendstil (German Art Nouveau) and Art Deco objects and furniture dating from 1890 to 1940. These are displayed in period room settings and may be seen on Tuesdays through Sundays from 10 a.m. to 6 p.m.

Berlin Dahlem and the Grunewald

Museum fans, gardeners, and anyone who enjoys a walk in the woods will love this easy daytrip, which combines culture with nature in one of Berlin's most delightful suburbs.

Even though it is home to some of Germany's greatest museums, world-class botanical gardens, and a leading university, the idyllic village of Dahlem still retains its rural Old World atmosphere. Located near the southwest corner of what had been West Berlin, next door to the lakes and forests of the Grunewald, this picturesque little *Dorf* dates from at least 13th century and remained a private estate until about 1900.

Beyond the village, the tour includes a stroll through the forest to the 16th-century lakeside hunting lodge of the ruling family, then another walk in the woods to a small museum of Expressionist art before returning to central Berlin.

GETTING THERE:

Begin by taking the **U-Bahn** subway (route U-2) to the Dahlem-Dorf station. This line can be boarded at Wittenbergplatz near Europa Center, and connects with other lines en route. Travel by **bus** is slow and requires several changes along the way. See page 299 for general transportation information.

PRACTICALITIES:

The entire museum complex at Dahlem is closed on Mondays, as is the hunting lodge at Grunewald. The Brücke Museum of Expressionist art closes on Tuesdays. Be sure to wear comfortable walking shoes on this trip. For further **Tourist Information** see page 300.

FOOD AND DRINK:

Some good eating places along the route are:

Alter Krug (Königin-Luise-Str. 52, near the Dahlem-Dorf station) A classy German with a garden terrace. On weekdays it's open in the evening only, so you might enjoy it after the tour. Phone (030) 832-5089. X: Mon. $$$

Forsthaus Paulsborn (Am Grunewaldsee, just southwest of the hunting lodge) A rustic lodge with German cuisine, noted for game dishes. Phone (030) 813-8010. X: Mon. $$

Luise (Königin-Luise-Str. 40, just east of the Dahlem-Dorf station) A friendly beer garden near the museums. $

Dahlem Museums Cafeteria (in the museum complex, near the Lansstrasse entrance) Light meals at reasonable prices, with outdoor tables in fine weather. X: Mon. $

In addition, there are several *Imbiss* stands by the Dahlem-Dorf station, and a McDonald's at Clay Allee and Königin-Luise-Strasse.

SUGGESTED TOUR:

The **Dahlem-Dorf U-Bahn Station** (subway) (1), with its thatched roof and timbered walls, reflects the rustic character of this most attractive village. Just a block to the northwest on Königin-Luise-Strasse is a genuine holdover from medieval times, the **St. Annenkirche** (2), a brick church built about 1220 with additions from later in the Gothic period. If it's open, step inside to admire the 17th-century Baroque pulpit and gallery, the beautifully carved altar, and the remains of some medieval murals.

Stroll one block southeast of the station to the star attraction of this trip, the ***Dahlem Museum Complex** (3). Here, seven important museums are housed in a maze of interconnected buildings, all using common entrances on both Lansstrasse and Arnimallee, and all joined together internally. You won't be able to see everything in a day, so pick up a diagram at the entrance, choose carefully, and try not to get lost. A combined day-ticket covering all seven museums is available. The complex is open on Tuesdays through Fridays from 9 a.m. to 5 p.m., and on Saturdays and Sundays from 10 a.m. to 5 p.m. It consists of:

The ***Gemäldegalerie** (Picture Gallery), which has one of the best collections of European paintings in the world. It covers the period from the 13th through the 18th centuries, and is rich in works by such German, Dutch, Flemish, Italian, French, and Spanish masters as Dürer, Cranach, Holbein, Memling, Bruegel, Rubens, Van Dyck, Vermeer, Hals, ***Rembrandt**, Botticelli, Giotto, Titian, Tiepolo, Canaletto, Poussin, Watteau, Velázquez, and Goya—to name but a few. *There are plans to move the Picture Gallery to another location in Berlin in the near future.*

The **Skulpturengalerie** (Sculpture Gallery), which displays two floors of European works from the early Christian era to the late 18th century. It is particularly noted for its German Gothic carvings by Tilman Riemenschneider and others; and for its sculptures of the Italian Renaissance, especially those by Donatello and della Robbia.

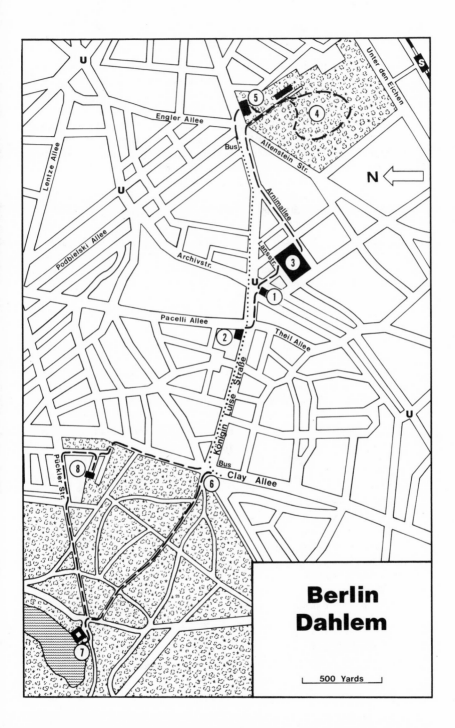

Berlin Dahlem

500 Yards

The **Kupferstichkabinett** (Cabinet of Copper Etchings), hidden away on an upper floor, is a treasury of drawings, prints, and graphics from the 15th through the 20th centuries. Works by Rembrandt, Dürer, Holbein, and Cranach are featured.

The ***Museum für Völkerkunde** (Ethnographic Museum) has separate sections spread all over the complex, dealing with life in pre-Columbian America, the South Seas, Africa, and Asia. Among the outstanding items on display are ***boats from the South Pacific**; native dwellings from New Guinea; artifacts from the Mayan, Aztec, and Inca civilizations; and African bronzes from Benin. The rest of the complex is occupied by the **Museum für Ostasiatische Kunst**, which specializes in art from the East Asian countries of China, Japan, and Korea, dating from prehistoric times to the present day; the **Museum für Indische Kunst** with its superb collections covering nearly 4,000 years of Indian, Himalayan, Central Asian, and Southeast Asian art; and the **Museum für Islamische Kunst**, which features art objects of the Muslim countries from the time of Muhammad to the present.

Leave the museum complex via the Arnimallee exit and follow the map to the nearby ***Botanischer Garten** (4), one of the largest and most attractive of Europe's botanical gardens. Over a hundred acres of land are laid out in geographic zones, with woodlands, hills, fields, and ponds adding to the overall beauty. Many rare and exotic species are featured, especially in the delightfully old-fashioned hothouses. The gardens are open daily, from 9 a.m. to sunset.

Botanists will surely enjoy the adjacent **Botanical Museum** (5), although others may find it more than a trifle bit dull. The only institution of its kind in Germany, it displays the evolution and propagation of all kinds of plants throughout the world. It is open on Tuesdays through Sundays from 10 a.m. to 5 p.m., remaining open until 7 p.m. on Wednesdays.

Cross Königin-Luise-Strasse and take bus number 17 back through Dahlem-Dorf as far as Clay Allee, where the **Grunewald Forest** (6) begins. This broad avenue was named after General Lucius D. Clay, the American military governor during the historic Berlin Airlift of 1948–49. Over 12 square miles in area and literally littered with lakes, the forest was once a royal hunting reserve but was opened to the public in the late 19th century. Some 70% of its trees, mostly pine and birch, were cut down to use as heating fuel during the hard times following World War II. These were since replaced with more appropriate species such as oak, ash, and beech.

A wide woodland trail leads in less than a mile to the **Jagdschloss Grunewald** (7), a 16th-century royal hunting lodge on the edge of a small lake. Enlarged and altered over the years, this elegantly simple lodge is surrounded by a courtyard and modest service buildings dec-

Jagdschloss Grunewald

orated with antlers. With its period furnishings, it now serves as a small museum of paintings by German, Dutch, and Flemish artists including Lucas Cranach the Elder and Rubens. Visits may be made on Tuesdays through Fridays from 10 a.m. to 2 p.m., and on Saturdays and Sundays from 11 a.m. to 4 p.m.

Now follow the map carefully onto another broad woodland trail that eventually becomes Pückler Strasse. When you come to a group of suburban houses, turn right on Fohlen Weg and right again onto Bussardsteig. At the end of this is the low, modern **Brücke Museum** (8), where works by a group of early-20th-century Expressionist artists called "Die Brücke" (The Bridge) are displayed. A complete break with past traditions, this movement was the beginning of modern art in Germany, and was the contemporary equivalent of French Fauvism. The group broke up in 1913 after each of the artists began to go his own way. Among the most interesting works shown are those by Karl Schmidt-Rottluff, Erich Heckel, Ernst Ludwig Kirchner, and Emil Nolde. The museum is open on Wednesdays through Mondays, from 11 a.m. to 5 p.m.

Now follow the map back to nearby Clay Allee and return by bus to the Dahlem-Dorf U-Bahn Station (1).

*Sans Souci Park and the Royal Palaces

Sans Souci means "without a care," and that's how King Frederick II, known as the "Great," liked to live at his sumptuous complex of palaces on the outskirts of Potsdam, in what had been East Germany. The name refers not only to the most lavish of the palaces but also to the 716-acre park itself, which is fairly riddled with an intriguing assortment of highly unusual buildings.

Both the park and most of its palace structures were created for Frederick the Great, the enlightened despot who ruled Prussia from 1740 until his death in 1786. He selected this site as his summer residence in preference to the ancestral palaces in Berlin, following a precedent set by his ancestor Frederick William, the "Great Elector," who had built a palace in Potsdam as early as 1660. Frederick the Great's successors, however, showed little interest in Sans Souci until the middle of the 19th century, when Frederick William IV added several dreamily romantic buildings to complete the park's ensemble.

Sans Souci should be seen in its totality rather than as a visit to just one or two of the palaces, as all of its components work together beautifully to form one harmonious whole. Exploring it at a leisurely pace will take the better part of a day, so it is best not to attempt combining a visit here with one to adjacent Potsdam.

GETTING THERE:

S-Bahn commuter trains on routes S-3 or S-7 connect central Berlin with **Potsdam-Stadt**, the end of the S-Bahn line. From here you can take a public bus or the special A-1 tourist bus to Sans Souci. A Berlin Ticket is valid for the entire trip, but does not cover the special tourist bus. You could also walk from the station to Sans Souci, a distance of 1½ miles.

By car, head to the southwest corner of Berlin on the A-15 Autobahn *(Avus)*, then turn right at Wannsee on the Königstrasse into Potsdam.

PRACTICALITIES:

Sans Souci Park is open daily throughout the year, although some of its attractions are closed on a few days as noted in their descriptions. The local **Tourist Information Office**, phone (0331) 29-11-00, is at Friedrich-Ebert-Strasse 5 in Potsdam.

FOOD AND DRINK:
Several restaurants and cafés within the park are:

> **Zur Historischen Mühle** (2 blocks northwest of Schloss Sanssouci) German cuisine with full service, indoors or out. $$
>
> **Schlosscafé** (in the Neues Palais) A stylish café next to the theater in the south wing of the palace. $$
>
> **Café im Drachenhaus** (near the northwest corner of the park) An historic structure in the shape of a Chinese pagoda, with a full-service indoor café and self-service section outdoors, both with light meals. $

SUGGESTED TOUR:

Leave the **Potsdam-Stadt S-Bahn Station** and either take a regular public bus or the special tourist excursion bus (Route A-1) to the **Main Entrance** (1) of Sans Souci Park, on Schopenhauerstrasse. If you decide to walk the 1½-mile distance, refer to the map on page 327. Enter the park and turn right at the elegantly terraced vineyards. There, rising in front of you, is ***Schloss Sanssouci** (Sans Souci Palace) (2), completed in 1747 and regarded as one of the finest rococo structures in Germany. Its low, single-story design and massive central dome were based on a sketch by Frederick the Great himself. This philosopher-king, very much a product of the 18th-century Enlightenment, was deeply involved with the arts and was both a talented composer and a noted flutist. He was also a friend of the French writer Voltaire, who lived in the Potsdam Town Palace from 1750 until 1753. Frederick is best known, however, as a brilliant military commander who kept his nation at war throughout most of his long reign, usually victoriously. It is said that he transformed Prussia from "a country with an army into an army with a country".

Walk around the palace to its entrance, framed by a semi-circular colonnade, from which there is a superb view of fake ruins atop a distant hilltop. ***Guided tours** through the magnificent interior of Sans Souci Palace are conducted at frequent intervals, daily except on the first and third Mondays of each month, from 9 a.m. to 5 p.m., closing at 4 p.m. in February, March, and October; and at 3 p.m. from November through January. The tickets are for tours at specific times, so be sure to get yours early.

Just east of the palace, at a slightly lower level, is the **Bildergalerie** (Picture Gallery) (3) with its marvelous collection of Renaissance and Baroque paintings by such masters as Caravaggio, Rubens, and van Dyck. Completed in 1764, it is thought to be the first building ever erected for the sole purpose of housing paintings. Its brilliant rococo interior has been well restored, with the pictures hung in the original old-fashioned manner. *The gallery is presently closed for restoration* *until sometime in 1996.* Return to the palace and continue on to the **Neue Kammern** (New Chambers) (4), just a few steps to the west. This was the palace's guest house since 1774, and is open daily except Fridays, from 9 a.m. to 5 p.m., closing earlier in winter.

Now follow the map through the Northern Gardens to the **Orangerie** (5), a late addition to the park that was completed in 1860 for King Frederick William IV. Designed to shelter delicate plants during the winter, this pseudo-Renaissance building is over a thousand feet long and contains apartments intended to house the king's sister and her husband, Czar Nicholas I, on their visits to Potsdam. You can climb the tower for a grand ***view**, and examine the 47 fake Raphael paintings in the hall. The Orangerie is open daily between mid-May and mid-October, from 9 a.m. to noon and 1–5 p.m.

A short stroll west through the woods brings you to the **Drachenhaus** (Dragon House) (6), a strange pagoda-like structure erected in 1770 as the royal winegrower's home. Happily, it now serves as a **café**, with additional self-service tables outside.

Turn south and follow a trail past the 18th-century **Temple of Antiquity** (7), a tiny imitation of the Pantheon in Rome. Just beyond this stands the grandiose ***Neues Palais** (New Palace) (8), built for Frederick the Great as a demonstration of Prussia's power and wealth after the end of the Seven Years War in 1763. Intended as a guest palace for visiting royalty, it was instead used as a summer residence by members of the royal family. You can visit the sumptuous interiors, including the fantastic Grotto Hall, on your own during the summer season or on guided tours all year round. An illustrated guide brochure in English is available. The palace is open daily from 9 a.m. to 12:45 p.m. and 1:15–5 p.m.; closing at 4 p.m. in October and February, and at 3 p.m. from November through January. It is closed on the second and fourth Monday of each month. Tickets are sold at the end of the south wing, and the entrance is at the center of the west façade. The theater next to the café in the south wing may be visited when not in use. If you have time for only one palace at Sans Souci, make it this one!

Walk east from the south wing to the **Freundschaftstempel** (Temple of Friendship) (9) of 1768, a circular Greek-style structure whose Corinthian columns bear reliefs of famous pairs of friends from ancient times. It is dedicated to the memory of Frederick the Great's favorite sister, Princess Wilhelmina of Bayreuth (see page 119), and a statue of her resides within.

Continue on to **Schloss Charlottenhof** (10), a small palace in the style of an Italian villa. It was built in 1826 for the crown prince, who became King Frederick William IV in 1840 and later went insane when he realized that the age of feudalism was over, even in Prussia. The

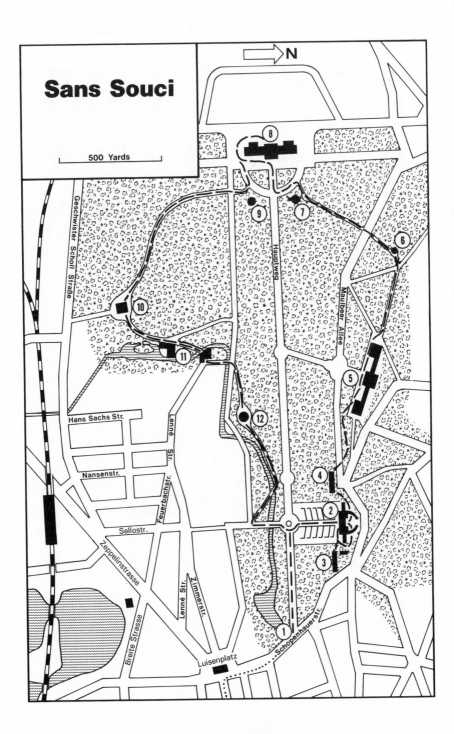

Figures outside the Chinesisches Haus

landscaped grounds around the palace are quite lovely, and the restrained interior may be seen on guided tours offered between mid-May and mid-October, daily from 9 a.m. to 12:30 p.m. and 1–5 p.m.

The path leads next to the nearby **Römische Bäder** (11), a highly romantic ensemble of fake Roman baths at the end of an artificial lake. The group includes the Italianate home of the court gardener, and is usually open during the same times as Schloss Charlottenhof, above.

Stroll across the tiny stream at the **Meierei**, an Italian-style dairy of 1832, and follow around to the incredible ***Chinesisches Haus** (Chinese House) (12), a dream-like circular structure from 1757. Its gilded walls support a tent-shaped roof whose cupola is topped with a golden mandarin sitting under a parasol. The gilded sculptures on the porches are fantastic, and inside there is a collection of Chinese and Japanese porcelains that may be seen from mid-May through mid-October, daily from 9 a.m. to noon and 12:45–5 p.m.

From here you can return to the park entrance or, better, wander around the park and discover some of its many hidden surprises.

Potsdam

Although it's close to Berlin and easy to reach, Potsdam is a very different place, and one that's filled with historic interest. Beautifully situated at a narrow point of the Havel River between two large lakes, its existence was first recorded as far back as 993 but it remained an insignificant backwater until the "Great Elector," Frederick William, built himself a palace by the riverside in 1660. After the electors of Brandenburg became the kings of Prussia they continued to come to Potsdam, especially Frederick the Great who began his nearby Sans Souci Palace in 1745.

Potsdam played a major role in more recent history, too. It was here that Hitler consolidated his power during the first all-Nazi parliament, held in 1933 right after the Reichstag in Berlin was set ablaze. Ironically, in 1945 it was the setting of the Potsdam Conference in which the victorious Allies carved up a defeated Germany, and in effect started the Cold War.

This tour explores the old part of town and visits the Cecilienhof Palace, preserved exactly as it was when the agreement to divide Germany was signed and Potsdam wound up under communist rule. Because it is so close, you might be tempted to include Sans Souci, described in the previous chapter, but this treat really requires an entire day in itself.

GETTING THERE:

S-Bahn commuter trains on routes S-3 and S-7 link central Berlin with the **Potsdam-Stadt S-Bahn Station**. A regular Berlin Ticket is valid.

By car, head to the southwest corner of Berlin on the A-15 Autobahn *(Avus)*, then turn right at Wannsee on the Königstrasse into Potsdam. You can drive to the Cecilienhof Palace instead of waiting for the bus.

PRACTICALITIES:

The Cecilienhof Palace is closed on the second and fourth Monday of each month, and two of the other sights on all Mondays. The local **Tourist Information Office**, phone (0331) 29-11-00, is at Friedrich-Ebert-Strasse 5, by the Alter Markt. Potsdam has a population of about 140,000.

FOOD AND DRINK:

Some good places for a meal are:

Schloss Cecilienhof (on the left side of the palace) Pleasant country dining near the lake, German cuisine. Phone (0331) 370-50. $$

Am Stadttor (Brandenburgerstr. 1-3, near the Brandenburger Tor) Solid German cooking, a good value. Phone (0331) 217-29. $

Gastmahl des Meeres (Brandenburgerstr. 72, east of the Brandenburger Tor) The best place in town for seafood. $

Klosterkeller (Friedrich-Ebert-Str. 94, 2 blocks south of the Nauener Tor) Simple food in comfortable surroundings. Phone (0331) 29-36-69. $

SUGGESTED TOUR:

Leave the **Potsdam-Stadt S-Bahn Station** (1) and cross the Havel River to the **Alter Markt** (2), which is where you'll begin if you're coming by bus or car. This old market square faces the **Church of St. Nicholas**, the Baroque former **Town Hall** of 1753, and the **Court Stables** of 1685. A modern hotel marks the site of the original Town Palace of the ruling electors and kings, built in 1660 and bombed out of existence in 1945.

Amble past the **Tourist Information Office** and along Friedrich-Ebert-Strasse to the **bus stop** at Platz der Einheit. Here you can board bus number 695 marked for Höhenstrasse, and ride it to the Cecilienhof Palace; or you could walk the 1½-mile distance.

*Schloss Cecilienhof (Cecilienhof Palace) (3) hardly looks like a real palace; in fact it strongly resembles a large English Tudor manor house. Perhaps this is because of its owner's heritage. Crown Prince Wilhelm, great-grandson of England's Queen Victoria and son of Germany's Kaiser Wilhelm II, built this lovely lakeside mansion between 1913 and 1916 as a home for himself and his wife Cecilie. The crown prince went into exile after the disaster of World War I, but soon returned to Germany and became an early supporter of Hitler. He lived here until March of 1945, when he and his family fled westward as the Soviet troops marched in.

The empty palace was seized by the Russians and quickly renovated in time for the **Potsdam Conference** held in July and August of 1945 to decide the fate of postwar Germany. Three delegations represented the United States, Great Britain, and the Soviet Union; and were headed by President Truman, Prime Minister Churchill, and Joseph Stalin. Late in July, Churchill was replaced by Clement Attlee after an upset victory by the Labour Party. It was from Potsdam that President Truman secretly ordered the atom bomb to be dropped on

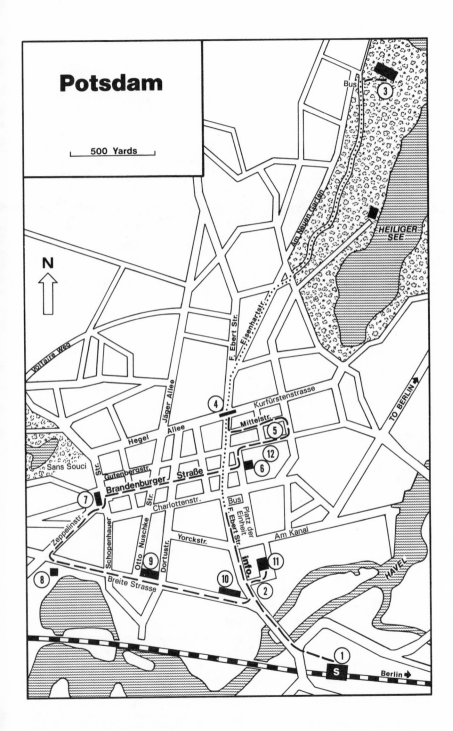

Schloss Cecilienhof

Hiroshima, putting an end to World War II before the Soviet Army could reach Japan.

The main part of the palace has been left as it was during the conference, and may be visited on frequent guided tours conducted daily from 9 a.m. to 5 p.m. (4 p.m. from mid-October through April) The palace is closed on the second and fourth Monday of each month. A rather charming country hotel and restaurant occupies the remainder of the palace. The grounds, fronting on two lakes, are part of the **New Gardens** and are a delightful place for a stroll.

Return by bus or on foot to the **Nauener Tor** (4), a large, crenellated Gothic-style gateway that was built in 1755 across Friedrich-Ebert-Strasse. Stroll through this and turn left on Mittelstrasse into the well-restored **Holländisches Viertel** (Dutch Quarter) (5). This neighborhood was developed in the mid-18th century for settlers from the Netherlands, whose gabled red-brick dwellings make it look like a corner of old Delft. Amble through it and return on Gutenbergstrasse, turning south past the Bassinplatz bus station to the **St.-Peter-und-Paul Kirche** (6), an interesting church from 1868.

Now head west on Brandenburger Strasse. Cutting through the heart of old Potsdam, this attractive pedestrian shopping street is lined with newly-burgeoning shops, restaurants, and cafés. At its end is the large, open **Luisenplatz** and the **Brandenburger Tor** (7), a triumphal archway dating from 1770, when Potsdam was both a royal seat and a garrison town.

Cross the square and bear left on Zeppelinstrasse past a shopping center to the **Dampfmaschinenhaus Moschee** (8) with its slender minaret, a very strange structure indeed. Built in 1841 to look like a Moorish mosque, it was actually a waterworks pumping station that supplied the fountains of Sans Souci. Today, its steam engines have been restored and the whole weird ensemble may be visited from Wednesdays through Sundays, 9 a.m. to 5 p.m., but not over the lunch hour.

Breite Strasse leads to the **Potsdam Museum** (9), whose exhibitions of the town's history are displayed in the former parliament house of 1770, and in its annex across the street. It is open on Tuesdays through Sundays, from 9 a.m. to 5 p.m. Just a bit farther down is the **Marstall** (Court Stables) (10), built as an orangery in 1685 and enlarged to house the royal horses in 1746. It is now home to the **Film Museum** (11), where the town's long connections with the movie industry are celebrated. Potsdam is a major film production center, with studios occupying over a square mile of the Babelsberg district. These may be visited on highly entertaining guided tours, conducted daily throughout the year. Ask about them here or at the tourist office. The Film Museum is open on Tuesdays through Sundays, from 10 a.m. to 5 p.m.

You are now back at the Alter Markt (2). in the center of the huge square stands the **Nikolaikirche** (Church of St. Nicholas) (11), the city's major church and architectural landmark. Built in the neo-Classical style in 1837 on the site of a Baroque church, it has a dome towering some 175 feet above its nave. Badly damaged in World War II, it was restored with help from West Germany and may be visited on Tuesdays through Saturdays from 10 a.m. to 5 p.m., on Sundays from 11:30 a.m. to 5:30 p.m., and on Mondays from 2–5 p.m.

From here you can easily return on foot to the nearby S-Bahn station (1).

Index

Castles and Palaces, Cathedrals, Lakes, Mountains, and Museums are listed individually under those category headings. *Names of persons are in italics.*

Daytrips

• OTHER TITLES NOW AVAILABLE •

Daytrips LONDON
Explores the metropolis on 10 one-day walking tours, then describes 40 daytrips to destinations throughout southern England—all by either rail or car. 5th edition, 336 pages, 57 maps, 94 photos.

Daytrips FRANCE
Describes 45 daytrips—including 5 walking tours of Paris, 23 excursions from the city, 5 in Provence, and 12 along the Riviera. 4th edition, 336 pages, 55 maps, 89 photos.

Daytrips HOLLAND, BELGIUM AND LUXEMBOURG
Many unusual places are covered on these 40 daytrips, along with all the favorites plus the 3 major cities. 2nd Edition, 288 pages, 45 maps, 69 photos.

Daytrips ITALY
Features 40 one-day adventures in and around Rome, Florence, Milan, Venice, and Naples. 2nd edition, 288 pages, 45 maps, 69 photos.

Daytrips ISRAEL
25 one-day adventures by bus or car to the Holy Land's most interesting sites. Includes Jerusalem walking tours. 206 pages, 40 maps, 40 photos.

Daytrips WASHINGTON, DC
50 one-day adventures in the Nation's Capital, and to nearby Virginia, Maryland, Delaware, and Pennsylvania. Both walking and driving tours are featured. 352 pages, 60 maps, 48 photos.

Daytrips NEW YORK
100 easy excursions by car throughout southern New York State, New Jersey, eastern Pennsylvania, Connecticut, and southern Massachusetts. 336 pages, 42 maps, 42 photos.

ABOUT THE AUTHOR

EARL STEINBICKER is a born tourist who believes that travel should be a joy, not an endurance test. For nearly 30 years he has been refining his carefree style of daytripping while working in New York, London, Paris, and other cities, first as head of a firm specializing in promotional photography and later as a professional writer. Whether by public transportation or private car, he has thoroughly probed the most delightful aspects of countries around the world—while always returning to the comforts of city life at night. A strong desire to share these experiences has led him to develop the "Daytrips" series of guides, which he continues to expand and revise. Besides this book, these now include London, France, the Low Countries, Italy, Israel, Washington DC, and New York. He pounds his word processor in rural Pennsylvania when not exploring new destinations or revisiting old ones.